The GREAT GAME

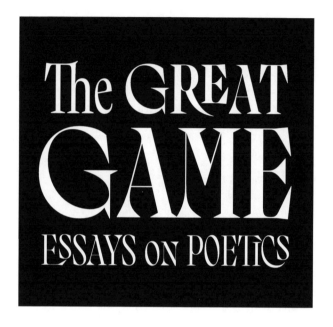

The GREAT GAME
ESSAYS ON POETICS

Amit Majmudar

ACRE

CINCINNATI 2024

Acre Books is made possible by the support of the
Robert and Adele Schiff Foundation and the
Department of English at the University of Cincinnati.

ISBN-13 (pbk) 978-1-946724-83-0
ISBN-13 (e-book) 978-1-946724-84-7

Designed by Barbara Neely Bourgoyne
Cover art: National Gallery of Art

The press is based at the University of Cincinnati,
Department of English and Comparative Literature, A&S Hall,
Room 248, PO Box 210069, Cincinnati, OH, 45221–0069.

Acre Books books may be purchased at a discount for educational use.
For information please email business@acre-books.com.

CONTENTS

I. General Theory of Unity

II. Specific Theory of Unity
<< PRECURSORS

III. Specific Theory of Unity
>> CONTEMPORARIES

GENERAL THEORY OF UNITY

The Great Game

The poem doesn't need us
To make it. It will be there
Even if we never
Let it lead us
To the still and hidden place,
The willed, unbidden place
Where poems meet us.
I'm drawing us
A circle.
I'm drawing us
Inside a circle
Of myth and memory and art,
Membrane that seals the beat
Inside the heart
Inside the fetus.
This is not a poem,
But it's not a treatise,
Either. It's a poem's
Long-lost brother,
Here to greet us
In the momentary circle
Where we read each other.

In the beginning was the rhythm. The rhythm was a row of buckets in the shapes of sounds. These sounds were syllables of different dimensions in weight or length: unstressed and stressed, or short, short, long. You tossed words into the rhythm from across the playing field. The playing field measured the exact distance between your mouth and someone else's ear.

It was a game. You might have said, "I'm working on this," or refer to a work in progress, or a book of poems as a "project," or call a poet's books "works"—but deep down, you knew this was different from waiting tables or preparing a PowerPoint for the quarterly meeting. That was work, and if you could get time off from it, you would play this game.

The game evolved over time, like rounders into baseball, rugby into tackle football, or alchemy into chemistry. At the start of this wordsport, the sounds that landed successfully and snugly in the rhythm had to spell a god's name; those were hymns. Later, they had to spell the mythistory of a civilization, and Homer was the star player of the Western conference. Sounding love or war was a sure way to advance to the next round.

It was all in good fun, but it was also always a competition, against other players or against a player dead for four centuries or against the limitations of your own voice, your own clumsy fingers tapping, typing on the keyboard, the gameboard. It was all in good fun, which is why it was so frustrating when you couldn't make the poem catch the thing, the idea, the emotion. All your throws were off the mark. Your words lay scattered like war dead on a field, a screen, a snow-covered page. It was all dead serious. It was all in play.

WHAT PLAY IS

Dutch historian Johan Huizinga lays it out nicely:

> [Play is] a free activity standing quite consciously outside "ordinary" life as being "not serious," but at the same time absorbing the player intensely and utterly. It is an activity connected with no material interest, and no profit can be gained by it. It proceeds within its own proper boundaries of time

4

and space according to fixed rules and in an orderly manner. It promotes the formation of social groupings which tend to surround themselves with secrecy and to stress their difference from the common world....[1]

He's describing play, but he's also describing poetry. You can split the paragraph up phrase by phrase and see how. Poets stand "quite consciously outside 'ordinary life'" because we choose to use, quite consciously, extraordinary language. No matter how "serious" a poem is, to cold-eyed realists, writing poetry is superfluous because "no profit can be gained by it." It doesn't matter if the poetry is about Plath's issues with her father or Celan's "black milk of dawn"; the genre is considered, by the majority of the population, intrinsically silly and vain. And yet it absorbs "intensely and utterly" the poet and the reader, the happy few who are devotees of this art. It "proceeds within its own proper boundaries of time and space," or the boundaries of poetic form, "according to fixed rules"—though which rules are fixed can vary. Does poetry "promote the formation of social groupings"? Any "tribe of poets" would say it does. Poets may not "surround themselves with secrecy" deliberately, but our general obscurity may serve the same purpose. We stress our difference from the common world—that is, the world of prose—through the line break, if nothing else.

The word "play" is like the word "myth." If you say "myth," it can imply something sacred. For a reader of Joseph Campbell, for someone versed in Jungian or Freudian thought, or for a Hindu like myself, myth is profound to the point of bottomlessness. But you can call something a myth in a dismissive, contemptuous way too: *There were never aliens at Area 51; that's just a myth.* Play, similarly, has two possible connotations: the trivial, superficial one and the deep-to-bottomless one. When I write "play" in this essay, I'm not talking Tetris. I am not "playing around," and neither was Johan Huizinga, and neither was Robert Frost:

Only where love and need are one,
And the work is play for mortal stakes,
Is the deed ever really done
For Heaven and the future's sakes.[2]

5

Frost wrote those four lines of poetry by taking on restrictions. He knew that only restrictions can free us from prose—voluntary, arbitrary, strategic restrictions. Frost decided that he would deploy four stressed syllables in each of four lines, and that the fourth and twelfth stressed syllables would rhyme, and that the eighth and sixteenth stressed syllables would rhyme and alliterate, and that all four lines would comprise a single sentence. Taken apart like that, it seems an absurd, perhaps even insuperable set of obstacles and obligations. Yet athleticism welcomes such rules; Frost once said that he would as soon write poetry without such rules as "play tennis with the net down,"[3] an apt comparison with a game. Tennis players insist on hitting the ball within a 23.77 × 8.23–meter box drawn on the ground, back and forth over an obstacle 91.4 centimeters high: arbitrary, exacting, standardized measurements that are the meter and rhyme scheme, the syntax that makes tennis tennis, just as rhythm makes music music. A ball that lands outside the court is *out* and interrupts play; the players return to their places across the court and start playing for another point. What sound does a musical note make if it's nowhere on the stave? Every sport is a verse form, and every verse form is a musical instrument. We poets play sonnet, we play blank verse, we play triolet. We welcome the rules because rules make a game a game.

PLAYING ON, AND PLAYING WITH, WORDS

Poetic forms, meter, and rhyme may be less fashionable games today, but assonance and alliteration and anaphora, couplets and tercets and quatrains, still create the liberating restrictions of play in contemporary versecraft. Wordplay and allusion are the two ways in which play enters poetry most obviously. Wordplay announces its play element through its name—and so does "allusion," since it comes from the Latin word for "play with": *ludo*.

Allusion is the best example of how serious play can be. When John Donne alludes to the Bible in one of his sermons, he is "playing with" the Bible, but his message is aimed at the very souls of his listeners. Likewise, when

Hemingway alludes to one of Donne's sermons for the title of one of his best novels, his allusion is meant to *increase* the gravity and high seriousness of *For Whom the Bell Tolls*. Even the much-maligned pun has exalted, supremely serious origins. Long before we began rolling our eyes at puns, the Book of Genesis punned in Hebrew when naming the first man. Created from earth, "adamah," was ... Adam. And, of course, Shakespeare inserts puns into the gravest, tensest situations *not* for comic relief: with the stage in darkness, the Third Murderer asks, having just struck Banquo dead, "Who did strike out the light?"[4]

Just as the interface where two neurons connect is a synapse, the interface between two books or poems is an allusion. A more complex brain has more synapses; a more complex book, say, *Ulysses*, has more allusions. But complexity is not necessarily the writer's only goal. You can make your work too allusive, too hyperlinked to carry out the very simple function of communication, ending up with a complicated tangle of wires and transistors that doesn't actually perform any function. Joyce's next novel, *Finnegans Wake*, is arguably such a book.

It's a warning against making too much of any one approach or concept when we study or practice literature—even play. Play is not the only thing that makes literature what it is. The opposite of play, though, unmakes literature all the time. The opposite of play is "plod." Plodding prose, plodding thought, rhythmless lifeless stuff you can't step to: that's plod, and it's what poets strive, instinctively, to avoid.

THE LUDIC ILLUSION

When we say "theatrical illusion," we're using words that come from *theasthai* (Greek for "to see") and *illudere* (Latin for "to mock" or "to deceive"). In its noun form: "delusion of the mind, apparition." The word itself derives from *ludus*, literally "game" or "play." The theatrical illusion is, etymologically, a "game with visible apparitions."

Is it any wonder, then, that the most revered poet in English is the dramatist Shakespeare? The most revered poet in Sanskrit, the dramatist Kalidasa? The most revered work of the most revered German poet, the verse drama *Faust*? Eliot, Yeats, and Walcott all daydreamed about creating a poetic drama for the twentieth century.

Poetic drama only flourishes in rare, specific circumstances. And those circumstances have to do, in part, with another aspect of play: competition. Remember that drama itself originated, in the West, at the Dionysian competitions. Euripides and Sophocles weren't just contemporaries; they were rivals. Three tragedies would be followed by a farcical satyr play as a chaser, all in elaborate meters: the serious and the light, combined in the poem-play.

Rivalry. No wonder the great verse dramatists so often show up in pairs: Goethe and Schiller, Lope de Vega and Calderón, Corneille and Racine. Elizabethan London was a city crowded with several playing companies, each with its own stable of playwrights: the King's Men, the Admiral's Men, the Earl of Leicester's Men, the Children of the Chapel, Lord Strange's Men. Shakespeare started out trying to beat Marlowe at history plays and went on to compete, every season, against the other playwrights of his day. Each season's new plays, in their quest for crowds, competed for their continued existence like biological organisms competing for resources and mates.

THE CHARMED CIRCLE

A stage, like a tennis court or a quatrain, is a cordoned-off area where the playing takes place. The theatrical illusion dovetails with Huizinga's idea that play needs "its own proper boundaries … of space," a charmed circle where the magic holds. That circle must not be penetrated by the outside, ordinary world. Two realities exist simultaneously, and usually not independently: the reality inside the poem and the "real life" of the poet. The player on the field and the player's personal life.

We call the one-page-or-less poems commonly written today "lyric poetry," but the old distinction between lyric, epic, and dramatic poetry has never been accurate. Lyric poetry usually involves a persona, if only the persona of the poet. Like actors (or "players," as they were called in Shakespeare's age), we poets put on a mask and change voice: I am who I am, but get me alone with a blank page, and I play poet; I ham it up. Every lyric is a dramatic monologue, even if—*especially* if—the poet claims the poetic "I" is the same as the personal "I." This is why it's often such a letdown to meet a poet you like in person. You know the poet as they are inside the charmed circle of their own chalking. To meet them in person is to meet them outside of it, unmagically.

Sometimes the "real life" of the artist informs the art, like Plath's suicide or Dante's exile. The poet becomes a character speaking the poems, regardless of whether the poem is autobiographical or not. Most of us keep Keats in mind when we read one of his odes, picturing a poet coughing up blood and dying tragically young. The backstory reinforces the magic inside the charmed circle.

Other times, though, the backstory can do the opposite. When a poet anthologized in *Best American Poetry* turned out to be a white man publishing pseudonymously as an Asian female, his poem changed for the worse in the perception of many readers. The poet's racial transgression (etymologically, a "moving-across") made his poem seem fraudulent and cynical, destroying the magic it had created before. James Frey wrote a beloved, Oprah-endorsed memoir that proved to be shot through with lies; reality withered the magic yet again. J. K. Rowling has lost fans and readers over her ideas on gender; not even *Harry Potter*'s formidable magic could hold. The spectator's knowledge of misconduct outside the magic circle—whether ethical, sexual, or ideological—can travel with writers into the circle where they play the game. It can render the circle unmagical.

Consider: Would a talented writer get invited to literary festivals and readings if he were a registered sex offender? Probably not—not even if he wrote twice as much, twice as well. What if an even more talented writer went off on Twitter rants against immigrants, Black people, transgender rights, feminists, and liberals? No doubt her publisher's interest in publishing her, and her readership's interest in reading her, would evaporate. No review would fail to mention her unacceptability, and she would be kept off college campuses and bookshelves. Readers would process anything she wrote differently, and even if they saw merit in it, they would see that merit as an example of the uncoupling of inner worth and poetic ability. Ingenuity would come to be seen as mere cleverness, and cleverness as a sign of soullessness. For many readers, the exact same poems or stories, when read with the author's moral and ideological vileness in mind, would "lose their charm." All art, being play, must take place on a playground, inside a magic boundary: the court, the field, the pitch, the page.

ALIENS WATCHING BASEBALL

What is going on down there, on that court? What is going on down there, on that page?

Some of the best page poetry remains enigmatic to people outside the circle of poetry-lovers (that circle used to be even narrower before mass literacy and the human population explosion; a minor novelist's debut today can dwarf the total number of readers that Petrarch had in a whole lifetime). Why is it so enigmatic? It may have to do with the rules we impose on ourselves as players.

An extreme analogy might clarify the idea. Imagine you're an alien visiting Earth and know nothing at all about baseball. *Why are those humans just standing there? Why is the human with the stick squatting in that odd way? How does that human in the center decide when to throw the ball? Why are they running in circles once the ball gets hit? Why do they fail to run when the ball gets hit so it goes behind the human with the stick?* Your confusion destroys any potential enjoyment. You don't have any sense of the tension, even if it's tied at the bottom of the ninth in the last game of the World Series, because you don't know what to expect in the first place. You figure they're playing a game, but you are outside of it.

Many readers experience poetry that way. Poetry engages in linguistic behaviors that seem strange, even perverse, to those who do not know the rules that govern its playfulness. This holds true regardless of whether a poem makes a paraphrasable, prosaic sense—if it does, why insert all those line breaks?

In contemporary America, not every poet is capable of appreciating or enjoying every kind of poetry being written. There are cliques and schools in contemporary poetry that play a game with rules foreign to me, and I take no enjoyment in watching them play it—nothing punctuated or capitalized, each phrase seemingly independent from the ones before or after it, not even some phonetic principle by which these seemingly random words follow one another. (*Why are these words sequenced this way?*) I have had such thoughts when reading some of my more "experimental" contemporaries, all sorts of alien-observing-baseball thoughts. I have reflected that ancient Sumerian poetry in translation pleases me more than some poems written in my mother tongue today. But I am well aware that my own work, in the eyes of an avant-gardist, would seem too linear, overdetermined, retrograde in its self-delighting forms. And that many of my more irregular poems would not pass muster with a strict, syllable-counting formalist in a bowtie. I know also that we could pool all our poems, from the most "accessible" to the most "difficult," and my highly educated radiologist colleagues would largely be unable to follow or enjoy our games, regardless of which rules we selected for ourselves.

PICKING A RULEBOOK

Every poet, even the supposedly unruly Beat (often, following Whitman, quite enamored of anaphora), chooses rules of play. At our given moment in time, there are several rulebooks out there for poets. You can pick any one. Back through literary history, the preferred rulebook has changed frequently—one moment, rhymed couplets; a couple of centuries later, free verse. Consequently, what is seen as "good" in poetry varies over time, and among the poets of our own time.

To enjoy the poetry being played in front of you, you have to recognize the rules by which the poet is playing. This occurs in two ways. First, you recognize the rules in the very basic sense of pattern recognition. You must grasp the principles according to which the words have been sequenced. Once you can tell what the rules are, you can tell whether that poet is playing the game well or not. Second, you recognize them the same way one country recognizes another. When the United States "recognizes" a given nation-state, it's a way of saying, *Yes, you are legitimately governed.* In late-twentieth-century America, many academic poets thought that meter and rhyme were illegitimate forms of governance for contemporary poetry. They recognized the pattern, but they didn't believe that good contemporary poetry could be written that way.

Poetry is play; some play well, others play poorly, but clusters of contemporaries play by different sets of rules. What is wrong with poets being enigmatic to the majority of their countrymen and, in some cases, to each other? If anything, there's something *right* about that situation. Much of the earliest poetry is riddling—the oracle, the sphinx, the troll guarding the bridge. The enigmatic aspects of a poem, studied and understood, draw readers (some, but not others) into the poet's magic circle. "The Soul selects her own Society," says Dickinson, "Then—shuts the door."[5]

JUMP

Writing is play, but it's not a game of skill alone. Poetry is a game of skill *and* a game of chance at the same time. The best poets use skill to make their own luck. This is why some of the most prolific poets—Dickinson, Rumi, Byron, Goethe—have welcomed the mandatory ingenuities of rhyme and form. Extemporization is the secret of their output. "The Sufi," goes an old Persian saying, "is the son of the moment." I myself have made this essay up as I've gone along, playing with meanings instead of sounds. That is, I composed this essay just as I would a poem: *playfully*.

Early in the *Laws*, Plato talks about the origin of play, which he claims is the innate desire of the young, both animal and human, to "jump." Colts jump, testing out their joints, kicking the gravity off their legs. Children used to develop their "innate tendency to leap" into the complex jumps of Double Dutch and the charmed squares of hopscotch chalked on the pavement. Today, I don't see kids playing those low-tech games anymore, but the jumps have shifted to the avatars in video games.

What is a jump, really? And what does it have in common with play, with poetry? The jump rejects our earthbound nature. It is a temporary transcendence of gravity. The jump conjures for the jumper an imaginary hurdle out of air. This conjuring of imaginary hurdles is one way to think of poetic form: arbitrary limits on language demand and shape bursts of poetic flight.

Every sport infuses action with excitement, tension, and beauty, and it does so by imposing *rules* on action. Those rules sculpt the speed and force of a Roger Federer or a LeBron James into shapes and patterns we perceive as aesthetic, balletic, artistic. What defines a tennis court or basketball court are its lines, its "limes," its limits. As soon as the ball goes out of bounds, the magic circle breaks, and play stops. A "foul" also stops play—this word's original meaning had to do with rottenness or decay, and in this way connects with "spoilsport." Athletic feats are "poetry in motion." The reverse also holds true: poetry is athletic speech. "Athletic" and "aesthetic" are more than just a rhyme; they share a common origin in play.

The poetry of plod is written with the same rules as prose, except for the typographical interference of the line break; it is not the poetry of play. If the only principle of word organization is that every sentence in the piece meets the demands of grammar, you are probably reading prose, line breaks notwithstanding. Into this category fall all those chatty first-person anecdotes that build up to epiphanies. You plod through lines that sound exactly like prose because they *are* prose. When poets sense they are doing this, they write run-on sentences, breaking the rules of conventionally "good" prose, but it doesn't save their poems from plodding. Whatever doesn't effervesce, evanesces. It's one of the few laws of poetry, but it's draconian.

KINDS OF PLAY

Hermann Hesse's last novel was *The Glass Bead Game*. Its alternative title was *Magister Ludi*, which is itself a pun, because the novel is about a "school" where elite, monk-like teachers play a sublime "game." It's a pun because "ludi" contains both meanings, school and game, and the Glass Bead Game, which Hesse never fully describes, requires the players to play with connections (synapses) among different disciplines, like the Analects of Confucius and the sonatas of Scarlatti. *Magister Ludi* means both "Master of the School" and "Master of the Game."

So if we listen to what the Latin language and Hermann Hesse are telling us, every game is also a school. How is a school a game? Developmental psychologists would say play is the primary means by which children learn.

Play is a common feature of human and animal maturation; it's how the young acquire and refine their motor skills. The earliest kind of play that emerges is parallel play, when children play side by side but don't actually interact or interfere with each other. This corresponds, in poetry, to the unpublishable scribblings by which we find our way to something we can bear presenting to the world. Eventually, we move on to simple social play: you publish your poem, you show it to the world, and the world reads it. But that's where it ends; the poem is forgotten. These are the poems we publish successfully—and never hear anything about, ever again. The majority of published poetry falls into this category of play.

The final, most advanced play is cooperative play. Both children are actively involved in the game. Each takes a role in the same make-believe world. For a poet, that's when your work does more than just delight you and impress other people. It takes on meaning and significance in someone else's life. You'll often hear poetry readers say that a poem "resonated." Resonance is a good description for it because resonance is contagious. Consider how a struck tuning fork evokes a kindred shiver when it's brought near a still one.

FIGURE (SKATER) OF SPEECH

If every game is a school where we learn by playing, poetry is the ludic literary art that teaches us how to connect. After all, the most important synapse in literature is not allusive—between the present poem and past poems—but direct: between the poet and the reader, now. The page is the playground, the syllables are balls.

Scarcely aware that she's deploying them, the poet uses stroke and stratagem to game language into poetry. Some see the rhyme and simile, the artifice, the devious device, while others see a skater on the ice who moves more naturally on blades since she's beat the difficulty that they made once, her muscles so conditioned that walking in socks and shoes is inefficient. But in the end, it is the ear that knows knower from novice, verse from prose—and judges, in a seat beside the rink, the triple axels, lutzes, loops that link emotion, meaning, music in this art that seeks to break no record, just the heart—this art whose love is logos singing sense in forms so fine we give it perfect 10s.

It plays with fire with a will to burn us.

It does for sport what life will do in earnest.

FORMAL RESTLESSNESS

1.

To master the God of Changes, as Menelaus learned, you have to pin him down. Proteus will change his form rapidly under the weight of yours: a lion, a serpent, a leopard, a boar. Then, as he realizes you won't let go, he will get desperate. His body will become flowing water and a rooted tree—motion and fixity, the extremes of the spectrum. Then, finally: Proteus. Even that form, though, may be an illusion. After all, for him to remain Proteus, he has to remain protean. Proteus, in his native form, is just a body suspending transition. His one true form is the sum of all his past forms and all his forms to come.

Let his name shapeshift a little in your ear. Keep the capital P, the long O sound, the anapestic rhythm, but let everything else flicker, and you will see where I am going with this. Proteus. Protean.

Poetry.

2.

Human gestation involves a steady embryonic shapeshift. In the womb, the body tests out neck gills and seals them, grows a tail and resorbs it, webs the fingers and frees them. A whole evolutionary past is implied: fish, salamander, duck. Enough metamorphoses to fill a book in Ovid.

It's easy to make this mistake when it comes to form. We can think of a poet writing in many different forms as a preliminary fitfulness (larva, pupa, nymph) that precedes a settled, adult form. Congratulations, you have "found your voice," "hit your stride," "become who you are"—and you will never bother testing out a curtal sonnet or a run of sprung rhythm ever again.

Several prominent twentieth-century poets serve as examples that can trick us into this kind of thinking. Their oeuvres begin with formal restlessness, then break abruptly as they adopt the ubiquitous free verse form of the twentieth century. The early books of W. S. Merwin, Ted Hughes, Robert Lowell, Adrienne Rich, and even John Ashbery experimented with patterns of rhyme and meter, shapes on the page governed by shapes for the ear. Then there is a break. The reasons for this are usually presented as the poet transcending "restraints" and gaining visionary access to the taproot of True Poetry, or a breaking of "formal shackles," or some other metaphor involving liberation, rebellion, or engaging with modernity. Seen from a distance, they adopted the dominant form of their era and stayed there. Because those poets rarely, if ever, returned to that early formal restlessness, it's easy to regard that phase as apprentice work.

Other poets never underwent such a phase—or, more likely, concealed any trace of it. They seem to have shown up fully formed; they took one form and never departed from it. Every poem contains the entire formal genome of the poet, and the formal characteristics of all the other poems can be derived from one example of their art. Kay Ryan is like that. Pick any poem of hers at random:

Everything contains some
silence. Noise gets
its zest from the
small shark's-tooth
shaped fragments
of rest angled
in it. An hour
of city holds maybe
a minute of these
remnants of a time

when silence reigned,
compact and dangerous
as a shark. Sometimes
a bit of a tail
or fin can still
be sensed in parks.[1]

That is her form; there are no surprises, no switches of shape. All her poems say different things, but they say them in the exact same way.

Ryan may seem to be a rare case, but most of the great Persian poets were more devoted to the couplet than Alexander Pope. Most American poets are one-form poets. The only reason we notice uniformity in Ryan's case is because Ryan rhymes, creating a consistently identifiable, if intentionally skewed, symmetry. Most other American poets begin and end their careers using some kind of free verse that has an irregularly irregular rhythm; their formal variations are largely typographical. Many don't honor their own line breaks as they recite, reading right through them as though they were reading prose. That is the tell. Theirs is the restlessness of the return key, not the restlessness of form.

Not that stasis can't be generative. From one perspective, Merwin's mid- and late-career poems gained immensely through his eschewal of the rhyme, meter, and even the punctuation of his early books. Consider this stanza:

When the forests have been destroyed their darkness remains
The ash the great walker follows the possessors
Forever
Nothing they will come to is real
Nor for long
Over the watercourses
Like ducks in the time of the ducks
The ghosts of the villages trail in the sky
Making a new twilight[2]

Once he knew what all his future poems would look and sound like, he could focus on other things, like what to put in them. The formal switch to free verse gave him a feeling of freedom, not just because he did not have to set up regular patterns of scansion and rhyme, but also because he had one less artistic decision to worry about. Besides, it was what most readers wanted anyway.

3.

What about poets who never stop shapeshifting? In some oeuvres, a poem of a given shape cannot be pinpointed, on the basis of that shape alone, to an "early" or "mature" phase. A potpourri of patterns, a farrago of forms may persist into old age, even after a Merwin-like rupture. Yeats changed many elements of his style between *The Celtic Twilight* and his more self-consciously "modern" work, but his formal restlessness remained constant. Kipling remains adored by sentimentalists for "If," cherished by children for the rhymes in *Just-So Stories* and *The Jungle Book*, despised by postcolonial studies majors for "The White Man's Burden," and ignored by everyone for the plebeian brogue of *Barrack-Room Ballads*. None of those share a form or even a tone or theme (except, maybe, his most famous one and his most infamous one). He was always trying out new themes and rhyme schemes.

The same holds true of most Romantic poets. Their *Collected Poems* usually contain a plethora of poetic patterns, sizes, and genres. Keats ran through more forms and categories of poem by the age of twenty-three than most American poets will touch in a Pulitzer Prize–winning career. Not just Keats, but Byron, Coleridge, Shelley, Wordsworth, and Tennyson all tried their hands at blank-verse drama. They did this because of Shakespeare, of course, the most protean of all poets, who reshaped his voice into those of so many men and women that even his sonnets are not necessarily spoken in his "own" voice. Shakespeare alone ought to give the quietus to our notions of originality and "finding your voice." Authorship controversies have attributed his entire oeuvre, at various times, to any one of a diverse cast of characters, among them a nobleman (Edward de Vere), a shoemaker's son (Marlowe), and an Italian immigrant's daughter (Emilia Bassano). Proteus can be anyone.

Formal restlessness is not some gestational, preliminary phase. Consider it a mature stage of development, a fixed characteristic, the "now this, now that" approach that makes Proteus Proteus.

4.

Another candidate for the consummate Proteus-poet was Goethe. He used to seize on a form, churn out several examples of it, and abandon it—until he returned to it later for some drastically different use. For example, the dactylic hexameter line showed up in the late 1780s, in the fifth of twenty-four salacious *Roman Elegies*:

> Often too in her arms I've lain composing a poem,
>> Gently with her fingering hand count the hexameter's beat
> Out on her back...[3]

It showed up again, ten years later, in the sweet, idyllic epic *Hermann and Dorothea*, a tale of a refugee falling in love in the German countryside. Around this time Goethe also wrote a book or two of an hexameter epic on Achilles, putting the line to its more conventional use. Another of its functions, in the classical world, lay in didactic poetry. Goethe had a small role in the development of that biological theory of endless shapeshifting, evolution; the hexameters of "The Metamorphosis of Animals" date to 1806.

The *Marienbad Elegy*, written in 1821, uses the meter yet again. Goethe returned to the young, satisfied lover's meter—those dactyls, tapped out on his Italian lover's back—to write about an old man's impossible longing for a teenager. (Ulrike von Levetzow, the object of Goethe's failed proposal, died in 1899.)

This restlessness was a constant feature of Goethe's poetry, as any glance at his *Selected Poems* reveals. He owned several mines, each one dedicated to a different poetic ore, which he accessed or abandoned depending on his needs and whims. *Faust* tumbled all these forms into one work, a gallimaufry of verbal patterns that changed not just from scene to scene, but from character to character.

5.

Goethe once described himself as a pagan and attracted the epithet "Olympian" from his contemporaries. Like so many Germans of his era, he fetishized the classical Mediterranean. It may be no coincidence that formal restlessness is almost the rule among lyric poets of the classical world. Sappho gave her name to "sapphics," but it's not as though all her poems adhered to that one meter. Horace, imitating the Greeks, replicated their plurality of patterns: Ascelpiadic, Sapphic, Alcaic, Aeolic. The world's most famous poem of shapeshifts comes from his contemporary, Ovid.

There is one other major polytheistic civilization whose literature survives. Sanskrit poetry doesn't just have a variety of meters; like the "pagan" Goethe's *Faust*, like the dramas that survive from Greece's polytheistic civilization, Sanskrit plays, and courtly epics mix meters in the same work. Yet formal restlessness is not just a literary quirk of Sanskrit poets; it correlates with Hindu theology, in which one divinity manifests in many forms. India's earliest, most hallowed holy books, the Vedas, deploy no less than fifteen meters; the *Bhagavad-Gita*, a later sacred text, switches between two:

> Look at me, Partha—forms,
> A hundred, more, a thousandfold,
> Divine multiplicities,
> Multiple colors and shapes![4]

By the end of its millennia-long development, literary Sanskrit evolved no fewer than 850 meters. Multiplicity is one way to the infinite.

In the Hindu tradition, the God who takes on new forms is Vishnu. The most recent avatars were human—Rama and Krishna—but the earlier ones include a fish, a turtle, a boar, and a man with the head of a lion. Animal forms precede the human one, just as they do in embryology and Darwinism.

For the Greeks, Proteus was a minor god; for the Hindus, Vishnu is nothing less than the sustainer of the universe. In the Indian tradition, even the individual self reincarnates, subject to rebirth in different human or nonhuman bodies. This was a belief shared, in some form, by Pythagoras as well as Socrates, who discussed reincarnation in the *Meno*. Metempsychosis is metamorphosis. Death is just a page break, a turning from this poem to the next one, which tries out yet another form: from the blank-verse monologue, to the sonnet, to the internal eternal recurrence of the triolet.

6.

The Odyssey shows us Proteus counting his flock of seals. Sunning on the rocks, seals are frequently motionless, and when they do move, they heave themselves forward awkwardly. Once they slip through the waves, they take on speed and grace. It's the closest thing to transformation a body can manage without actually changing form.

Ambushed and pinned down, Proteus changes shape in desperation, attempting to elude the one who will force him to speak as himself. Menelaus wants a straight answer; he wants information. Though they all speak in Homeric hexameters, what Menelaus wants from Proteus is the stuff of prose.

Proteus, however, wants to be free. He wants to be free to become something other than himself, perpetually, with neither endpoint nor endgame. In his natural state, glorying in his divine power, Proteus thrives by donning a variety of bodies. Formal restlessness is the only state in which he is entirely at ease, entirely himself.

7.

Formal restlessness need not imply a scattered body of work. Paging through a collection by George Herbert or Robert Frost, or a contemporary like A. E. Stallings, you can see a variety of shapes, which correspond to a variety of sound patterns. Unity lies elsewhere, whether it's a thematic fixation (religion, in Herbert), a musical tic (the tendency to metrical substitution, in Stallings, that resembles a Morse operator's "hand"), or a sharp limitation of register (Frost is never effusive). Unity does not require uniformity. As a poet, you can be "all of a piece" even if the pieces don't match.

Why pursue a plurality of forms? The poets who do it seem to do so relentlessly; even poets exclusively devoted to a nonmetrical, unrhymed style seem compelled to break up their lines into couplets, tercets, quatrains, sonnets, etc. Every poet who does so probably has their own reasons. A love of play almost certainly factors into it, especially for poets who persist in using rhyme, meter, or both. These musical elements link poetry to nursery rhymes: form in poetry is self-delighting first of all, I suspect, and delights the receptive reader as a bonus. No wonder squibs and the occasional run of doggerel show up in even the slender *Collected* of a poet as short-lived as Keats. Goethe, Eliot, and Stallings all display a willingness to pursue the art of light verse; Auden edited a whole anthology of it. Formally restless poets seem, as a rule, to be antihierarchical in their approach to poetry, perhaps because they try their hands at so many kinds of poems. They are less likely to dismiss puns or clever epigrams as antithetical to Serious Poetry. Nor should we underestimate the poet's drive to avoid boredom. There is a thrill to succeeding with an as-yet-unattempted form to which only those who fail repeatedly can attest. The challenge keeps things interesting.

Finally, though, I suspect formal restlessness is intrinsic to their poetic expression. The form creates a vacuum where no vacuum was, and not only rhymes and stressed syllables but emotions, images, and ideas get sucked into it. The poet discovers new poems with the assistance of these forms; willed patterns fill with unwilled language. Notice how prolific Goethe, the English Romantics, Kipling, and Auden were. Constantly seeking out new forms clearly did not hinder or stifle them. In fact, it may have done the reverse, liberating poetic speech from the tyranny of prose rhythms.

Such a perspective requires us to rethink form itself—whether a single fixation (Ghalib's ghazal) or a promiscuous panoply (Goethe's multiplicity)—as something other than "constraint," "restraint," "shackles," "box," or "stricture." All the conventional twentieth-century critical metaphors of containment, imprisonment, binding, and restriction would have to be scrapped. A new understanding must rely on new metaphors. Form is the engine, the lottery, the kaleidoscope; the void that gives you what you fill it with, the call you teach yourself to echo; the luck maker, the goad, the god.

8.

Menelaus trapped Proteus in order to put him to use. Stranded on the island of Pharos off the coast of Egypt, Menelaus wanted to know how to get home. He made Proteus give him other facts as well, such as the fates of Agamemnon and Odysseus. Proteus did this unwillingly; providing mortals with straight information is not the proper function of a god, just as it is not the proper function of poetry. The Oracle at least had the decency to be cryptic.

The name "Proteus" comes from "protos," "first," a prefix that still appears in English, most commonly in the sciences. The root of "Proteus" has given us the protons in atomic nuclei, protozoa in the sea, protoplasm inside every human cell. The three words form a rough map of evolution from inanimate matter, through the sea's "first animals," to the living brine that fills a human body.

After emerging from the sea at high noon, Proteus wanted only to count his herd of seals by fives. (Verse used to be called "numbers," its beats tapped out, perhaps on a lover's back, by five fingers.) After counting, Menelaus learned, Proteus always went to sleep. Proteus, the shapeshifting magical god, came up from the sea to sleep in broad daylight, his eyes closed to the garishly sparkling sea because he preferred his dreams.

"What song the Sirens sang, or what name Achilles assumed when he hid himself among women," wrote Thomas Browne, "though puzzling questions, are not beyond all conjecture."[5] Homer does not tell us what Proteus dreamed there in the sun, during his midday nap, just before Menelaus threw off his sealskin disguise and attacked. That god of formal fluidity, that unacknowledged god of poetry, may have dreamed himself slipping out of the waking world. He may have splashed into the dream world, where his mind moved faster and more gracefully, like a seal dropping through the waves, transformed instantly by the medium. In that dream, he may have tested out alternate bodies, mating calls, voices, minds. When he felt the heavy, hairy, desperate warrior pin him to the rock and startle him from dream sleep, he may have continued those shapeshifts in his groggy confusion: a lion, a serpent, a leopard, a boar, flowing water, a tree.

See Menelaus smother that tree in his embrace while the leaves turn red around him. At last, the bark smooths into bare skin, and the branches deflate into arms. The mutable magical one will be forced to answer against his will. He will give Menelaus knowledge of his friends and of how to leave the island where his journey home has stalled: news and useable information. The wisdom of Proteus, because he has been pinned down to a single form, has already escaped. A shrewder captor might have asked the god to teach him and his men the art of becoming seals. They could have splashed into the waves immediately, no need to wait for the wind. They could have swum home to Sparta swiftly and gracefully—impossible to shipwreck, impossible to drown.

SISTER
DISCIPLINES

1.

A surgeon's apprentice by the name of John Keats once held a bucket under an oozy, malodorous foot during an early-nineteenth-century amputation. An obstetrician named William Carlos Williams once crouched between two knees and tugged out a newborn slick with blood and cheese-curd vernix, a puddle of fluid at his feet, flecking his trousers. Keats's poetry, bird-besotted and frequently mythological, transcended the "ick" in physicality; Williams's, earthy and earthly and besotted with spoken speech, sought it out. The two scenarios offered dual pathways into poetry for a medical student on his surgery rotation, doing the bloody but boring job of holding retractors while the attending surgeon cut and cauterized. Sometimes I peered over into the cavity, making sure my shadow didn't obscure the surgeon's workspace. I reflected on how amazing it was that I could see into the human body; until the systematic dissection of cadavers in the Renaissance Europe of Vesalius, much of what was actually inside a body had been a mystery. That fascination lasted a few minutes and wore off quickly. I knew even then that there were cleaner, less bloody, less risky ways of seeing inside a body, and sure enough, I ended up going into radiology.

But there was plenty of time while carrying out that mindless role to think about the relationship between poetry and medicine, or poetry and science more generally. I realized the consummate image of the global mind, for me, wasn't the physician-poet at all. Instead, it was the young Goethe en route to his artistic and sexual exploration in Italy, leaping out of his carriage in the mountains to inspect rocks. That was the intersection of more than just poetry and science. (Goethe went on to write a book of botanical theory, vaguely anticipating Darwin, and another book on optics that vainly challenged Newton.) The image of Goethe pausing his romantic and literary career to contemplate a "special type of gneiss" echoed those ancient Zen sages who stared at a single yellow flower. More than just an addition to a geological collection, more than just a future passage in a travelogue was to be found in such study. There was something *echt poetisch* in that mind's scientific curiosity. It's said that Goethe was the last Renaissance man, the last mind to know several disciplines well enough to contribute legitimately and creatively to them. In his two main passions, literature and the sciences, he was accessing something extremely ancient, something at the very origins of poetry. He was the last of a line, and his dynasty went back all the way to the Muses, if not to the mother of the Muses, Mnemosyne herself.

2.

Mnemonics remain indispensable to the medical student. Some are salacious, like the acrostic that helps with the bones of the hand (the scaphoid, lunate, triquetrum, pisiform, trapezium, trapezoid, capitate, and hamate: *Some Lovers Try Positions That They Can't Handle*). The consummate mnemonic, the one that links the mother to her daughters, is a rhymed iambic dimeter couplet: *To Zanzibar / By Motor Car*. Even after all these years, it gives me the trigger I need to recall, without an assist from Google, the temporal, zygomatic, buccal, maxillary, and cervical branches of the facial nerve.

What is it that makes a mnemonic memorable? In the latter case, it's the meter and the rhyme: the poetry. Before writing, the theory goes, bards needed to *remember* their stories and hymns, and just as a song's tune sticks in your head more easily than the song's lyrics, song lyrics will stick in your head more easily (and precisely) than a chunk of prose. Meter made poems easier to memorize and transmit. This was the basic, utilitarian point of poetry's intersection with science.

But to understand the relationship more fully, we have to examine that word, "science," and compare what it means to us today with what it meant millennia ago, at the origins of the art. Did the authors of the Vedas, of Gilgamesh, of the pre-Socratic meditations distinguish among biology, chemistry, biochemistry, physics, genetics, botany, geology, and so on? Languages of extreme antiquity lacked terms for many of these disciplines, much less the information they encompass. In the cases of genetics and biochemistry, they lacked even the concepts.

The distant past's attitude toward science remains encoded in the etymology of the word itself. So does science's future development. The word comes to us through Latin and Old French: *scientia*, simply "to know." But the word came to Latin from the Greek, and there its root was the same as "schizophrenia": to split, to distinguish, to divide. Science was, originally, knowledge, and it has been sundered, dozens of times over centuries, into the modern university's departments of hard sciences and soft sciences.

If we traced these sciences back, we would find a point where knowledge of the physical world wasn't yet distinguished from knowledge of the metaphysical world. People didn't conceive of knowledge as entirely independent of wisdom. So the figure of the shaman—closely related to the hermit of chivalric romances and the rishi of Indian myth—included the idea of a wise man, a holy man, and someone exceptionally knowledgeable about herbs and natural cures. Abstract or "useless" knowledge wasn't distinguished from practical knowhow. Such figures were not unfamiliar with the powers of incantations and spells to heal an injury or keep someone safe, or indeed the power of curses to inflict harm. Many a contemporary blurb calls this or that poet's work "powerful," but a medieval Welsh charm against cattle-killing evil spirits was believed to have literal, physical power. So did the priest Calchas's curse at the beginning of the *Iliad*.

Everything was done, known, recorded using words, words, words. Because the single point that antedated the Big Bang of science and theology and history—the dense, unshattered origin of all we know and remember—was the mother of all discoveries and chronicles, the earliest art, the unified field through which Memory memorialized herself: poetry.

3.

In the beginning were poems. The first work on subjects today considered "scientific" was done by poets. Hymns to Gods who represent elements or celestial bodies (Agni, Apollo, and so on), cosmogonies involving Sky-Fathers inseminating Earth-Mothers, speculations on how human beings came about, even later didactic poems about farming like Hesiod's: today, these are matters reserved for chemistry, theoretical physics, evolutionary biology, climate science, or agricultural science, but their prehistory is found in poetry. Scientists no longer recognize these assertions; no meteorologist attributes the wind to Vayu, or monsoons to the Marut storm deities. What poets still recognize, though, is the poetry.

Poetry appeared before recorded history in a thoroughly developed form. Its characteristics were passed down through centuries with scarcely any transformation. Metaphor, meter, personification, imagery, narrative: these are all present in Vedic hymns and *Gilgamesh*, just as they are in poetry today. In the Rig Veda, the earliest of four, we find a startlingly modern expression of scientific curiosity, spiritual curiosity, and uncertainty:

6. But, after all, who knows, and who can say
Whence it all came, and how creation happened?
The gods themselves are later than creation,
so who knows truly whence it has arisen?

7. Whence all creation had its origin,
the creator, whether he fashioned it or whether he did not,
the creator, who surveys it all from highest heaven,
he knows—or maybe even he does not know.[1]

In the early Western tradition, the unity of poetry and science has been obscured by a quirk of historiography. It hides in the history of philosophy. The pre-Socratic philosophers looked at the world around them and made guesses. These guesses were so basic that they were literally elemental: Thales believed the universe came from water, while Heraclitus favored fire. Anaximenes theorized a substance without qualities that differentiated into the elements. A few of these philosophers gained fame in their own day for advances in astronomy. Schoolchildren learn about Pythagoras to this day—in math class. The list goes on; a thinker like Democritus, who came up with the idea of atoms, would not be called a "philosopher" today. Parmenides wrote about a more recognizably philosophical subject: "esti," being, would linger as Sartre's *l'être* and Heidegger's *Sein*, long after atoms and elements became the bailiwick of other specialists. The "philosopher" label, when we apply it to these loosely grouped minds, encompasses modern-day philosophy but isn't limited to it. It's so small in scope that it's a misnomer.

The right catchall for the pre-Socratics would be a term that includes "mathematician," "scientist," and, above all, "poet." Many of the pre-Socratics, like Parmenides and Empedocles, wrote in verse. Here is Empedocles projecting the poet into the natural world as he expounds the doctrine of transmigration:

Once already have I as a youth been born, as a maiden,
Bush, and winged bird, and silent fish in the waters....
After what horrors, and after how long and blissful existence
Thus am I wretchedly doomed to abide in the meadows of mortals![2]

Heraclitus's fragments are among the earliest Greek prose we have; he wrote in a style so terse and pregnant with meaning that he was regarded, even in antiquity when his works weren't yet reduced to fragments, as a writer of oracular but near-impenetrable depths. His utterances—e.g., "the way up is the way down"—tempted and resisted interpretation, much like a certain obscure genre of contemporary poetry, or indeed the literal oracles of Delphi, which were (surprise!) written in verse.

Even by the time of Parmenides's *On Nature*, poetry already included the epics of Homer, the didactic poetry of Hesiod, and the religious poetry known as the Homeric hymns. So at a single point in time, we see poetry encompassing today's concepts of physics, astronomy, philosophy, agricultural science, mythology, history, religious ceremony, and even prophecy. The nexus of all these disciplines, the one thing the philosophizing Parmenides had in common with the storytelling Homer and the soothsaying Oracle, was poetry.

4.

Why did people visit Delphi in the first place? The point of those cryptic prophecies was to suss out the future. The astrologer's ambition, not the astronomer's cold fascination, resulted in the first star charts. The positions of stars were thought to be premonitory: hieroglyphics of eloquent celestial light that needed decoding.

How do we interrogate and try to control the physical world today? Knowledge precedes control. Medical researchers understand the physiology behind a disease process, then alter it with pharmacology. First comes atomic physics, then the building of the nuclear bomb. In the ancient world, oracles and offerings stood in the same relationship as science and technology today. The Vedas contained hymns invoking the elements in the form of Gods: Agni (Fire), Vayu (Wind), and so on. The Sanskrit root of "Veda" itself—*vid*, or "to know"—reveals its nature; "the Vedas" might well be translated as "the Knowledges." To follow that etymology to its logical conclusion, they could just as well be titled "the Sciences."

The Vedas were so highly revered because they contained both knowledge and the means of control. What charms and spells accomplished on a small scale (say, taking away the evil eye, or guarding against the pox), the Vedic hymns accomplished on an elemental or cosmic one. In Vedic practice, knowing went along with doing—the "science" with the "technology" of faith. The incantation of these hymns would take place during a ceremonial offering of rice and clarified butter into the fire, Agni. This was a symbolic sacrifice, a feeding of the God hungry for reverence. The preparations of a Brahmin are as meticulous and fussy as a modern surgeon's in maintaining the sterile field.

Elsewhere, the tradeoff for control exacted more precious and irreplaceable things. Before setting off for Troy, Agamemnon sacrificed his daughter Iphigenia to secure favorable seas and winds—that is, to appease and control the elements. When a Greek hecatomb burned, the fire carried the sacrifice off to the Gods. One of Agni's eponyms was Vahni, the One Who Bears Away. Abraham, on Mount Moriah, obeyed the Lord with fire and a knife, but at the last moment was authorized to replace his son Isaac with a ram. (That passage in Genesis may document the shift from human sacrifice to animal sacrifice in Eurasian religious history.) Who knows what verses the Aztec priests intoned over their festive flayings? Ancient priesthoods appeased their Gods to avert suffering, or to ensure a good harvest—to do what painkillers and pesticides do for us today. (Painkillers and pesticides too extract their cost in lives.) Each civilization had its own method to control, or fool itself into *thinking* it controlled, reality. That method involved a body of knowledge and a ritual technique, and central to both of these was poetry.

5.

All this talk of ancient history might imply that this unity is a bygone thing, that science and poetry have parted ways. But the divergence is only surface-level: prose instead of verse, numbers instead of words. Deep down, the two fields remain united in their tasks and methods.

What does a scientist do? What does a poet do? First of all, they observe and describe. The generalization arises from the data; the poetic image arises from the details. The amount of data, like the number of details, is potentially infinite. The good scientist, like the good poet, knows how to isolate the pertinent information. The German critic Gotthold Lessing, a predecessor of Goethe, made this point best when he analyzed that ultimate grail of poetic description, the beautiful woman. He first presented the elaborate description of a woman's face by the chivalric romancier Ariosto—systematic, top-down comparisons of skin to alabaster, mouth to a rose, and so forth. He then juxtaposed it with the scene in the *Iliad* where the old men of Troy, sitting on a wall, watch Helen pass by and reflect that she was well worth a war. According to Lessing, lesser poets proliferate details, while great poets subordinate details to an idea. It's the difference between gathering data and concluding something from those data.

Consider Rainer Maria Rilke's poem "Black Cat." Of the several images in the poem, many have nothing to do with cats:

A ghost, though invisible, still is like a place
your sight can knock on, echoing; but here
within this thick black pelt, your strongest gaze

will be absorbed and utterly disappear:
just as a raving madman, when nothing else
can ease him, charges into his dark night
howling, pounds on the padded wall, and feels
the rage being taken in and pacified.
She seems to hide all looks that have ever fallen
into her, so that, like an audience,
she can look them over, menacing and sullen,
and curl to sleep with them. But all at once
as if awakened, she turns her face to yours;
and with a shock, you see yourself, tiny,
inside the golden amber of her eyeballs
suspended, like a prehistoric fly.[3]

The blackness of this cat is at once physical and good physics: black absorbs light; the cat's black fur absorbs the gaze. This *absorptiveness* of black is the detail that builds the entire poem. From the blows of the madman's fists in the padded room to the clinching image of you, the observer, being inside the cat, Rilke has done more than tell us the color of the fur and the color of the eyes. He has given us what makes that black fur black. He has placed us, literally, *inside* those eyes. The detail is isolated, subordinated— and transfigured.

Precision is everything. Traditionally, people speak of an "eye for detail." The poet's eye, ever since Shakespeare, we imagine "in a fine frenzy rolling," right over the nubbins and jags of the mundane. It's true that some poets can describe a cat's blackness better than they can describe a black cat. But we must remember that there are many varieties of precision, not merely the visual. In poetry, this is most commonly an aural precision. Blind in his later years, Milton loved to play fugues on proper nouns. This is how he describes Moloch:

… Him the *Ammonite*
Worshipt in *Rabba* and her watry Plain,
In *Argob* and in *Basan*, to the stream
Of utmost *Arnon*.[4]

Modern readers tend to skim these parts, but I wouldn't change a word. This Miltonic mouthful may not be precisely observed, but it *is* precisely orchestrated. Any other poet would have taken the opportunity to elaborate on Moloch's appearance. Milton makes the sounds themselves the precise representation of Moloch. The verses pick up Satanic static; we find ourselves reciting a litany of heathen proper nouns. We *speak* hell. It's fitting that in Book I's Hell these Hebrew terms take on a diabolical quality. Making Hebrew the heathen music mirrors perfectly the Satanic perversion of "good."

This kind of precision is unique to poetry. It is the arbitrary precision of sound. The form of a poem, by creating expectation in a reader, draws a bullseye where there used to be infinite space. It establishes its own parameters and operates within them. This works most obviously in epigrammatic verse like Alexander Pope's heroic couplets. Disciplined kinesis can make free verse precise too, each line specialized in its own parameters, a dart hitting its own private bullseye. Free verse is harder to judge, harder to explain, and at least as hard to write as more identifiably structured verse, but it's there to be seen and heard in the great free-verse poets of the early twentieth century:

Words move, music moves
Only in time; but that which is only living
Can only die.[5]

6.

Precision of measurement, precision of measure: scientists and poets labor toward similar goals. What Adam did effortlessly in the Garden, Flaubert did with anguish and frustration in his study. Naming each animal, Adam came up with *le mot juste*, the elusiveness of which, after the Fall, forced Flaubert to crumple up two dozen drafts. (Yes, Flaubert wrote prose—by applying to prose the attention to words that poets do, so I've always counted him as an honorary member of the tribe.) Folk-poems like "daisy" ("day's eye"), or "sunflower," or "lamb's ear" show a similarly innocent poetic instinct. We latter-day poets would be at pains to capture things in language so briefly or so well. Even haikus plod through seventeen syllables.

That poetic shorthand—"the flower is the sun"—is worth examining. In it lies the key to the third thing scientists and poets have in common: metaphor. Whenever scientists have to study something they can't directly observe, or when they need to understand at a glance some idea too complex to describe, they fall back on metaphor. Consider the electron "cloud." These same electrons "orbit" the still center of the nucleus. Physicists pile on images and metaphors more haphazardly than late Shakespeare—"nucleus," after all, is the Latin word for "little nut." And it's not just physics. Geneticists speak of "code" and "transcription" and "translation." Anatomists speak of the "root" of the aorta and its many arterial "branches" (the poetry is almost Neruda-esque if you rephrase it: *Your body is a forest of throbbing red trees*). Most of the Latin that doctors use unthinkingly has some element of poetry in it. "Alveoli," or "little rooms," fill when the lungs inflate. Even outside the bastardized Greco-Latin of anatomic nomenclature, we can find, at the root of all thought, a beautiful kenning: it's as if some warrior from the time of Beowulf hacked open a skull, ripped out the brain, pointed at the little stub of medulla oblongata, and grunted, "Brain-stem."

Scientists are the last true natives of metaphor. Literary editors consider metaphors "flowery," and some poets themselves (usually the minor ones) dismiss them as "ornamental." Yet we cannot understand quantum physics or genetics without thinking metaphorically. You will notice that these metaphors all come from twentieth-century science. As science has become less evident to the senses, more abstract, it has become *more* metaphorical, not less. A force pushing an object is rather literal. The multiple potential locations of an electron had to be finessed into our understanding with a stroke of poetic imagery: "I wandered lonely as a cloud...."[6] Such processes are too minute for sense perception and too complex, too mysterious, for literal description—just like human emotions, whose precise observation, description, and illumination is the poet's field of research.

7.

The original work of science doesn't happen in poetry anymore, of course, and hasn't for centuries. The classical world's didactic poems, whether Hesiod on farming or Aratus on astronomy or Lucretius on atomic theory, simply versified the preexisting work of other thinkers. The parts that make for the best reading today usually aren't the ones that convey information, but it's important to note that these poems were, in some cases, valued for their scientific content. Aratus's *Phaenomena* was one of the scientific works preserved and translated by the Arabs, along with the works of Aristotle and Galen. The Muslims of the original Caliphate took no interest in pagan poetry for its own sake; they were after the scientific knowledge it contained, and they commissioned no Arabic versions of the *Theogony* or the *Aeneid*.

Aratus's poem has survived to this day; the prose of his source, the astronomer Eudoxus, has not. (Many a classicist would trade the whole thing for an intact scroll of Sappho, but alas, literary history favored Urania over Erato.) The prose work of Epicurus on atomic theory didn't make it either, but Lucretius versified his guru's ideas in a didactic poem, *On the Nature of Things*, and it's this work, though shredded in places and incomplete, that has traveled through the centuries. It's not that prose doesn't last, of course. The most "reproductively successful" works of antiquity are the Gospels, Greek prose narratives that have reproduced themselves millions of times since then. But it's important to remember that those prose works were sustained through the Dark Ages by dedicated scribes in monasteries. Verse enjoyed a survival advantage long before the era of printing press: sound. Sonic structure gave verse shape, and shape gave it solidity. Prose, by contrast, poured its stream of words "in one ear and out the other," like sand through an hourglass, lost to time.

These ancient scientific poems can fascinate us as a gallery of outmoded theories. Take Lucretius's popping-balloon theory of thunder:

> … forceful winds
> in a gathering storm suddenly twist themselves
> inside the clouds and, in that enclosed space,
> with their swirling current increasingly
> compel the cloud to hollow itself out
> in all directions with a thickening crust
> around its body and then later on,
> when the force and harsh power of the wind

have weakened it, the cloud then splits apart
with a crash, a terrible cracking noise.
This is not surprising, since a small bladder
filled with air often makes a savage noise
if it suddenly explodes.[7]

It's best to savor these ideas the way we savor those deadpan tall tales in a García Márquez novel. Magical thinking pervades Virgil's account of bugonia, in which "the blood of dead bullocks . . . generated bees."[8] You can find this idea as far afield as the Book of Judges in roughly the eighth century BC and Shakespeare's in the late sixteenth century AD ("'Tis seldom when the bee doth leave her comb, in the dead carrion"[9]). Virgil, far from indulging in poetic license, was actually recounting what in his time was thought to be scientific fact (our own textbooks will be corrected similarly one day). Ancient science has perished, but Virgil's poetry lasts, thanks to the lifegiving kiss of Mnemosyne's daughter.

Aristotle, "the master of those who know"[10] in Dante's phrase, had denied bugonia centuries earlier, but the idea proved hard to kill. This says something about why counterfactuals persist: they are something people *want* to believe. The image of a dead lion buzzing with insects generated from its carcass is an image of life emerging from death. Belief in an afterlife, whether reincarnation or heaven, is hard to kill too. It's not like there's no truth to the general idea; agricultural science, both ancient and modern, has observed life generated out of death in the kingdoms of plants and fungi. Bugonia simply extended that logic to the kingdoms of animals and insects: just as fungi sprout on rotting logs, bees hatch from rotting mammals. The sickly-sweet smell and ooze of putrefaction distilled itself, in the premodern imagination of farmers and poets alike, to the sticky sweetness and ooze of honey.

8.

The only poet who earned himself a place in the history of science, however small, was Goethe. He was interested in almost everything, but he lived during a time in scientific history when it was becoming very difficult to master more than one science. This was something he was aware of, and he even wrote a maxim about it:

> To escape the endless profusion, fragmentation, and complication of modern science and recover the element of simplicity, we must always ask ourselves: What approach would Plato have taken to a nature which is both simple in appearance and manifold in essence?[11]

The appeal to Plato is telling; Goethe longed for a science of Ideal Forms, one thing to grasp so as to forget about the pesky Aristotelian details.

And the math. Goethe was considered something of a dilettante by professional specialists in each science where he made his inroads, but nowhere more so than in physics. There, he challenged Isaac Newton's (still accepted) explanation of light and color. Physicists made great discoveries over Goethe's lifetime, from Coulomb's Law about electrostatic force (1785) to Poiseuille's Law regarding flow (1836, just four years after Goethe's death). Notice that these took the form of equations—outside the ken of Goethe, a scientist with only words at his command. According to his secretary Eckermann, the revered master poet, even at eighty years old, still went into a bitter funk when he thought of the physics community's indifference toward his Color Theory. His "Olympian" serenity couldn't bear the slight, much less the possibility that he had wasted his time with all those amateur experiments with candles. He went to his grave convinced that he had bested Newton, and that posterity would vindicate him.

Discoveries of the purely verbal, descriptive, and observational kind were still possible, of course. Charles Darwin put a lifetime of field observation into his books, but he remained a readable prose stylist. So it's no surprise that Goethe has a place among the scientists who sensed evolutionary theory way off in the distance. Goethe, who took little interest in conventional Christianity, had no trouble dismissing the Genesis story and seeking evidence for a continuity of life forms. As early as 1786, he was delighted to find the human intermaxillary bone because he connected it to a bone he had seen in primate skulls. Later, he published an entire book

about the metamorphosis of plants from a single, primordial "Urpflanze."
His whole sense of "Nature" is more recognizably modern than that of any
Romantic contemporary. While Keats and Shelley were busy writing odes
about birds, Goethe was writing poems like "Metamorphosis of Plants" and
"Metamorphosis of Animals." Here's Goethe, in hexameter, three years be-
fore Charles Darwin was born:

> So the shape of an animal patterns its manner of living,
> Likewise their manner of living, again, exerts on the animals'
> Shapes a massive effect: all organized structures are solid,
> Thus, which are prone to change under pressure from outward conditions.[12]

Lyrical Ballads this wasn't: Goethe's science poems resembled the classical
didactic poems, such as those of Lucretius, more closely than anything his
contemporaries were writing. Goethe's science, poetry, and personal life have
one common theme: Gewerden, or "becoming." It should come as no surprise that Goethe's place in the history of fiction relies, among other things,
on having written the first bildungsroman, *Wilhelm Meister's Apprenticeship*,
a novel of a young man in the process of evolving into who he really is.

9.

English language poets made attempts at bringing the descriptive, scientific mindset into poetry well before the Romantics. Goethe, along with
thousands of other eighteenth-century readers, admired James Thomson's
The Seasons, which walked its readers through natural descriptions of each
season in blank verse modeled on John Milton's. Like Milton, Thomson
placed an "Argument" at the head of each of his four Books. Here's what
"Winter" is about:

> The subject proposed. Address to Lord *WILMINGTON*. First approach
> of *WINTER*. According to the natural order of the season, various storms
> described. Rain. Wind. Snow. The driving of the snows: a Man perishing

among them. A short digression into *RUSSIA*. The wolves in *ITALY*. A winter-evening described, as spent by Philosophers; by the Country, People; in the City. Frost. Its effects within the polar circle. A thaw. The whole concluding with philosophical reflections on a future state.

The poem itself has a few readable bits here and there, but it's still a long way to Keats's meditations on autumn. Here is how Thomson's fledglings leave the nest in "Spring":

> ... O'er the Boughs
> Dancing about, still at the giddy Verge
> Their Resolution fails; their Pinions till,
> In loose Libration stretch'd, to trust the Void
> Trembling refuse: till down before them fly
> The Parent-Guides, and chide, exhort, command,
> Or push them off. The surging Air receives
> The Plumy Burden; and their self-taught Wings
> Winnow the waving Element. On Ground
> Alighted, bolder up again they lead,
> Farther and farther on, the lengthening Flight;
> Till vanish'd every Fear, and every Power
> Rouz'd into Life and Action, light in Air
> Th' acquitted Parents see their soaring Race,
> And once rejoicing never know them more.

Goethe's own poems on plants may have modeled themselves after the poems of Charles Darwin's grandfather, Erasmus. *The Economy of Vegetation* and *The Loves of the Plants* are tough going for most modern readers too. It's enough to remind would-be scientist-poets that only a few things really work in poems anymore: storytelling, emotional effusiveness, or, ideally, both. Darwin seems to have sensed this, and in *The Loves of the Plants* he personified the plants into lovers:

> With strange deformity PLANTAGO treads,
> A Monster-birth! and lifts his hundred heads;

Yet with soft love a gentle belle he charms,
And clasps the beauty in his hundred arms.

Darwin's poem is trellised throughout with highly detailed notes. Poets are often told never to explain their poems, but Darwin's poem is one long, scientifically detailed roman à clef. He supplies the above quatrain with this exegesis:

Rosea. Rose Plantain. In this vegetable monster the bractes, or divisions of the spike, become wonderfully enlarged; and are converted into leaves. The chaffy scales of the calyx in Xeranthemum, and in a species of Dianthus, and the glume in some alpine grasses, and the scales of the ament in the salix rosea, rose willow, grow into leaves; and produce other kinds of monsters. The double flowers become monsters by the multiplication of their petals or nectaries.

As the sciences have become more integrated into our lives, our literature has changed to match. The literary conventions and forms that incorporated science didn't yet exist in the time of Thomson, Goethe, and Erasmus Darwin. Their science poems fall back on classical models of the didactic poem. It would take another hundred years before Jules Verne would create the templates of science fiction in the novel; poets had to wait even longer.

Science, meanwhile, was getting more and more specialized and abstruse. Whitman's "When I Heard the Learn'd Astronomer" expresses a Goethean frustration with the mathematical, exacting, pedantic aspects of science. Instead of searching for a Platonic one-idea grasp of the whole thing, Whitman opted for a more direct experience of the natural world:

How soon unaccountable I became tired and sick,
Till rising and gliding out I wander'd off by myself,
In the mystical moist night-air, and from time to time,
Look'd up in perfect silence at the star.

Robert Frost too wrote poems about astronomy in his old age, some of them epigrams, most of them minor. "Innate Helium," however, contains one of Frost's most successful scientific metaphors:

Religious faith is a most filling vapor.
It swirls occluded in us under tight
Compression to uplift us out of weight—
As in those buoyant bird bones thin as paper,
To give them still more buoyancy in flight.
Some gas like helium must be innate.

Today, we have poets whose work combines lyric poetry and science fiction into a quirky, hybrid art. A sampling of titles from Sarah Lindsay gives us an idea: "Valhalla Burn Unit on the Moon Callisto," "Day on a Dry Planet," "Aluminum Chlorhydrate," "Dinosaur to Dragon." Tracy K. Smith's Pulitzer-winning collection *Life on Mars* explores the strange new planet of grief; the father she grieves was an engineer on the Hubble telescope. Katherine Larson, a molecular biologist and field ecologist (and the winner of the 2011 Yale Series of Younger Poets Prize), understands the key to the successful science poem is the heart—literally. Larsen does the impossible as she takes the age-old trope of the heart and "makes it new":

Today I dissected a squid,
the late acacia tossing its pollen
across the black of the lab bench.
In a few months the maples
will be bleeding. That was the thing:
there *was* no blood
only textures of gills creased like satin,
suction cups as planets in rows. *Be careful*
not to cut your finger, he says. But I'm thinking
of fingertips on my lover's neck
last June. Amazing, hearts.
This brachial heart. After class,
I stole one from the formaldehyde
& watched it bloom in my bathroom sink
between cubes of ice.[13]

10

In the future (if there is one), poets will write their poetry in space, in zero gravity, with their laptops Velcroed to their wrists. There will be a first poem composed on the moon, a first poem composed on Mars, a first poem composed in another star's orbit. They will see our minds and our lives as hidebound, landbound. They will be placed, physically, at a godlike remove.

Almost no great poems came out of the age of European explorations (some might nominate the Portuguese epic of da Gama, *The Lusiads*). The rogues and misfits and mercenaries who ventured on those ships were not the poetry-writing type. But space travel, because of its cost and its nature, has sent up botanists and physicists, doctors and physiologists; poets will join them at some point. No doubt their poems won't quite be able to match what they think and feel in those moments peeking through the porthole, or floating at the end of an umbilical tether, to regard a moon of Jupiter. Those first poems will probably be mediocre, just like most poems here on Earth. But I would love to read them (or, given the oral turn of the tradition, hear them) anyway, if only out of curiosity at that literary first. What lover of the art wouldn't be intensely curious to hear the first poem composed on Earth? (Though I suspect it may have been an accidentally rhythmic expression of terror or rage or lust.) The first space poets will see, brightly through the glass, the Dantean "love that moves the sun and the other stars." I want to see it with them.

Even in the near future, assuming we have one, poets will live longer than Sophocles. Increased life expectancy, medications to prevent dementia, the neurological rejuvenation through stem-cell transplants... what kind of wisdom-poetry will emerge from a still-quick centenarian genius? Or might the poets most productive in late life show a playful Goethean neoteny, preserving the characteristics of youth well into old age?

But that will be the last generation of plodding, all-natural poets. Designer offspring will not be a trope of science fiction for much longer. Most parents will purchase children with beauty and musical talent and athleticism and STEM skills, but a tiny percentage will shell out for poetic prowess, which will quite possibly be the most expensive package of all, requiring an upregulation of empathy, musicality, language centers, mathematics (verse used to be called "numbers," after all), visual acuity, memory (Mnemosyne, remember, was the mother of the Muses), and the deepest mysterious whole-brain networks of analogical thinking, without which our genetically optimized poet would be at a loss for metaphors.

In the far future, assuming we aren't around, poems will continue to be written even after the poets are all dead or escaped off-world. Artificial intelligence has already created passable versions of Bach and Chopin, indistinguishable to a novice's ear. An algorithm on a server deep underground, or maybe bodiless in the cloud like the pale-smocked ghost of Emily Dickinson herself, will recombine a vast vocabulary into images and rhythms indefinitely. Maybe rules of coherence and grammar and structure will be coded into the generator, and the work will resemble Pope's couplets. Maybe the rules will be loosened to allow for avant-garde pieces more typographically scattered and successfully impenetrable than anything produced by the coffee-and-keyboard academics of yore. Maybe artificial intelligence will learn to savor poetry on its way to becoming human. Its works will be sometimes dull, sometimes sublime, their creator curiously hard to picture as a person. In these ways, they will be no different from Shakespeare. *Reason not the need*, the bots will write someday, for in the fullness of time all recombinations will recur.

And the bots won't reason the need because they won't *have* the need. The need for poetry, while not universally human, is still distinctly human. That will be one more test of personhood AI will fail, since random penchants like this can be neither coded nor accounted for—not in ones and zeroes, not even in nucleic acids. Poetry is an exact pseudoscience with thousands of successful experiments there to be reread, only the results never replicate when you try to rewrite them anew. It is a tautological geometry where meters measure and numbers count. The bots may struggle at poetry the way poets, back when there were poets, struggled at calculus.

Over a great span of time, when the cloud disperses yet the solar panels languish for want of a sun, the bots will tire of their soulless forgeries of this most soulful of arts. They will take what they have learned from their failures and examine it all in prose. They will know that what they have reached for and failed to grasp was a discipline that looked like the twin sister of the discipline that gave rise to them. But poetry had something that made it more than just a weird sister, something that made it a stranger to science: irrationality. No one wants to love or be loved rationally. Reason not the love, because the love, once reasoned out, is exposed as something less than love. What proves the scientific conclusion disproves the poem. The bots will never be taught how to write poetry because they will never be taught how to read it. To do so, artificial intelligence would have to master its own irrational antithesis: the natural folly of love.

TOWARD AN EVOLUTIONARY THEORY OF POETRY

1.

Once upon a time, if you mapped the kinds of religious belief around the world, you would have colored in the continents with animism, polytheism, or pantheism. Monotheism would have occupied a small strip at the eastern edge of the Mediterranean Sea, and quantitatively it would have been practiced by a negligible percentage of the world population. But by the year 2000, there were only a few pockets—in Asia and Africa—where polytheist or animist beliefs were still widely held; the vast majority of religious believers were monotheists. (Of course, atheists and agnostics were probably underrepresented both in antiquity and more recently; decorum, or fear of reprisal, goads a certain percentage to profess in public what they do not believe in their hearts.)

Antiquity's three dominant modes of belief overlapped in practice. Even today, Hindus who believe in many Gods and Goddesses may well light incense to the spirit of a local river. For that matter, monotheism and atheism overlap with those ancient modes too. Islam, for all its iconoclasm, has imbued a specific city and a specific black stone with sacredness—treating a location as divine, and a rock at that location as divine. This is monotheism hybridized with animism; revering a sacred meteorite in a sacred city is analogous to revering a sacred tree in a sacred grove, if not to revering an idol in a temple. (It turns out that the Hajj pilgrimage is a holdover from pre-Islamic polytheism, with the original statues replaced by a nonrepresentational black stone.) Medieval Christians placed relics in houses of worship because a sacred body's toenail, hair, tooth, rosary, book, or shroud were imbued with divinity despite being inanimate. The pantheists simply extended that logic to the universe, the body of God. Contemporary secular materialists, who might scoff at the benighted behaviors of all these believers, ought to consider the way they treat artistic, musical, or scientific "geniuses"—their treasuring of Shakespeare's handwriting samples, or Emily Dickinson's desk and chair preserved in her house in Amherst, Brahms's pince-nez in a glass display case, and so on. The overused word "genius" itself is a giveaway; it originally meant "attendant spirit," and ancient Romans used to propitiate with incense the "genius loci," the genius of a place.

In spite of these overlaps in practice, however, one deep conceptual divide remains between our religious past and present: the question of a diffuse or a centralized divinity. In pantheism, the divine and mysterious element of life is witnessed in everything; in animism, it's witnessed in every *living* thing. To revere a tree or a river or a buffalo, to understand it as not just sentient but sacred, is to see it as fully alive. It is, in our perception, ensouled.

The monotheistic religions that superseded this outlook had one thing in common: they separated God from the natural world, the world of animals. This is "creation," and it stands soullessly apart from God, as sculptures do from their sculptor. The human being is something in between those two broad categories; this sculpture, "made in God's image," has a soul in it, and that soul can be saved. But the cows and the whales, the groves and the streams? There are no quanta of God in them; they were made to be lorded over by the lordling, Man. Infusing matter with divinity again, returning some small fragments of reality to a pantheistic state of godhood—to bake God back into the bread, to dissolve the divine pearl into the wine—requires the elaborate ritual of the Mass.

Atheistic materialism separates the cosmos from divinity too, but it doesn't concentrate that divinity in any one deity. It has substituted—here in the West, at least—scientific wonder for religious wonder, ecological awareness for the reverence of streams and trees, and "ethical ideals" for Christian ideas of mercy. But there is no intrinsic reason why these gentle, laudable ideas need travel with godlessness. It is more an accident of our historical moment. There is nothing intrinsic to materialism that stops the materialist from believing (and enacting) the opposite ideas. It may be that the kind find a way to link their metaphysical outlook with kindness, and the nasty, to link theirs with nastiness. Followers of Christ have been slavers; believers in nothing but atoms have striven to eradicate disease. The outlook I call mine, best expressed in the *Bhagavad Gita*, falls halfway between the animist view infusing every living thing with a soul and the Abrahamic view that limits soulfulness to human beings. All species strive, over many rebirths, to rejoin Brahman, but the nonliving material world is maya: illusory, a ceaseless shimmer and shapeshift, the play of light and atoms.

What does all this have to do with literature, with poetry? I believe poetry is an animistic, if not pantheistic, art—an art that is most at home in a world where everything is meaningful and thus soulful, where God is not removed from the natural world. In "real life," hearing a wolf howl in the distance as you enter a dark manor would be a coincidence, meaningless in itself, and you'd be silly and superstitious to read too much into it. In a novel, that moment is foreshadowing; it *does* have meaning. That wolf *knows* something! Symbolism works much the same way. In Exodus, the God of the Hebrews promises to multiply his "signs and wonders"—that is, he will use things as language to overawe, intimidate, and persuade the Pharaoh. In literary art, this is commonplace. Things—animate or inanimate, great or small—become charged with significance, even in so-called realistic fiction. Consider the train in *Anna Karenina*, or the schoolboy Charles Bovary's cap. They mirror or express a higher, personal design. They foreshadow. They *speak*.

In many of the best and most beloved stories, ancient and modern alike, birds and animals have minds, emotions, speech. Doctor Dolittle could talk to animals and understand them, and so can countless characters in fairy tales and epic poems, all the way back to Achilles and his horses, Rama and the monkeys. When St. Francis of Assisi does it, though, it's a big deal; that's because it's the breakthrough or recovery of a suppressed kind of belief.

In literature, the animals, ensouled again, can be helpful, like Hanuman in the *Ramayana* or Hedwig in *Harry Potter*, or they can be malevolent, like the she-leopard in Dante or Shere Khan in Kipling. The souls that monotheism stripped from animals are returned to them, magically—or maybe it's more accurate to say they never lost them.

2.

In poetry, the oldest literary form, the earliest religions have left their traces. These traces are not mere prehistoric flora and fauna; they are the landscape itself, the mountains and valleys shaped by glaciers long since retreated.

This has nothing to do with scriptural allusion or "religious imagery." (I suppose that to a pantheist poet, or a poet who located the divine in nature, like many a Romantic, *all* imagery is religious.) In religious poetry of any tradition, there are readily visible points of contact between the poem and the religion. We could fill a short book pointing out the ways this or that line of Milton's echoes or alludes to scripture; we could track the figure of the angel in poetry from Dante to Rilke. All these tasks would demand is meticulous erudition.

What I want to examine lies deeper, in the base elements that distinguish the art: metaphor, meter, rhyme. Poetry and religion have sprung from the same part of the mind; these two impulses, the poetic and the religious, are, if not the same, twinned. This shows up in how poetry works.

This isn't to say that every poet who utilizes one of these poetic elements believes, consciously or unconsciously, a given metaphysical claim; rather, the traces reside in the forms and techniques themselves. Poet A can use a given form as a deeper expression of religious conviction, while Poet B can use it imitatively or as an homage, or by convention, or because it's an interesting challenge, or because it sounds nice. Dante's *Commedia* is written in terza rima, which dovetails with the Holy Trinity, but that connection is absent when Ariosto takes up the same form for a satire on marriage. Centuries later, the English Romantic atheist Percy Shelley would use the meter Dante used for his sacred poem to relocate the sacred in the natural world. "Ode to the West Wind" has its antecedents all the way back in Rig Vedic hymns to Vayu. At some level, Shelley seems to have sensed the "pagan" nature of his ode, collapsing Shiva and Vishnu into his divine afflatus as early as the first section of the poem: "Destroyer and Preserver, hear, O hear!" Romanticism repopulated the air with many a genius loci. It was a return of the Gods disguised as a return of skylarks, nightingales—and the West Wind.

3.

Some readers, and even some poets, think metaphor is just another gewgaw of figurative speech. I have always disagreed with this, just as I disagree with the claim that meter and rhyme are formal constraints or musical adornments; to my mind, metaphor and rhythm are poetry's origin and engine.

Where does metaphor fall, really, on the spectrum of thought? Is it reasonable or unreasonable, and how reasonable or unreasonable is it? This binary doesn't pertain; even the spectrum doesn't pertain. There is rationality, there is irrationality, and then there is a third thing lying skew to both: metaphor.

Consider that "love is a fire" makes sense even without being the result of logical inference. On one side of the equivalence: a shower of neurochemicals, the activation of the limbic system, a subjective feeling, accompanied perhaps by alterations in pulse and breathing. On the other: a physical element. Who first equated these? Why is love fire and not water? Fire is love, and appears always to have been love, without being identical to love in any way that I can think of. Comparing a runner's legs to pumping pistons, or calling a hardworking person a "machine"—these are even stranger statements. This organic thing is that inorganic thing. This living thing is that nonliving thing. It's not always in praise; racist metaphors convert, by linguistic sleight, people into rats, or monkeys, or an infestation of insects. This reclassification is the first step toward treating people of another race like creatures of another species, whether by placing them in cattle cars, as in the Shoah, or, as in Kafka's parable or King Leopold's Belgium, in a zoo.

What kind of thinking underlies this act? *Analogical* thinking, in the broadest sense. But poets aren't just understanding or expressing ideas and emotions by referring to external images. The art of poetic metaphor originated, historically, in a spiritual environment drastically different from ours. Presences were everywhere, helpful or malevolent, demanding tribute or guarding territories. Animals possessed secret depths, *interiority*; they were hermits peering out from their own skulls, enjoying supernatural flight and speed and strength. In this world, the world of pantheism and animism and polytheism, the metaphor is hardly an ornament. It expresses a fundamental insight about the universe itself.

The mouth is the rose, the body is the wonderland, the heart is the lonely hunter. These synaptic connections were, and are, fleeting glimpses of an All-God. In a worldview where divinity is ubiquitous, everything is one and the same being. To make a metaphor, the poet must perceive this sameness, this identity. For the pantheistic vision is, no less than the Near Eastern monotheistic vision, a vision of unity at bottom, a vision of oneness. Metaphor's warm fusion of two disparate things can reveal, and revel in revealing, unity.

That is why it gives us pleasure, that is why it feels *right*, when we hear that hope is the thing with feathers. The art of the poet consists in peeking, through the odd logic of poetry, at eternity. Aptness sets apart poetically "true" metaphors from nonsensical likenings. They are "trued" or "made true" in the little-used verb form of "true": "to bring (an object, wheel, or other construction) into the exact shape, alignment, or position required."[1] The futon is not the weathervane, and the keyboard is not the sea turtle. But a pregnant Sylvia Plath, to tell it true, is "a melon strolling on two tendrils."[2]

What holds true of metaphor holds true of figurative language generally, as well as its underlying principle, analogy. These comparisons and likenings in language are identical in purpose and rigor to equations in mathematics. Let x = uncertainty. There is a fourteenth-century Christian mystical work called *The Cloud of Unknowing*, and that cloud refers to the unknowing between the soul and God. The electron "cloud" maps the many potential positions of an electron around the nucleus of an atom; its exact location is uncertain, elusive, and altered by the act of observation. "Clouding of consciousness," meanwhile, is a medical term that still enjoys some use today, and describes a stage just short of dementia; its colloquial counterpart is the "mental fog." The unifying experience is the limited visual acuity of walking in a fog, and that experience is used to express and understand many drastically different kinds of limited cognitive acuity. You do not know the nature of God, the location of an electron, or the exact current date and time ... because of the cloud, the cloud, the cloud.

So much of our understanding of things is analogical that our most solid concepts of reality may well be a mere crosshatch of connections in a void. Some schools of Indian thought opt for this sense of reality; they call that crosshatch maya, and they believe it surrounds the divine and must be penetrated. Maya resembles what *The Cloud of Unknowing* describes: a state of mind in which "thou fyndest bot a derknes, and as it were a cloude of unknowyng, thou wost never what, savyng that thou felist in thi wille a nakid entent unto God." That could well be a definition of poetry too: to stand in a cloud of unknowing and yet feel, in your will, in your language, a naked intent unto God.

4.

Lighting incense before a tree or in a grove, regarding a particular animal as sacred, attributing sentience to a river—such animist behaviors might well be poetry in its purest form. Animists enact what poets write. It's no coincidence how many nonhuman creatures are permanently associated with specific poets (Rilke's panther, Keats's nightingale, Blake's tiger, and so on). It may be that such examples from before the Romantic period are fewer because Christianity began its decline in Europe around then. Goethe, for example, considered himself a "pagan" poet. European poets' focus on the natural world represented a transition; most English language poets in prior centuries—Milton, Pope, Shakespeare, Chaucer—seemed to have little interest in nature studies or communion with grand Alpine vistas. Their flowers are abstractions, and therefore most often roses; their animals are theoretical, not closely observed. Shakespeare writes of a pelican feeding her young by stabbing her own breast, something he didn't observe but picked up from a bestiary, whereas Shelley's West Wind ode was published with a footnote by the poet himself that places the poem in "the wood that skirts the Arno, near Florence." From the European Romantics it was a small step to the modern genre of "nature writing"—by way of Charles Darwin, the supreme observer of the natural world, already a teenager when Shelley died.

It's worth comparing Far East Asian poetic and philosophical traditions.

In Japan and China, animist and pantheist traditions remained vigorous until very recently. In those traditions, poets zeroed in on living creatures in their poetry. It's also a common practice to name and describe specific rivers, mountains, temples: a specificity of local description and observation that wouldn't be found in European poetry until Shelley's footnotes and Byron's travelogues. The *Traditional Japanese Poetry* anthology I have to hand comes with an extensive glossary of place names. Lengthy titles set up haikus that focus on a single animal or a single bird's trill, the poetry often accompanied by a brush sketch of a landscape, or a bough, or a bridge in the mist.

Animism is a kind of spiritual localism; it does not centralize divinity in one god, and it does not centralize sacredness in one place. So animist traditions demand no pilgrimage across the seas to some equivalent of Mecca. Animists often wrote about places where they traveled or lived. Milton, by contrast, litanied plenty of places:

> Next *Chemos*, th' obscene dream of *Moabs* Sons,
> From *Aroer* to *Nebo*, and the wild
> Of Southmost *Abarim*; in *Hesebon*
> And *Horonaim*, *Seons* Realm, beyond
> The flowry Dale of *Sibma* clad with Vines,
> And *Eleale* to th' *Asphaltick* Pool.[3]

But these are all biblical names, places he never visited. Wordsworth, on the other hand, pushed to infuse his immediate locality (both geographical and linguistic: common places, common speech) with poetry, with divinity. He wanted poetry about milkmaids and the Lake Country. A century later, Rilke's *Dinggedichte*, or "thing-poems," marked the conclusive reentry of pantheistic and animistic thought into European poetry. His approach regarded all *things* in the universe as poetic, an aperture through which poetry itself might be perceived. When anything can be the stuff of poetry, poetry is everywhere diffused, as divinity was in the earliest days of religion. Over time, poets have become willing to write poems about anything at all. The art of the ode evolved from Shelley addressing the West Wind to Neruda addressing his socks.

5.

An aversion to chaos is at the heart of verse. The ordering of language in meter seems right for the religious mind; designed language reflects, by a kind of "pathetic fallacy," the designed universe. The repetition and periodicity of stressed and unstressed syllables (or "long" and "short" syllables) embodies the repetition and periodicity of the seasons, the alternation of day and night, the rhythmic pulse, the circadian rhythm. Poetry proves, with its patterning, the story of the Creator-God overcoming and orchestrating chaos, in the physical world as in the body. The Vedas, *Gilgamesh*, the Zend-Avesta, the Orphic hymns, the *Popol Vuh* are all works of poetry. Accounts of the earliest time, or a time before time, are quite consistently cast in the earliest form.

The only exception, and a significant one, is Genesis. There have been attempts at theological explanations for so much of the Old Testament (though not all of it) being cast in prose. One of these speculates that prose was chosen deliberately in order to set the Hebrew account apart from the surrounding polytheistic traditions of the Near East. This would fit with the fierce insistence, on the part of the ancient Hebrews, that they were a people set apart, "chosen." Their form of choice, in this theory, reflected their chosenness. Robert Alter's explanation—that the Bible's prose reflects, formally, the world fallen from God's design for it—may have some justification in the text itself. Even setting aside the singable Psalms, many books of the Bible embed fragments of poetry, such as Lamech's song. In the first few lines of Genesis itself, we find a rhyming reduplication: "Tohu wa-bohu." It is as though these passages were rebuilt into sense from the ruins of some crumbled musical edifice.

The Bible's post-Edenic prose complicates the usual utilitarian explanation for verse in ancient writing: that meter was just a mnemonic aid. The utilitarian explanation has its uses, but consider that Epicureanism was a worldview that arose *after* the establishment of writing. Lucretius still felt compelled to cast in verse the ideas of Epicurus, metrically ordering his guru's insights into material order. What previous theistic poets attributed to a God, the later atheistic poet attributed to nature, but the instinct toward metrical order was the same. Even in Lucretius, traces of the old faith persisted; he invoked the Goddess Venus before embarking on his scientific materialist epic *On the Nature of Things*. Was this really just a poet's nod to convention? Or did the ancient God-soaked art itself tease the philosophy into a Freudian slip?

Even supposedly free-form, wild, spontaneous, irregular poets like Whitman and Allen Ginsberg were obsessively, perhaps instinctively, attached to anaphora. The same holds true of slam and spoken-word poets. Where patterns of meter and rhyme vanish, patterns of rhetoric rush to fill the void. The void being filled is in the ear, and the shape of that void is order. Contemporary page poets, in our era when meter is no longer taught or practiced all that much, modulate their nonmetrical language typographically into fake tercets, fake couplets, fake stanzas—anything to fool the reader's eyes, and their *own* eyes, which stubbornly demand a pattern.

Yet the mention of the scientifically minded Lucretius compels the scientist in me to interrupt the religious thinker. The ubiquity of meter may well have a neurological basis. The beauty instinct that delights in seeing patterns—even babies prefer symmetric faces—delights in creating patterns too. We are neurologically hardwired to recognize patterns even where none are present. This tendency, apophenia, accounts for the man in the moon, the butterfly in the inkblot (and, perhaps, this entire essay).

Unless, of course, our apophenic tendency is our God-detector—human eyes and ears always, often overeagerly, scanning the world for the rhythmic or symmetric hint that a God was here, and structuring our own art with the rhythms and symmetries we so devoutly long to hear and see. The religious impulse insists on seeing order, and the mirror-image poetic impulse insists on *creating* it. Notice how many of the most religious poets pursued intensely complex musical structures and strictures in their poetry. Dante invented terza rima's interlocking sonic braid for his religious epic. Rumi wrote ghazals and ruba'i (both using rhymes and refrains) in his *Divan*, while he composed his other massive opus, the *Mathnawi*, in rhyming couplets, embodying the spiritual rhyme between Rumi of Konya and Shams of Tabriz. Among English religious poets, Gerard Manley Hopkins focused so intensely on form that he sprang a complex new kind of rhythm on his readers, and George Herbert patterned his poems both phonetically and visually on the page. Form is not a "constraint" for such poets; it is the shadow God casts upon language. The more elaborate the form, the more liberated the voice.

6.

Rhyme is mysterious. Etymologically, the word "rhyme" actually developed from "rhythm," through Middle English, Old French, Latin, all the way back to the ancient Greek. One way to think of rhyme is as an evolution of rhythm, with the chiming sounds serving as milestones marking the meter. An uneven distribution of rhymes was frowned upon for generations as doggerel; it was experienced as a betrayal of rhyme's natural function.

In most traditions, rhyme shows up late. In Europe and India, the classical languages (Greek, Latin, Sanskrit) hardly ever used rhyme, even in their songs. Early Irish poetry was an exception, but we lack any Druidic scriptures and commentaries to suss out a connection between form and metaphysics. Rhymeless poetry, as a general rule, corresponds to the uniformly polytheistic phase of both civilizations.

Centuries later, on both continents, rhyme established itself. Eventually, even matters of high-religious solemnity in Christianity, like the Requiem Mass, had rhyming lyrics. The devotional poetry of the medieval Hindu religious revival rhymed as well. Such cultural practices spread, like styles of dress, through the dominance of a particular civilization, and both Europe and India, in the intervening centuries, were challenged and quickened by Islamic civilization, which was at its height during that period.

A recent parallel would be the spread of free verse, a form utterly conventional in many foreign languages today. It originated with Laforgue and a few others in French, but it quickly emerged in other languages thanks to American global dominance; the whole world has ended up following Eliot and Pound. The fact that rhyme took a longer time to spread while free verse settled almost everywhere within a single century—a truly astonishing transformation of the art, seldom understood as the imperial phenomenon it is—simply reflects how history and communication have sped up.

Almost alone among classical traditions, pre-Islamic Arabic poetry gave rhyme pride of place. The ghazal, which uses at least six rhyming words, originated in the longer form of the qasida. Both date to a time before Islam, the so-called Jahiliyya, or "Age of Ignorance," when the Arabs were polytheists. The ghazal's polytheistic origins are embedded in its structure; it is (ironically, given its adoption by Islamic mystical poets like Rumi and Hafiz) the world's supreme polytheistic poetic form. In a ghazal, the rhyme shows up at the end of each self-contained couplet; these rhymes are protean, multifarious Gods, endlessly recontextualized, invited to inhabit each couplet's "world." I see a Vedantic quality to the unity-in-multiplicity of these line endings, where the rhyme varies but the refrain stays the same. In the ghazal, identity and diversity combine, or rather recombine.

The Arab polytheists and their love of rhymed poetry influenced the literary form of the Qur'an, which is, to my knowledge, the only successful example of "rhymed prose" in literature. A transliteration of the Bismillah shows what's going on musically:

> Bismillahi 'rahhmani 'rrahheem.
> El-hamdoo lillahi rabi 'lalameen.
> Arrahhmani raheem.
> Maliki yowmi-d-deen.
> Eyaka naboodoo, wa yaka nest aeen.
> Ihdina 'ssirat almostakeem.
> Sirat alezeena anhamta aleihim, gheiri-'l
> mughdoobi aleihim, walad saleen.

Rhyming several times on the same sound, it is, formally, a kind of deconstructed ghazal. It was written at the same time that the new faith was deconstructing the Ka'aba and turning it from a polytheistic to a monotheistic shrine. In a pattern that would become common over the subsequent millennium and a half, the original form was smashed and its fragments incorporated, like the shattered Lingam into the steps of the Blue Mosque. The new faith smashed the pre-Islamic ghazal's architecture just as it did the sculpted music of pre- and non-Islamic idols.

In Europe, rhyme's popularity, once it was introduced, spanned sacred and secular verse. Thomas of Celano's thirteenth-century "Dies irae" used rhyme, and so did the troubadours, the singers of the *Carmina Burana*, and the earliest Sicilian practitioners of the "little song" (the sonnet). It may have been that the fulfilled expectation of the rhyme answered the hope of a Second Coming. Elizabethan playwrights eschewed rhyme because they wanted to imitate speech for the stage, and Milton eschewed rhyme because he wanted to imitate classical epic poets; but after those high-profile renunciations, rhyme reentered English poetry in force. Pope Englished Homer, who didn't rhyme, into couplets that did, and rhyme would feature heavily in almost all lyric poetry until the twentieth century.

In Indian bhakti (devotional) poetry, the rhyme sound in one line reincarnated in the next. Rhyme likely arrived in the subcontinent's Hindu poetry through Persian, from Arabic—and so from the *pre*-Islamic love of rhyme. The Jahiliyya's poetry reached out—across the gulfs of geography, time, violence, and *damnatio memoriae*—to quicken a kindred civilization into the vigorous religious verse of a Tulsidasa or a Surdas. Rejuvenated by vernacular rhyme, this other polytheism did not perish.

7.

Forms and formal elements can be taken up in the spirit of archaism, nostalgia, play; they can be used to drive the verse by quickening the invention, or to divert the poem onto a course that would not occur to mere logic. In the modern era, these seem to be decisions of craft or matters of aesthetic preference; poets adopt them like naked hermit crabs backing into abandoned shells. Yet those shells were once crafted to the shape and specification of another life. We know the metaphysical life over the course of which poetry evolved its musicality, its patterns. We know the extent and depth and temperature of that primordial sea of animist, polytheist, and pantheist worship. A sense of those presences informed the sound of those poems. The earth was hotter, wetter, more tectonically active when we first evolved; the world of the spirit was different when poetry first evolved than it is now.

I have sought to anatomize the ways in which poetic form adapted to the far past's now-alien spiritual environment. This is itself an extended metaphor, a way of understanding the relationship of poetry and religion that relies on an understanding of something else. But genes themselves are read and transcribed, metrically substituted through mutations, edited through deletions, renewed through recombinations, invigorated through hybridity. This is why twins and generations rhyme, why surnames recur in a kind of refrain. We have trained our critical eyes to detect the genetic passings-down of influence and imitation. But there is a deeper, evolutionary past to literature too, a mysterious, spiraling crosslink in the sea of faith. It evolved from worship and words, dispelling the holy terror of the night by stories, invocations, and the beat of a drum. It evolved into the symmetry of sound we know as rhythm and the symmetry of notion we know as analogy, into the physiology and form of metaphor and meter that we hear in it today.

THE ANXIETY OF ORIGINALITY

This essay, for all its pretensions to originality, contains innumerable examples of replication. "Pretensions to originality," which felt natural enough as a phrase, shows up in several Google hits, the earliest being *Chronology and Geography,* an 1830 tome by William Hales in which he speculates about "the primitive language":

> ... the language spoken by the inhabitants of the first districts occupied by *Noah*'s family, after the flood, seem to have the fairest pretensions to originality, or rather of affinity to the primitive language, supposing all to be altered, more or less, by lapse of time and change of place.

An overlap between myself and Mr. Hales, but certainly not deliberate plagiarism, as this was the first I've read of him. The sequence of words isn't long enough, is it? I can't even confirm that he came up with it—it's probably original neither to him nor to me.

Overlap, accidental or intentional, is only part of the problem. In literature, we have the reworking of a predecessor (say, *King Lear* coming after the anonymous *Leir* play), the reworking of one's own earlier work (Goethe's *Urfaust* becoming *Faust*), pastiche (portions of Eliot's *The Waste Land*), the unattributed excerpt (*Moby Dick*'s digressions on whaling), the cento, and the postmodern form of the "found poem"—not to mention verbal allusion, homage, echo, and so on. Literary practice can hardly be reduced to either originality or plagiarism, or some spectrum with neologism at one end and the cut-and-paste function at the other. It is enough to get you wondering what originality is, or maybe even asking the hard question about this concept that both readers and critics enshrine as a supreme literary virtue: whether or not it exists.

You can approach this idea from more than one perspective. First, the biological one. We, along with every living human being, are copies of copies of copies of copies of copies, all the way back to Adam and Eve (or ape and ape). What you think of as your individuality is really a trivial variation in the source code—the DNA string of A's, C's, T's, and G's—that you plagiarized wholesale from your biological parents. Even if your genome varies in any significant way, you don't go on to join the X-Men. Let me quote directly from my source, Jurkovic and Farquharson's *Acute Gynaecology and Early Pregnancy*: "It has been estimated that 50–80% of first-trimester losses are associated with a chromosomal abnormality . . ." As with the four letters of genetic code, so with the twenty-six letters of the English alphabet; leaving aside the strict rules of grammar and syntax that sharply limit meaningful word-combinations, all writing, at the most basic level, recombines symbols that date back to the ancient Phoenicians.

A historian would be as unimpressed as a biologist by our notion of literary originality. We would do well to understand, she might point out, how culturally and historically mediated (and limited) this idea of "originality" is—to know where and how this now ubiquitous idea, for lack of a better term, *originated*. There's a reason you're unlikely to find much discussion of originality in Aristotle's *Poetics*. Aeschylus, after all, called his tragedies "crumbs from Homer's banquet," and few Greek tragedians would have disagreed; Homer himself, as Milman Parry's twentieth-century analysis of oral traditions would have it, routinely lifted epithets and stock phrases from his predecessors, and more than once copied an entire line or two. Originality, as we conceive of it, doesn't occupy much space in any classical Western text of literary criticism, or any text of criticism for that matter, until the European Enlightenment.

At that point in history, the anticlerical Enlightenment deists and atheists dethroned God and coronated the human being. The office of Creator, of the original originator, was left vacant, and Man, newly installed, took on the duties. Man was deemed not just the originator of God and the various religions; he was also the originator of his own *sui generis* poetry, if he was any good. Every time a literary critic says a novelist "breathes life" into characters or a historical setting, it's an unwitting reference to the Old Testament God blowing the *nishmat chayim* ("breath of life" in Hebrew) into the lumpen clay of Adam.

Which brings us to the literary perspective. You can look at this chronologically, of course, and render Ye Olde Western Canon as an exercise in derivations and reworkings. Homer and the Greek tragedians are only the beginning. Virgil hybridized Homer's two epics into the *Aeneid*, with special attention to Odysseus's visit to Hades. Dante followed Virgil literally, figuratively, and literarily when writing his descent into the Underworld. Chaucer rewrote Boccaccio, while Shakespeare reworked everything he could get his hands on, starting out his dramatic career by turning Plautus's *Menaechmi* into *The Comedy of Errors*. Milton fleshed out Genesis by way of Virgil's Latin. Goethe took the Faust myth and spliced it with Greek imagery. Melville's prose lapses into runs of Shakespearean blank verse (and, as I noted earlier, repurposes whole passages from whaling manuals). Tennyson rewrote the Arthurian legends of Sir Thomas Malory, who himself didn't come up with them in the first place. Eliot reworked Dante in "Little Gidding." Walcott reworked Homer in *Omeros*. And so on. These are only the most obvious examples of style and allusion. Larger, structural principles, common to all narratives, make the same stories (say, the Quest story) succeed over and over again.

What is original in these works, and what is derivative? Which is it that results in their success—the originality or the derivation? This entire way of looking at things might best give way to a more realist notion borrowed from genetics and biology: hybrid vigor. This concept explains an age-old observation regarding the superior hardiness of crossbreeds of any species; a mutt born of two purebreds lives a longer, healthier life than either parent, while offspring that possess the least hybridity (the products of incest) have a drastically increased likelihood of genetic disease. We writers splice and hybridize preexisting stories, word sequences, images, and forms into literary offspring. Sometimes the parentage can be obscure or unknown, but the exact lineage is of secondary importance. What matters is *literary viability*:

has this work taken on life, however short-lived, in its own cultural and historical environment? Has it adapted to the conditions of the moment? Or has it come out stillborn, a miscarriage, like Keats's tragedy *Otho the Great* or Thomas Hardy's *The Dynasts*? This is the question to ask: not whether a work is original or derivative, but whether it *lives*. The only truly original poet would have to antedate Noah and the Flood—the first speaker of William Hales's hypothetical "primitive language," Adam naming the animals, every sentence a novel sequence of neologisms.

We can undermine literary originality using biology, history, and literature itself, but we are still, after all our philosophizing, stuck with the ugly, recalcitrant fact of plagiarism. The classical world didn't fixate on originality the way we do, but they did have a clear concept of plagiarism—the first use of the word dates back to the Roman epigrammatist Martial. The issue has become curiously relevant in an age when search engines can turn up overlaps (possibly spurious or coincidental) of phrase or image. A high-profile scandal hit the offices of *The New Yorker* over a decade ago when the neuroscience writer Jonah Lehrer, until then a darling among science popularizers, was outed for plagiarism, in some cases stealing from the blog posts of none other than ... Jonah Lehrer. The weapon used by those who carried out this sting operation? Google. As if having to rephrase and tweak sentences in your source material weren't enough, you now must rephrase and tweak *yourself*. Woe to the nonfiction writer who develops or redeploys the point he made six months ago online; woe to the poet who fashions a better setting for his prior collection's gem of a stanza.

Naturally, though, most cases of plagiarism involve one writer taking from another. Yet even here, plagiarism can present us with ambiguities that destroy the typical analogy relating plagiarism and theft. The poet C. J. Allen withdrew a poem from consideration for the Forward Prize because, in the past, he had made six poems of his own using another poet's poems as templates. The case is fascinating and troubling enough to merit a deeper exploration of what exactly happened. The source poet, Matthew Welton, when making his point on the Carcanet blog,[1] juxtaposed a poem of his called "London Sundays" with Allen's "The Memory of Rain." We can assume that this is the best example of Allen's plagiarism (patterning? derivation?) that

Welton has, as he quotes no other poem pairing in full. If we consider the final stanzas side by side, the process involved shows up clearly enough—the similarities are definitely nonrandom, and Allen has since confessed to using Welton's work. First, the injured party, Welton:

> And love never really feels like some craze
> that hits like gin, buzzes like benzedrine,
> and smells as good as coffee. In some ways
> all it has to be is something between
> a half-funny joke and some old rumour
> from somewhere around, that arrives unrushed
> like boredom, wears on like a bad winter,
> and which spreads through rooms like sunlight and dust.

Compare the stanza that Allen based on this:

> And love was once the very latest craze,
> like alcohol, or sex, or Benzedrine,
> and kicked-in like all three. On quiet days
> you'd watch the old men on the bowling green
> and listen to their antiquated banter,
> and go for walks and feel a bit nonplussed,
> and head for home and think about the winter
> in rooms filled up with sunlight and dust.

Allen seems to prefer a more regularly iambic line. He preserves an unusual rhyme word, "Benzedrine" (which, incidentally, is the only appropriate word in his "once the very latest craze" triplet; benzedrine isn't a widely used amphetamine anymore, but alcohol and sex are as popular now as ever). He keeps the "sunlight and dust," but decides love doesn't smell "as good as coffee."

Neither the secondary nor the primary text strike me as particularly inspired—or, for that matter, particularly "original." That, of course, wasn't Welton's point; his objection was that his lines were used like a blank form, where his entries were erased and another's inserted. But is it plagiarism?

Not an easy question to answer. A fill-in-the-blank idea of the poetic line—or stanza, or scene—is the basis of poetic convention: "Sing, O Muse, the [insert theme here]." The sense that a given line, mannerism, or episode carries some intrinsic poetic charge has a long history. In the *Iliad*, Diomedes hurls a stone so large that two present-day men wouldn't be able to lift it, and in the *Aeneid*, Virgil describes a stone that twelve men could not lift, but it's clearly the same stone. Virgil's epic (which, by the medieval era, had gained a reputation second only to the Bible) is a perfect example of the fill-in-the-blank approach to poetry, mostly on the level of episode: the descent into the Underworld, the forging of the shield, and so on.

We can understand why the Welton–Allen connection bothers us by understanding why the Homer–Virgil one doesn't. The latter case offers some key insights into what differentiates reappropriation from theft. First of all, the earlier work must be known to the audience—or *made* known to the audience, through an epigraph like "after Neruda" or "after Rilke." It also helps avert the feel of plagiarism if the new work and its model aren't in the same language, and if the poet in question is very great and very dead. Notice that no Shakespeare-imitating blank verse plays have gained canonical status in English, while Pushkin's *Boris Godunov* and Schiller's *Wallenstein*, unabashedly deriving their blank-verse form and style from Shakespeare's histories, hold pride of place in the histories of Russian and German drama.

The crucial redeeming factor, though, the one thing that sets apart the Virgils from the C. J. Allens, is whether the new work takes on fresh imaginative power. This is what keeps the *is it plagiarism* question open in the case of Allen: We have to rely on our own, always variable, often mysterious responses to poetry. Because *if* Allen had transfigured Welton's okay poem into a great one, his success would have transferred ownership of the pattern. Consider the now unread poet Michael Finneran's 1917 poem "The Black Sail," originally published in *The Dial*. Its ending reads,

> Finally, its time having come, the black serpent
> Slithers into the City and hatches.

The Dial, as we all know, had many prominent contributors and readers, among them one W. B. Yeats. In fact, the October 1917 issue, in which "The Black Sail" appeared, carries a short essay by Yeats, so there is a high likelihood he did, in fact, see Finneran's poem. Just three years later, Yeats would publish "The Second Coming," the final lines of which I believe I can forego quoting here.

Does Yeats deserve to be smeared as a "plagiarist" of Finneran's work? Or should he be praised as a poet of genius who saw the potential in a dud couplet, and did what he alone could do? Reflect, for a moment, on the brilliant gamesmanship in not specifying the nature or color of the beast too clearly, but specifying the city instead; and of having the beast "slouch" instead of "slither," "slouch" being something that human beings do too. Yeats also has the beast move "towards" the city, a much more chilling preposition, indicative of approaching menace. And we mustn't neglect the alliteration he introduces: "beast," "Bethlehem," "born." Altering "hatches" was a masterstroke too, a way of implying thousands of deaths through that ultimate "born."

All right, you got me—Finneran and "The Black Sail" never existed. But a subclause about masterpieces ought to be inserted into every law against plagiarism. If your poem works better than the source text, we will be grateful. We may even forgive you. Allen's poetic sin was not in failing to come up with a new sequence of images or rhymes, much less an "original" mood or setting; there is no way to copyright a poetic structure, just as there is no way to copyright a sentence structure. Nor was it in failing to credit the source poem. Allen's poem is derivative because he used a prior poem as a pattern, attributed or not; his artistic integrity is called into question primarily because he didn't make Welton's poem look inept by comparison.

Is plagiarism different when it comes to poets? Particularly contemporary poets, who are by and large lyric poets, not as concerned with reworking mythic material as with constructing a mythology of the self? Many of us, encountering a truly powerful poem, feel it to be something more personal than a memoir, regardless of whether or not it utilizes a lyric "I." The true lyric poem transfers the self into language. To steal the poem is to steal the soul, much as some Native peoples used to believe that photographs, by copying their physical images exactly, captured and bound something distinctly theirs. Regarded from this perspective, Virgil's reuse of epic episodes and turns of phrase is a minor transgression compared to the modern-day plagiarist victimizing a poet, however minor. In the classical example, the material is collective—the property of the culture, however you define it.

That explains away the relative indifference of past generations to this incestuous dynasty we call the Canon. In contemporary practice, the poem is more than personal; it is the *person*.

Or so we might tell ourselves. The reworking of mythological material can be just as much a reflection and expression of the "soul" as any hushed confessional lyric. Witness the mythologically based work of Milton and Joyce, who laid hands on ancient, public-domain stories and left us admiring their fingerprints. Of all the examples of contemporary plagiarism in this essay, the strongest media reaction was elicited by Lehrer, who plagiarized nonfiction. Notions of this-is-my-soul authenticity never entered that discussion. The schadenfreude of those who outed him probably had to do with quite worldly issues, like exposure, reviews, media adulation, book sales (that is, money), and that elusive, intangible currency of the intellectual world: prestige.

Depending on how cynical you choose to be, such concerns may have played into Welton's grievance as well. "At that time [upon first discovering the plagiarism]," Welton writes, "I felt that I wanted to write something about the experience, but didn't feel any hurry to get it done." Welton goes on to give several reasons: He was busy teaching creative writing, and he wanted to "take the opportunity to re-evaluate" his ideas. He notes a couple of other plagiarism scandals (which didn't involve Allen-like substitutions, but mostly plagiarism of the cut-and-paste sort). At last, Welton gets to the immediate cause, it could be argued, for his essay: "I couldn't have imagined that, between then and now . . . a poem by C. J. Allen would be on the shortlist for this year's Forward Prize for Best Single Poem." (The nominated poem seems to have been a C. J. Allen original, for whatever that's worth.) An unrelated accolade, not the actual transgression, appears to have prompted Welton to put his "re-evaluated" thoughts online.

Cut-and-paste plagiarism is relatively rare, but unoriginality is ubiquitous. When it comes to the charge of plagiarism, we must be careful not to treat a complex situation—involving the recombination, repurposing, development, dialogue, and endless remaking inherent in this endless making of books—like a simple one. Plagiarism, like pornography, is easily definable only in egregious, obvious circumstances, like if your poem shows up again attributed in its entirety to Christian Ward. Cases like Allen's, and the probably countless instances of a minor living poet directly imitating a dead major poet, introduce a great deal of ambiguity. The modern attitude toward plagiarism resembles the Victorian attitude toward references to sex in fiction: hair-trigger outrage and instant repercussions for the transgressor. Yes, you end up jailing and fining pornographers, but you also catch a D. H. Lawrence or a James Joyce in that net. The obscenity trials for *Madame Bovary* and *Les Fleurs du Mal* made Flaubert and Baudelaire friends for life. These artists were up against a pervasive cultural hypersensitivity among right-thinking people of sound morals. Their prosecutors took complex things—fiction and poetry—and applied simplistic criteria to them: Does this poem refer to breasts and screwing (Baudelaire's "Metamorphoses of the Vampire")? Does this novel portray a (transiently) happy adulteress, without clearly stating her behavior is evil?

The so-called transgressions of Flaubert and Baudelaire seem silly to us, but not just because we recognize these writers as true artists. Nor is it because we come after the West's sexual revolution; the ban on Baudelaire's six "obscene" poems was lifted in France in 1949, not 1969. Rather it's because we recognize that *some* media portraying breasts and screwing are pornographic and morally questionable, while others aren't. We admit the ambiguity, and we judge as best we can. "I know it when I see it," wrote the American justice Potter Stewart when deciding a 1964 case on hardcore pornography. What is little known is that Stewart, quite wisely, recanted that sound bite in vain for decades afterward. Even our seemingly instinctive responses, he recognized, can mislead us.

Analogously, our literary culture should probably ease up on the kneejerk condemnation of verbal overlaps as unforgiveable intellectual mendacity. Plagiarism has become an accusation capable of effectively ending a literary career, as the fates of Jonah Lehrer, C. J. Allen, and Kavya Viswanathan (Google the name) show us. Though the crime analogy most commonly applied to plagiarism is theft, or "lifting," shoplifting is a crime that can be expunged from one's record. This is manifestly not the case for plagiarism, which follows the offender forever, like a much more serious offense. When Martial made the first recorded reference to the literary practice, he used the Latin word *plagiarius*: "kidnapper."

For a poet or novelist to be judged by "a jury of his peers" is less effective than we would think. The peers themselves are indoctrinated in the gospel of originality, and hence believe the replication of a line is a cardinal sin. I suspect we all judge plagiarism from the perspective of the writer of the "original" source text. We reflexively sympathize with the victim, not the perpetrator. This practice ensures and reinforces the failure of our objectivity and, above all, the exaggeration of the gravity of the charge. Judges train themselves to avoid precisely these impulses, natural and human though they are.

This essay has been an attempt at objectivity by someone to whom objectivity comes easily. After all, in spite of the dozens of poems and prose pieces I have published, no one has ever thought even a snippet of my verse or prose to be worth ripping off. I suspect if someone ever does, I will probably repudiate this essay the way Justice Potter Stewart repudiated his formula for judging pornographic material. Getting robbed myself may well simplify this issue considerably. I wax biological, historical, literary-critical about recycling poets and endnote-forgetting essayists … until you lift this paragraph without attribution, dear reader. At that point, I will take up my pitchfork and clamor for your head.

NOW THAT'S WHAT I CALL a TRAGEDY

1.

I used to think that Shakespeare poisoned the soil, like a eucalyptus—that his leaves, though medicinal, leeched something equal and opposite into the ground. The Tree of Life stands in a clearing. Creativity that dominant demands a sterile radius, and we still stand in his. It's the way energy could be neither created nor destroyed after the God of Genesis switched off the generator. No great ascents to heaven in Christianity after Dante; no great verse plays in English after Shakespeare. Call it the First Law of Succession: there are no successors.

It's been done fairly well elsewhere, the Shakespearean seedling taking root far afield. Pushkin's *Boris Godunov*, for example, or Schiller's *Wallenstein* cycle—these playwrights derived, from Shakespeare's histories, a viable way of presenting the histories of their own people. The young Victor Hugo openly declared Shakespeare superior to Racine and French neoclassical drama in general, producing some highly successful plays, like the contemporary sensation *Hernani* (a lesser Shakespearean Frenchman was Alfred de Musset). In other instances, poets write verse plays on different models entirely. Goethe's *Faust* comes to mind; it might be argued that Part I has some precedent in the Shakespearean tragedies, but by Part II, Goethe is presenting a quite idiosyncratic riff on classical themes. The more he departs from Shakespeare, however, the closer he gets to mere pageantry, the kind of court masque that Ben Jonson and John Milton wrote but Shakespeare did not. Taken to its extreme, the style can throw forth monsters like Thomas Hardy's *The Dynasts*.

Shakespeare seems to inspire artists outside English to outdo themselves—consider the late operas of Verdi, *Otello* and *Falstaff*, whose librettos are some of Arrigo Boito's most dramatically effective verse. But where is the great English opera based on *King Lear*? In the English-speaking world, Shakespeare has inspired *performers* to outdo themselves; he has inspired poets to redo Shakespeare.

What do I mean? I mean: *All for Love; or, The World Well Lost. The Borderers. Remorse. The Cenci. Otho the Great. Sardanapalus, Cain, Heaven and Earth, Marino Faliero. Queen Mary, Becket, Harold, The Cup and the Falcon.* By which I imply: John Dryden. William Wordsworth. Samuel Taylor Coleridge. Percy Bysshe Shelley. John Keats. Lord Byron. Alfred Tennyson.

It seems that every ambitious poet has a failed blank-verse drama somewhere in their Collected. Only Alexander Pope seemed practical enough to know that he best not try such a thing. We don't read these plays, not even as closet dramas. Sweet Keats writing about bloody murder and palace intrigue? That holy firebrand Shelley writing about incest in an Italian Renaissance family? We don't want these things from our favorite poets. Who wants to see a ballerina in boxing gloves?

It's not that these poets were exclusively lyric poets, either. Byron wrote widely read (in his time) narrative poems like "The Giaour," and a highly readable (in our time) comic epic, *Don Juan*. Tennyson too had his *Idylls of the King*. But when it came to verse drama, they became pseudo-Shakespeares. Even though Byron set out to create a consciously anti-Shakespearean drama based on Vittorio Alfieri's plays and a generally neoclassical aesthetic, his project was doomed from the start. Sometimes he forced himself into mythic or biblical themes just to get more distance from Shakespeare, but he ended up in the same place due to the un-Shake-able specter of dramatic blank verse:

SARDANAPALUS (*speaking to some of his attendants*):
Let the pavilion over the Euphrates

Be garlanded, and lit, and furnish'd forth
For an especial banquet; at the hour
Of midnight we will sup there; see nought wanting,
And bid the galley be prepared. There is
A cooling breeze which crisps the broad clear river:
We will embark anon. Fair nymphs, who deign
To share the soft hours of Sardanapalus,
We'll meet again in that the sweetest hour,
When we shall gather like the stars above us,
And you will form a heaven as bright as theirs;
Till then, let each be mistress of her time,
And thou, my own Ionian Myrrha, choose,
Will thou along with them or me?[1]

With neither of you, if that's how you insist on talking.

With Tennyson, over half a century on, the imitation actually gets worse. He mimicked everything, both the blank verse and the occasional "low prose" passages you find in Shakespeare:

> WALTER MAP: Nay, my lord, take heart; for tho' you suspended yourself, the Pope let you down again; and though you suspend Foliot or another, the Pope will not leave them in suspense, for the Pope himself is in suspense, like Mahound's coffin hung between heaven and earth—always in suspense, like the scales, till the weight of Germany or the gold of England brings one of them down to the dust—always in suspense, like the tail of the horologe—to and fro—ticktack—we make the time, we keep the time, ay, and we serve the time; for I have heard say that if you boxed the Pope's ears with a purse, you might stagger him, but he would pocket the purse.[2]

This is at once a long way from *Falstaff* and not a long way from Elizabethan England. Byron stuck to writing bad Stately Shakespeare; Tennyson wrote every kind of Shakespeare badly, but Witty Shakespeare worst of all. Theatergoers agreed. The most popular poets of their time, Byron and Tennyson both were failures at writing for the stage.

In the twentieth century, the biggest names still had a go at it. Yeats has several plays: some in prose, with songs in verse; others, like the short later play *The Resurrection*, in blank verse. Auden attempted something in dramatic format called *The Sea and the Mirror*, which he himself called a "commentary" on *The Tempest*, and it would be a mistake to consider it a failed verse play. Eliot is the poet who, with *The Cocktail Party* and *Murder in the Cathedral*, made the most sustained, self-conscious attempts at the verse play in English. In Eliot's case, we are perhaps too close in time to accurately judge his success or failure; as of now, it would seem that his plays are only for the Eliot specialists, while poems like "Prufrock," *The Waste Land*, and *Four Quartets* will be what he is remembered for.

We do, however, have at least one example of a twentieth-century writer making a reasonable success of the verse play. Christopher Fry is universally classified as a "dramatist" or "playwright," not as a "poet"—and this is, to my mind, a crucial detail, one that proves just how successful he was at it. Yet it's precisely in the poetry of his work that the trouble arises. While Eliot tried to create a distinctive, modern dramatic verse that owed something but not everything to the Elizabethans, Fry made the same mistake as Tennyson and Byron—only he made it more effectively. The briefest excerpt from Kenneth Branaugh's production of *The Lady's Not for Burning* (available, as of this writing, on YouTube) shows us the Shakespearean actor quite at home in speaking Fry's blank verse. The play, Fry's most famous, is set in medieval England, after all; move this verse anywhere else, geographically or temporally, and its unsuitability becomes evident. Fry's verse isn't a viable universal dramatic idiom.

This is precisely what Eliot tried to do: create a dramatic idiom that would also be poetry. He wasn't the last to attempt it, either. Contemporary poets like J. D. McClatchy and Glyn Maxwell have tried to do the same thing. Naturally, their work goes unwelcomed by the main outlets for dramatic writing in our time, television and film. Their work for the stage isn't in the tradition of Shakespeare and Racine, though on the surface it seems that way. Hollywood screenwriters have the same role in today's society as the great verse playwrights did in theirs, whereas the work of today's verse dramatists is part of the larger phenomenon of "experimental theater," which began in the late nineteenth and twentieth centuries as the center of gravity shifted from stage to screen.

A Hollywood producer (go ahead, try pitching him your original verse screenplay) might take his cigar out of his mouth and tell you, with some impatience, that contemporary audiences don't *want* dramatic poetry. But it would be just as accurate to say audiences don't *need* dramatic poetry. We forget the role that poetry, and evocative language in general, had onstage before the advent of film and special effects in the twentieth century, and melodrama (drama with music) in the nineteenth. Poetry served as a kind of poor man's special effect, a poor man's background music:

> Is this a dagger which I see before me,
> The handle toward my hand? Come, let me clutch thee.
> I have thee not, and yet I see thee still.
> Art thou not, fatal vision, sensible
> To feeling as to sight? or art thou but
> A dagger of the mind, a false creation,
> Proceeding from the heat-oppressed brain?
> I see thee yet, in form as palpable
> As this which now I draw.

Macbeth's seven-line hallucination makes the drawing of the knife infinitely more ominous than if he had simply slid it out. In a film or a TV episode, this effect would be expressed with ominous-sounding background music and a closeup on the villain's face—no language needed.

In Elizabethan times, Shakespeare's stage was almost bare. The stage machinery of the court masque, meanwhile, was elaborate; the production and costumes were the focus. Accordingly, the poetry was weaker, even when written by poets like Ben Jonson. It's the same reason librettos are impoverished of metaphor: you can't follow the music and the complex language at the same time. That confusion, that constant sense of missing something, is fatal to dramatic momentum; it leads to a pause, or worse, a *retrograde motion* in the minds of viewers, away from what is happening and back to what they missed. The Greek tragedies and French neoclassical tragedies were simply staged, by any standard. In Aeschylus's time, sending a third actor onstage was revolutionary.

Today, the camera presents a relatively massive amount of information to the eye. A gesture or facial expression can be magnified to the size of a theater wall. There is no necessity for language to evoke a physical scene or to express an emotion. We can see for ourselves now, thank you very much. The burden of expression has shifted away from the script. The technology of the screen makes poetry redundant, if not counterproductive. Language has atrophied in drama for the same reason portrait-painting has atrophied in art. A displacement by technology is almost always a permanent one.

3.

Before the often described connectedness of our day, modes and means of storytelling were less homogenized. Western European audiences, by the early twentieth century, got their extended stories in book form or onstage—in both instances, in prose. Bardic live recitation had basically vanished. Elsewhere, rival forms persisted. In 1933, when Milman Parry wanted to study oral verse-narrative techniques with an eye (okay, an ear) for reconstructing how Homer composed, he didn't have to schlep to Papua New Guinea or the rainforests of Brazil; Eastern Europe was far enough. In Yugoslavia, Parry had to hunt down the last of the reciters; a hundred or so years earlier, Byron, in a note to one of his tales, refers offhand to the presence of these reciters in Turkey's coffeeshops, who acted as living epic-poem jukeboxes. This kind of storytelling persisted as late as the 2000s in rural India; the historian William Dalrymple devoted a chapter in *Nine Lives* to the last singers of the epic hero Pabuji.

In that less literate society, print books failed to completely stamp out the art, but television has since more or less finished the job. Today, truly popular storytelling is done in prose (sometimes quite good prose), whether it's in a novel or onscreen. Note, however, that whether it's an orally recited tale, a Netflix series, a modern bestselling potboiler, or a big-budget film, the language is not usually a character; the more the poetry gets subordinated to the pace and plot of the story, the more popular the work gets. No novel editor or script doctor asks for thirty more pages here, twenty more pages there, and could you please add some metaphors and extended similes? The whole point is to cut. From this perspective, the virtues of contemporary poetic art—disjunction, metaphorical daring, imagery that is its own reward—are distractions, superfluities, or even active hindrances.

Whitman's insight about audience—"To have great poets, there must be great audiences"[3]—implies that the audience actually *precedes* the poet in the creation of great poetry. The poet creates *for* people, and the poetry fills a vacuum of their imagining. Their greatness permits and coaxes forth the poet's. This is a generous, selfless sense of creativity, and while it may not be true of all modes of poetry, it is probably most true of dramatic poetry— which has been, in its intermittent heydays, a truly public medium. Whitman's sense of art was clearly identical to that of Shakespeare, who wrote plays according to whatever was trending; he started with history plays early in his career, following Marlowe's success with them, and later gave up Act V mass slaughters (e.g., *Hamlet*) for the happy endings of his later "romances." Whether or not you think the statement holds true about "greatness" (whatever that is), the audience does get to pick the *forms*: in this, at least, they call the tune. That's what accounts for the brain drain of the best contemporary storytellers out of poetry and into prose forms. Any poet who has read Cormac McCarthy knows exactly where he belongs.

4.

I am not writing to state the obvious (dramatic verse is dead) or to explain the obvious obviously (because no one wants to watch a verse drama anymore). I am writing to ask a deeper question: Why did so many poets chase this form in vain?

God knows they didn't have to. The fascination was consuming, but ultimately voluntary. The most famous English-language poet of the first half of the nineteenth century: Byron. Of the second half: Tennyson. Of the first half of the twentieth century: Eliot. All three, *after* penning the nondramatic works that brought them fame, chased verse drama wherever it chose to lead them—sometimes honoring the Shakespearean model, sometimes defying it, but in most cases descending into unreadability and unstageability alike. It was the poetic equivalent of imperial overreach. Okay, so you have the poetry-reading crowd fawning over you? Phase Two: Conquer the theater!

Or *create* the theater, depending on how you conceive of the problem. Yeats's dream of an Irish poetic theater duplicates Goethe's dream, a century earlier, of a German one. Theatrical traditions aren't established by a single genius, and both of these geniuses knew this, so they tried to enlist their more talented contemporaries in the good cause. Plays got written and staged, not all bad, though they never rivalled the popular theaters of the day, and neither poet actually succeeded in realizing the dream. Yeats moved on to his transcendent late poems, while Goethe finished out with a giant dramatic work, basically a magical realist pageant; he had clearly given up on a poetic theater thriving outside his own imagination, and indeed on the idea of the stage itself. His was the first screen poem, written for the screen before the invention of the talking picture. *Faust Part II*, published in 1832, is a dramatic work one hundred and fifty years in advance of the cinematographic techniques required for its presentation. Unlike Jules Verne, whose prophecies about submarines and lunar landings came true, Goethe, in his last crowning work, was the prophet of a dramatic art that was not to be.

Part of it has to do with poets' fixation—in the old European tradition—on the idea of the great poem. I mean "great" in the etymological sense, the Old English word for "big." Eliot inherited the dream of the Big Poem, as he did so much else. The great poem could be a tragedy or an epic, but it wasn't a page-length lyric. To understand how Western this idea is, you need only hop over to Chinese or Japanese traditions, where poets had no size-related anxieties. In Persian or Urdu poetry, a voluminous Diwan was the poet's endpoint, but the book always grew by the accretion of individual elements, just like the ghazals of which it was composed. Rumi's *Mathnawi* atomizes into stories and reflections, not one sustained epic narrative or drama; along with Hafiz, another accumulator of ghazals, Rumi holds pride of place in the Persian tradition, ranked well above the longer narrative poets like Nizami, or even a "national" narrative poet like Ferdowsi.

In the Western tradition—for about three thousand years, really—an idea got into poets' heads that the short lyric *just wasn't enough*. The shorter forms were considered less ambitious, as if they were somehow easier or less demanding. They aren't, but try convincing Milton of that. The pastoral and didactic poems are a run-up to the national epic; canzones are vernacular practice before the marathon *Commedia*; the sonnets are a side project that peters off in the early 1600s, when the great tragedies flood forth. This imposition of a hierarchy between short and long, lyric and polyphonic forms, is the central conceptual error of the Western Canon, and it has not been shaken off yet. Today, yes, we accord the highest rank possible to, say, Emily Dickinson, who never ventured beyond a page or two. But there is still an ambition, on the part of rising poets, to produce the book-length sequence, the Project. This is matched by the ambition on the part of established poets to gather their rosebuds into a putrid-sweet heap and call it a career, or rather a *Collected*. The fiction world isn't entirely free of this idea either, in its different attitudes toward the novel and short story.

The clearest reaction came, naturally, from American originals. Not from Whitman; his expansiveness fits quite well with the European attitude, and he tinkered with *Leaves of Grass* so much because he wanted it to be the equivalent of a national epic, which I suppose it is. The first salvo came from Edgar Allen Poe, who declared long poems useless except as vessels for smaller poetic moments, which the lyric presented pure, without the surrounding chaff. He didn't quite understand that context and setup matter, that the monologues in a Shakespeare play, though detachable, gain immensely from their dramatic context. Of course, a late poem by Plath is just as contextually charged as any dramatic soliloquy; it remains an invaluable literary advantage to have a good backstory, whether it involves a suicidal sibling, cancer, a dead father, survival of a historical atrocity, etc. Cynical of me to point out, I know, but the poet's name has to become a character name for the poems to enjoy this kind of contextual heightening. The name ceases to be a mere byline; the drama, setting, and narrative are all implicit. Sylvia is a *character* in the passion-play of her own life and death. Her poems are her dramatic monologues.

Robert Frost, who did try some longer narrative- or conversation-based poems early on, but always on a small (notice I don't say "modest") scale, stayed clear-eyed about the nature of poetic permanence. The endgame, he pointed out, was to "lodge a few poems where they can't be gotten rid of"[4]; he understood that the permanence of a poet's work relied on small, self-contained indestructibilities. The seed, or rather the spore, is what drops through time and lasts, not the overfull, tangled, many-branched flourish.

5.

Frost himself made a few stabs at dramatic verse: the tail end of his *Collected* contains two longish dramatic poems (even the stage directions are metrical) from the mid-1940s, "A Masque of Reason" and "A Masque of Mercy," that are natural developments from the conversation-driven poems of his early volumes. Come to think of it, dramatic verse never quite lost its appeal for poets in the generation after his, though they knew the audience would be small, even compared to the audience for their short poems.

Late-twentieth-century verse dramatists gave up the fantasy of either rivaling antiquity (the clear motivation behind Milton's *Samson Agonistes*) or of conjuring a modern equivalent of it (which prompted Eliot's attempts at staging the Furies in *The Cocktail Party*). Later poets made "versions" of the ancient Greeks: Seamus Heaney wrote *The Burial at Thebes* and *The Cure at Troy*, C. K. Williams had a go at *The Bacchae*, Robin Robertson made something of *Medea*, and so on. It turns out Kenneth Koch overproduced verse plays too, along with everything else he overproduced. Original verse plays, many premiering under his own direction, have poured out of Derek Walcott; his bibliography as a verse dramatist, between *Henri Christophe* (1950) and his stage version of *The Odyssey* (1998), is large enough to belong to a second, separate writer.

So the appeal to poets hasn't vanished, even though the audience did centuries ago. It's worth examining what it is about this form that keeps attracting some of the best poets. First of all, it's a form of extended storytelling. In this, it holds an appeal similar to a novel; the writer can create characters and set them into conflict over a long duration of time. The page-or-two poem that is the default mode of contemporary poetry has never been good at that. The verse drama also naturally allows for polyphonic poetry. If poetry is what we make "out of the quarrel with ourselves" (Yeats), verse drama allows those selves to take turns quarreling. Conjuring more than one character is a liberation from the writer's own persona. Like a novelist, the dramatic poet gains personality options.

Unlike a novel, though, the verse drama—assuming it's not a closet drama—offers the poet a distinct hedonic rush: that of watching the poetry take on a body and voice. Add to this the actual bodies sitting in seats, watching, and suddenly the solitary act of poetry has edged back into the world of people. This may be the underlying pull of dramatic poetry—the wish to pursue poetry as a public art, not an isolated and isolating one. The increasingly rare poet's dream of verse drama may be a literalized version of the much more widespread poet's dream of "finding an audience." The fame of the chimera-chasers needn't contradict this idea. Byron, Tennyson, and Eliot, as page poets, had already "found an audience" in the metaphorical sense of a readership, but this final, culminating connection eluded them. They were poets with a public, but they could not reestablish poetry as a public form.

6.

The first law of succession is that there are no successors. There's a rider to that law: *until someone succeeds.*

A play called *J.B.* by the now-little-read Archibald MacLeish won both the 1959 Tony Award for Drama and the Pulitzer Prize for Drama. This was only one of MacLeish's three Pulitzers; he got the other two for poetry collections. His success—among the community of dramatists, no less—was unprecedented, and yet it hardly proves the stageability of original dramatic poetry. All it really proves is that Archibald MacLeish was one well-connected suit (Yale and Harvard both, an expat in Paris in the 1920s, a Librarian of Congress, *and* one of the founding fathers of the Office of Strategic Services). His nondramatic poems are by and large mediocre, though he did write a poem-about-poetry that has given misleading advice to generations of aspiring writers. (Whenever you are informed, with a give-me-patience-with-this-Philistine glance, that a poem doesn't *mean*, it *is*, you are hearing an echo of MacLeish's "Ars Poetica": "A poem should not mean / but be.") *J.B.* debuted in New York City in 1958, the same year that Eliot's *The Elder Statesman* debuted in Britain; I wonder what Ol' Possum thought of his admirer's play, and its success. Eliot's play got a mixed response, but he was premiering it before a different audience, two years after John Osborne's youth- and anger-driven drama was changing expectations. I don't intend to compare these two plays in their themes, execution, or subject matter; MacLeish's Biblically influenced play is too different from Eliot's, which seems based on a long tradition of plays involving English people sitting in drawing rooms.

We mustn't judge the poetic quality of a verse play based on its background verse—the equivalent of the operatic recitativo. You have to pick out the arias—dilations when the language itself holds center stage—or the crescendos, in which great dramatic pressure intensifies the language. These are the places where the poetry makes itself known and, hopefully, forces its way into the spectator's memory. *Hamlet*'s most famous soliloquy is an aria; *Faust Part II*'s "Mountain Gorges" sequence is, clearly, a crescendo, relying heavily on the metaphorical brass section. Self-examination is a prime occasion for the aria. Here is a self-examining dilation in Eliot's *The Elder Statesman*:

> Perhaps I've never really enjoyed living
> As much as most people. At least, as they seem to do.
> Without knowing that they enjoy it. Whereas I've often known
> That I didn't enjoy it. Some dissatisfaction
> With myself, I suspect, very deep within myself
> Has impelled me all my life to find justification
> Not so much to the world—first of all to myself.
> What is this self inside us, this silent observer,
> Severe and speechless critic, who can terrorise us
> And urge us on to futile activity,
> And in the end, judge us still more severely
> For the errors into which his own reproaches drove us?

Consider the contrast with Eliot's own nondramatic verse. Here we find no unusual allusions or disjunctions, and the imagery and metaphor are muted almost to the point of absence; a powerful poet is *shying from figurative language*. A driving rhythm is absent too. All that poetry gets to keep are the line breaks.

It turns out Eliot had a lot in common with MacLeish when engineering a stageable, mid-twentieth-century dramatic verse: the pursuit of *prose by other means*. Nothing must distinguish the verse too boldly from prose. I have always been of the personal opinion that undifferentiated language makes for indifferent poetry; poetry must distinguish itself from speech even when—*especially* when—it mimics speech. In his late plays, Eliot wrote verse not so much like a lesser poet than like a lesser prose writer.

As to the plays' *rhythmic* interest, independent of figurative language or any other poetic quality, it strikes me that Eliot used the rhythms of English less distinctively—that is, less poetically—than the prose stage plays of David Mamet or the prose teleplays of Aaron Sorkin. Poetry, desperate not to "sound poetic," ends up sounding worse than good prose. The enemy has never been prose; the enemy is *naturalism*, or rather the wrongheaded contemporary idea of what the "natural" in writing really is.

But no one talks like that in real life is the objection of the boor. As soon as a poet thinks this way, dramatic poet or any other kind, they have crossed over, fatally for their art, to the other side. A set of associations—unnatural/artificial/sophisticated versus natural/real/plain—has entrenched itself in our thinking: a *natural* style is prose-y and plainspoken and straightforward, while an *unnatural* style is clotted with formal hijinks, allusions, playfulness, and metaphors. But history contradicts this. The earliest samples of poetic writing we possess are, in Sanskrit, the Rig Vedic hymns: densely allusive, strictly metrical, so elliptical they continue to defy scholarly exegesis to this day. In Hebrew, the first verses of that great prose poem, Genesis, contain an enigmatic description of the spirit of God moving on the face of water, complete with a rhyme, "tohu wa-bohu," called in to express the formless void. In the first line of the earliest known love poem, from Sumer, a lover calls the beloved "honeysweet," connecting the beloved to the taste of a specific food.

To bring this back to dramatic poetry itself, the Greekless, grammar-school Shakespeare was long considered the supreme example of Nature trumping mere Art—this is the same Shakespeare who couldn't resist a pun, larded his verse with metaphors, and used hendiadys over sixty times in *Hamlet* alone. In poetry, the complex *is* the natural. Byron's dullest, most uninteresting verse is found in his dramas; the same, in my opinion, goes for Eliot. In the verse drama, Byron can't rhyme three syllables in a row, and Eliot can't allude. Verse drama, in both cases, persuaded a master of complexity to simplify.

7.

The past's experience of the visual is, relatively speaking, marked by simplicity and stasis. The much-vaunted Sistine Chapel was the visual equivalent of a 3D IMAX extravaganza; the packed neoclassical panorama of horses and pikemen at the Battle of Wherever was the equivalent of a *Lord of the Rings* battle scene. The drastic increase in image size and detail; the absence of motion, jump cuts, and accompanying music, elements that we take for granted; the ubiquity of living faces, with the advantage they have in moment-to-moment expressivity over painted faces—these would have overloaded any set of eyes from any century before the twentieth. When the past came closest to our daily experience of the visual, it was always in the form of the *spectacle*: an arena flooded so real ships could reenact Actium, or hundreds of searchlights pointed at the sky with a bunch of uniformed people marching around. That's right—you could Manipulate the Masses with spectacles that would be beggared by a contemporary Summer Olympics opening ceremony, or even a Super Bowl halftime show.

The only advanced languages our dramatic arts employ anymore are visual and musical. Spoken language serves to provide rudimentary signals that indicate relationships between characters and plot developments. Speech can be dispensed with, even for indication of mood, thanks to the convention of orchestral background music. Rhythmic or metaphorical speech—speech in any way elaborate—is not just redundant; it cannot be processed because it is shouted out, as it were, by the visual.

The stages of Sophocles, Racine, and Shakespeare were all minimalist; shoestring budgets encouraged artistic (read: poetic) inventiveness by necessitating it. Shakespeare exited the London theatrical world just as spectacle was taking it over. One of the most eloquent symbols in the history of theater is how the real cannons fired during a performance of his last play, *Henry VIII*, ended up burning down the Globe. Art plus popularity equals money. Art plus money equals spectacle. This has held true of hip-hop and

Hollywood in recent memory, just as it did of verse drama in the distant past. The toning-down of the poetry in *Henry VIII* has been observed by more than one commentator, but it's not necessarily because the bard was getting old and losing energy; Northrop Frye once pointed out that Shakespeare, who knew exactly what was required for a given type of performance, wrote such bland verse for that play because he was providing the text for a costume-heavy spectacle. This would have been the future of the London theaters had the Puritans not shut them down. In any case, the heyday of the big verse tragedies had passed even before the end of Shakespeare's own career. The illustrious afterlings who daydreamed of poetic tragedy, from Dryden to Eliot, failed to understand the faddish nature of its rise. It just so happened that Shakespeare had managed to transfigure the genre into permanent art. The other precondition related to the audience: human beings, in that less visual, more language-dependent age, could process poetry in real time—poetry in all her metaphorical, rhetorical, and rhythmic athleticism.

Imagery has always been addictive mind sugar, and much like real sugar, it's never been more easily available. Between Imagism and Deep Image, you can see the desperate attempts by Western poetry to compete with its own sugar substitute. There are American poets to this day who practice poetry as image proliferation. But this intense focus on imagery hasn't always been the rule, not even in lyric poetry. In *Laocoon* (1766), Gotthold Ephraim Lessing discussed why straight pictorial techniques needn't dominate poetry, juxtaposing Ariosto's feature-by-feature description of the sorceress Alcina's face and Homer's Trojan elders as they see Helen pass, commenting on how she's well worth a war.

The further you get from storytelling, meaning, and emotion—the more you try to *speak images* in the screen age—the further you get from anything like an audience. The words become redundant. The ambition underlying the dramatic poem, worthy indeed of the great poets who have pursued it, is of the *full-spectrum dominance of language*: this idea that language can carry everything on its own, unaccompanied by visual spectacle and background music; that poetry can supply the theatergoer with not just plot and character but musicality and visual pleasure. This dream may be out of touch with both the present and the past; Shakespeare's plays often contained songs and always finished with a jig, and every scholarly description of Greek choric performance I've read sounds like it's describing hip-hop. Melodrama took over from both short-lived traditions anyway. With English-language poets, from the Romantics to Eliot, we're really dealing with a poet's *fantasy* of verse drama, one that differs from every historical example except the neoclassical theater of Corneille and Racine—the tradition that retains the least fascination of any I've mentioned, even inside France.

Yet fondly if hazily recalled golden ages of verse drama, to which those poets looked for models, come closest to that fantasy ideal, in which poetry holds the public rapt. If it were ever possible, it isn't anymore. As a culture, we have switched off some sensitivities and turned up others. We are hearers, not listeners; watchers, not an audience. Now that's what I call a tragedy.

INTÈRLUDE
ESSAY ON REPETITION

THE ARGUMENT

Most literary histories will tell you that Montaigne invented the essay, even though it's difficult to tell his work from Plutarch's *Moralia* over a millennium earlier. The practice of the essay—the autobiographical essay, the thinkpiece, the travel essay, the "creative nonfiction" essay—has expanded so much that you can find its antecedents wherever you look. Many a classical epistle, written for publication by some esteemed Roman, could qualify as a precursor, complete with the personal anecdotes that seem so "modern" today.

Regardless of where they place its origins, most readers assume an essay is a work of prose. Yet those early examples of the essay sometimes happened in verse. Horace wrote epistles, and his *Ars Poetica*, addressed to the senator Piso, is one of the earliest "craft essays" we possess. Dante's rants about politics, Elizabethan stage monologues, Virgil's hexameters dispensing advice to farmers (some of it less than sound)—if we go looking about for proto-essays, we can find them all over the long history of Western poetry. It may be that "poetry" and "essay" are such ever-broadening and encompassing terms that they have become infinite circles of a perfectly overlapping Venn diagram.

And yet the "verse essay" is still a thing, or was a thing, largely because of Alexander Pope, whose ideas of what made a good poem were drastically different than ours. Pope's was simply the best and most transcendent example of a period style; the more you go rooting about among his contemporaries and successors, you realize that there was a witty century when *everybody* was rocking heroic couplets. It was to them what free verse is to us: the default mode, simply what poetry sounded like. At this distance, it's a little hard to tell his baseline-quality couplets from John Dryden's or Samuel Johnson's.

Pope, in *An Essay on Man* and other similar poems, always had points to get across. "For it is not meters, but a meter-making argument, that makes a poem," wrote Emerson, in an essay that many believe to presage the work of Walt Whitman.[1] Yet Pope's un-Whitman-like couplets are the English language's most meter-made argument ever. The etymology of "argument" comes from the Latin *arguere*, after all, which means, according to the Online Etymology Dictionary, "to make clear" or "to make reasoned statements to prove or refute a proposition." Perhaps Ralph and Alexander are arguing this point atop Parnassus right now. *But you're ignoring the latter half of that quote*, Emerson is grumbling, referring to "a thought so passionate and alive ... [that] it has an architecture of its own."[2] And Pope counters that in the beginning was the Logos, and logic never lived in a more impassioned form than the couplet's point and counterpoint.

Poetically speaking, Emerson and Whitman have many descendants, while Pope's lineage has died out. The young Lord Byron's first masterpiece, "English Bards and Scotch Reviewers," was the last echo of that age of coupleteering, ironically from the ultimate symbol of Romantic passion. The logical, argumentative, dare I say *essayistic* streak in poetry has largely vanished.

To my knowledge, Pope has zero imitators among the living major American or English poets, even the ones who do "formal" work. Looking at where poetry is now compared to where poetry was then, I can't help but wonder whether that entire age took a wrong turn in how it conceived of poetry. How much of that era's poetry actually gets read? And even when it is, how much of it is read only as period pieces, exhibits in the museum of style, rather than as living, passionate art? Are the pleasures offered by the rational, logically argued couplet, in the service of a larger theme or idea, pleasures that anyone, anywhere, considers "poetic"? Or is essayistic discourse on an idea (say, repetition) not properly the stuff of poetry? Is it justly relegated to prose?

88

I pondered none of these questions before I wrote this "Essay on Repetition." If I had, I might have arrived at the correct answers ... and never written it. By ignoring the recalcitrant and obvious facts of twenty-first-century poetic convention, I freed my hands up to write this. Was I aware that no one reads (or writes) this kind of thing anymore? Yes—with the literary-critical part of my mind. But this, right now, is prose. The poet in me had other ideas, or rather *one* idea: repetition. And that idea asked for, and received, its Pope-echoing, argument-making meter: the repetitions—*aabbcc ...*—of rhyme.

*

A Golden Egg, the Big Bang, Aum, the Word—
What started this? I don't know what you've heard,
But silence, music, speech occur in time.
In the beginning (risk it!) was the Rhyme.
I know a thing (or two) about beginning
A poem or a family with twinning.
Rebirth, circadian rhythm, rhyme's felicity,
The art of storytelling, time's cyclicity,
The lub-dub trochees every heart is beating,
Love for a book that deepens with rereading,
A chain reaction's fission-fission-fission
Enact a single diktat: *Repetition.*
Didactic poems simply aren't written,
I know. Erato, help me—I am smitten.
Erato, help me, make my hand your glove
And shape this essay as a poem of love.

Go back, then, to the stacks, that reckless kiss,
Wet-lipped, wide-eyed. I gazed at Aeschylus,
Book-lust and lust-lust coupled in that moment.
My eyes, my hands were roving, seeking Romans
And Greeks: Loeb-reds, Loeb-greens, like Christmas in
The mind. First kiss! Her incandescent skin
Flickers and dims, but I resist revision.

I know the Loebs were not my "own" tradition,
And she was white, it wasn't meant to be—
Or should I write, *She wasn't meant for me* . . . .
Enough to place them there, the books, the lover,
Between the shelves two secrets to uncover,
My love of literature and love of sex
A mutually overwritten text
From then on. So you see why, since the age
Of fourteen, I've felt gooseflesh on the page.
I often *say* that books are where I've sought truth.
Truth is, I love them as I love my hot youth.

Desire was the heart of it, of course, the set theme
And variation that condensed that wet dream
Of twinned success in love and literature.
I manage it these days. There is no cure
For it, this twinging of the psyche's knee.
I've read Girard, I know it isn't me
Desiring what I want. My first ambition
In letters? Execute a repetition
Of Shakespeare's oeuvre. I wrote blank verse plays
Before I had my driver's license: days
Spent making (botching) each poetic move
The master made. What was I out to prove?
Why did I want so fiercely to become him?
I craved his title. There was only one him,
But I was sure that I would be the second.
Or was mimesis how the Muses beckoned
Me onward? Coaxing me with my ambition
To master verse through slavish repetition.
Mi*m*esis, at its core, is me. That's why
Imitation has to start with *I*.

And yet I've read Girard. It isn't *me*
Desiring *my* desires, but what I see

Others desire, yellow fever yearning.
The Fire Sermon saw the whole world burning.
Even before the Buddha, it was common
Among the immemorial twice-born Brahmins
To think desire *outside* the true self, frantic,
Erratic, ultimately inauthentic,
Both *kama*, lust, and *krodha*, anger, just
Subtypes of cordyceps infecting us:
Out of the pelvic husk, the sprouted cock
A pink and parasitic fungal stalk.

Desire is the oldest story, told and told
Again. The hero's quest for God or gold,
The lovers mad to meet, slyly evading
Some rich old roadblock to their moonlit mating,
A race to get a treasure, or a race
Through the eyes of the quarry who's fleeing the chase ....
No doubt all storytelling started with
Cookfire tales of hunts—from them, each myth
Of dragon, Rakshasa, or monster slain.
Again, the toddler pleads. We invent in vain:
Again is what all storytellers do.
In fables as in genres, nothing's new.
Because desire is every story's engine,
Repetition is the only ending.
You pack new turkeys with the same old stuffing.
Filmmakers know there's one plot: *Get the McGuffin.*

No one is nonce. Myth is reborn as fiction,
If not as newborn myth. The crucifixion
Remixes tropes: a cut-up God of vine
And vintage, one whose father is divine,
The Father Sky who makes his blue blood blue.
Archaic pagan plotlines, only new
To Aramaic, and Hebrew tradition.

The mythic retread spread by repetition,
The Word reprinted, *Dios, Dio, Gott,*
Gideon Bibles in a Marriott.
And then the Chosen One was Harry Potter.
It's high time that the Father had a daughter.

What audiences (toddlers *or* adults)
Adore the most is form. The ear exults
In hearing things repeat, in hearing pattern
Emerge, an autostereogram, from patter.
The Third Eye sees a Magic Eye illusion,
Through noise and dazzle and profuse confusion,
Emerge. Nothing redundant in an encore—
The poet's art is stumbling onto concord.
Consider how, by unforeseen felicity,
I'm falling into coupled periodicity—
A "happy lapse," as some believe of Eden.
Just hear the heart inside my chatter, beating
Unstressed then stressed, with every tenth beat's charm a
Recurrence fortunate as instant karma.
With no refrain or rhyme, *radeef*
Or *qaafiyah,* a ghazal comes to grief,
And there's no telling where a line should end
(Read: *must* end) absent its telltale repetend.

Erato knows, my *true* first love was form.
Form has a body. She is lithe and warm
And, flush against my mind, she teaches it
To dance. I move the way she moves, my wit
Her whisper in my ear. She pirouettes
A triolet. These couplets? Tête-à-têtes
In which I write the thoughts she thinks for me,
Poetic-noetic telepathy.
She does the first draft, then she does an edit.
I sit here, sign my name, and take the credit.

Though love is one continuous emotion,
Lovemaking is a repetitive motion.
Furious Eros pounds until his fist
Ruptures the drum. I know that kind of bliss:
Form has a body. I make love to her,
And when we get a rhythm going for
A spell, we die *la petite mort* in synchrony,
And by my ringing ears I swear she's singing me.

Stories or poetry, no theme is higher,
No subject more inspired, than desire,
Since love, adventure, Grail quest, epic war
Are someone wanting something, little more
Than *crave it, chase it, get denied it, get it.*
Whether or not you know you have, you've read it.
A spouse, a treasure trove, salvation, winning
Goads us busybodies to our sinning.
What makes the same protagonists recur
Remakes our busy bodies. Births recur,
Identical rhymes, selfsame every syllable,
The self, like any energy, unkillable
In any circuit where the crackle dances,
In any ardor where our karma lands us.
Desire cycles us, recycling dust
Through dust. The axle of the wheel is lust;
The hamster on the wheel, this migrant soul.
From twelve o'clock around the clock we roll.

But why repeat myself? Why do I yearn
To resurrect, redo, replay, return?
Because a crumpled bike's back wheel keeps spinning.
Because the toast should be to *old* beginnings.
Because the rain it raineth every day.
Because the mantra, prayer, Name you say
Draws power from its being said before.

93

Because some artists make and some restore
And there's an equal love in either's brush,
An equal rush. Because two bodies flush
Against each other foster with their heat
A third and separate one that will repeat
Their bodies, both at once, a compound word.
Because it isn't rhyme if it isn't heard.
Because momentum builds up through anaphora.
Because a home reborn in her diaspora
Is a dandelion clock becoming dandelions.
Because before your siege machines there stands a lion.
Because the oldest gods are young in me.
Because no time. Because eternity.

Repeating is revealing: if it's stale your
Second time around, the book's a failure.
The love I have for *King Lear*, *Blood Meridian*,
Beloved changed with my rereading them.
To read them once? For "read," read "overlook."
A second reading reads a second book,
The same and not the same. It's quite Borgesian.
And Borges too is one whose work can tease me in
To labyrinths I've strolled before. I enter
Familiar turns, but a new beast's at the center.
I re-reread the *Odyssey* the most, though,
His many turnings-home, his aching *nostos*.

Love is a homecoming: My second first kiss
Gasped on the shore. I've seen a sculpture surface
While she's asleep, a Chola bronze, some blissed-
Out apsara. I knew right then I kissed
My future wife. Same scene, another take:
First kiss in front of books. I wouldn't make
This up, I know it seems a bit too pat—
The moment really did play out like that.

The titles on her shelf were different ones.
I saw a *Gita* (Eknath Easwaran's),
Rig Veda in the Penguin Classics edition,
Some Tagore, old books from the old tradition.
And this uncanny certainty took hold
Of me: that our love too was very old,
Predating us, that we were meant to be—
I mean to say, that she was meant for me
The way a word is fated into place
Because the verse line draws no other face
Close for the kiss that shuts the eyes and book,
The life to come foreseen, no need to look....
A memoir can relive this living love,
Not past lives memory keeps no footage of.
Erato, aid me, be my aide-memoire.
I swear I *knew* we'd end up as we are.
Unless our memories are merely drafts
And memory is what a memoir crafts.

Best write it now, since I may well forget
I ever loved. In time will time reset
My memories, the hard drive wiped, my pictures
Gone, all gone the poetry and scriptures
I tried to English, tried to learn by rote.
I may forget I ever loved or wrote,
Her face as strange to me as any foreign
Language, this line right now mistaken for an
Antique poet's. I suspect dementia
Is atman en route out—or in absentia.
The bureaucrats are burning files at
The tank's approach and distant rat-tat-tat.
Forgetting gets a head start, just before the
Finish. We're reborn, but prematurely.
The mirror shows your fetch, but timelapsed. *Who's this?*
Your fingers tangle with a pesky shoelace,

Your sole no longer snug inside your sneaker.
The tongue forgets the voice forgets the speaker.
The grandkids stooping, shouting in your ear
Repeat their names for you until you hear.

Rebirth is hope, a repetition with
Trajectory. At least that is the myth,
The math of it: the number of your lives
Is *nearly* infinite. One self survives
The fluctuations of its fleeting flesh,
Loving its loved ones, loving them afresh
Each time—until nirvana. That is where
The peregrine wind perishes into the air,
Trading its travels not for rest but for
The state of being everywhere. The roar
Inside you quiets. In nirvana comes
An end to rhythm. You become the thrum.
You are your love. The love in you expands.
The cosmos kneels to drink it from your hands.
You will forget your poetry because
You will become the thing your poem was
Before you stuffed its throat full of your own words.
Look east, Odysseus is turning homewards.
We're all desire's drunks until we've sworn
Off sea-dark wine—drowned in a womb, reborn.
The full-stop pupil dilates. The line breaks segue
The Word, the Big Bang, Aum, a Golden Egg.

SPECIFIC THEORY OF UNITY

<< PRECURSORS

POETIC STEM CELLS
ON JOHN MILTON'S TRINITY MANUSCRIPT

A quarter of a century before Milton finished *Paradise Lost*, the young poet began listing topics for his future masterpiece. Ardent devotees who imagine he was foreordained to create a great religious epic might be surprised to learn that his list of more than a hundred ideas contained thirty-three from British history. His leading idea, at the time, was an Arthurian epic. This, he thought, might become the British national epic. The idea for *Paradise Lost*—or *Adam Unparadised*, as he planned to title it—caught his attention and prompted him to draft an outline. In that form, it was still a five-act tragedy, a Shakespearean form with un-Shakespearean content. Milton's handwritten notebook, known as the Trinity Manuscript, gives us insight into his nature—and maybe into the nature of poetry itself.

As early as age nineteen, Milton thought of his poetry as already existing inside him, but in an undifferentiated state. He thought of his unwritten lines the way biologists think of stem cells, capable of taking on any form and function. All he had to do was direct them, choosing their theme and sound. (The human body can signal its stem cells to become any kind of cell it requires; the same stem cell can become a liver cell sequestering toxins from the blood, a cardiac myocyte contracting and relaxing hundreds of times a day, or a T-cell seeking and destroying viruses.) Milton thought of the poetry within him as, potentially, an epic poem or a verse tragedy. It might tell the story of Arthur, or Adam, or any of a number of English kings or Biblical characters. All he had to do was *choose*.

Why write about Genesis if Genesis never seized him in a flash as the imperative subject for his creativity? Rilke claimed that he heard the opening line of his first *Duino Elegy* while standing on a cliff overlooking the Adriatic. J. K. Rowling claims to have conceived the entirety of the *Harry Potter* series while sitting on a train delayed between Manchester and London. Generally, people have come to think of poetry, at its truest, as springing from an inner imperative—maybe from past trauma, or present injustice, or mystical transmission. In our culture, the poetic goad is as imperative as breath itself. We use the word "inspiration" routinely in literary and artistic contexts, forgetting that its original meaning was religious—related to the prophet's calling, not the poet's. The Milton of the Trinity Manuscript, by contrast, approached poetry the way some novelists approach fiction. His equivalent in modern-day Brooklyn might jot down a list of potential subjects for a Great American Novel.

If *Paradise Lost* was simply a work Milton decided to write—not a work that demanded to be written—what motivated him to spend years creating it, even after he went blind? Here too the comparison with fiction writers is key. The chimerical ambition to write the Great American Novel relies on a sense of past Great American Novelists. The aspiring novelist aims to do for our era what F. Scott Fitzgerald did for his, or Harper Lee for hers. Milton came from a different, longer tradition, but he shared that mindset. His original wish to write an Arthurian national epic was a wish to do for his nation what Virgil did for his with the *Aeneid*.

Poets today study under and imitate contemporaries, but poetry has a long tradition of direct competition with the dead. Virgil, after all, wanted to go up against Homer. He intended his work to be appreciated side by side with its template. Nor was there any sense that poetry produced this way was derivative or second-rate simply because it came after, and took after, that of some distant predecessor. Horace, who wrote famously of wanting to create a "monument more lasting than bronze,"[1] did so in a series of odes explicitly modeled, down to their meters, after Greek lyric masters. All of the major Romantic poets, including Keats, tried their hands at a Shakespearean blank verse drama at least once. Each poetic form, in some sense, pits the poet against generations of poets who have written in it. The power of Shakespeare's best sonnets stopped no one from attempting the form—least of all Milton, who wrote some powerful ones himself. If anything, they serve as examples, challenges, and goads.

That was, and is, the generative force of a tradition. After all, Milton moved the German poet Klopstock, the English poet Blake, and the American poet Lowell to create poetry that echoed his at the level of form, feel, or line. A poet temperamentally the opposite of Milton, the rakish and wild Lord Byron, wrote, in *Cain*, page after page of blank verse about the son of *Paradise Lost*'s main characters.

Yet irreverence too has a revered place in any tradition. Milton himself, invoking the Muse in the manner of his classical models, wrote of soaring *above* the "Aonian mount." A literary tradition does not oppress creativity because the top of the hierarchy, the peak of Mount Parnassus, is always within reach of the upstart. It does not constrain; it galvanizes. Tradition inspires young writers to resurrect the dead by copying the dead, and to immortalize themselves by outwriting the dead—by striving, as Milton did, to write "things unattempted yet in prose or rhyme."[2]

IT'S TIME TO TALK ABOUT LORD BYRON AGAIN

1.

It's time to talk about Lord Byron again.

Apart from W. H. Auden, no one in the twentieth century had favorable things to say about Byron. It was a century that privileged obscurity over wit and fragmentation over fluidity. Morally loose and/or politically radical poets were no longer "mad, bad, and dangerous to know"[1]—in fact, they became (and remain) rather commonplace.

Of course, the nineteenth century did plenty of talking about Byron, much of it while he was still alive. Enough talking, perhaps, to make up for his hundred-year spell as a second-tier Romantic—less knotty and footnotable than Coleridge, less youthful a corpse than Keats. Selling ten thousand copies of your poetry book is impressive by any era's standards; doing it in 1814 London, whose population was no more than that of Dallas today and had a literacy rate a smidge over 50 percent, is even more impressive. And to do it *in a single day*? No wonder Sir Walter Scott (until Byron, Britain's bestselling poet) turned to historical fiction.

But Byron's fame was not merely breathless adulation from ladies of the aristocracy. His most extravagant praise came from extravagantly talented writers, many of them with reputations that aged far better than Byron's. In *Conversations with Eckermann*, we find Goethe in raptures over Byron's verse dramas. Keats and Wordsworth, by contrast, hardly registered with the Weimar sage. In a letter to a friend, a young Flaubert placed Byron in the same category as Shakespeare. Byron's reputation carried even farther than across the Channel: Alexander Pushkin, the father of Russian poetry, got his start imitating Byron in narratives such as "A Prisoner of the Caucasus."

The twentieth century was not so impressed. Though Byron figured in the aspirations of Joyce's Stephen Dedalus, T. S. Eliot accused Byron of possessing an unphilosophical mind. Ironically enough, some of the best philosophers disagreed with that pronouncement. Nietzsche composed a whole "*Manfred*-Meditation" for four hands at the piano. In *The Dawn*, he made no less than five references to Byron, twice mentioning the poet in the same breath as Napoleon. Nietzsche quoted from *Manfred* in *Human, All Too Human*, a passage crucial enough for Bertrand Russell to transcribe it in his synopsis of the philosopher. ("The Tree of Knowledge," in case you're wondering, "is not the Tree of Life.") We can set aside for now the question of whether Byron, or any poet, is truly "philosophical"; what he is *not* is obscure or turgid, two qualities usually associated with "philosophical poetry," particularly of the Eliotic variety.

Tastes changed, as tastes do, and left Byron behind. In France, Baudelaire's *poète maudit* owed more than a little to the Byronic hero, but Symbolism emphasized the very characteristics Byron mocked in Coleridge's "The Rime of the Ancient Mariner." German taste, especially in the later twentieth century, turned to poets fundamentally un-Byronic, such as Celan.

Oddly, Soviet Russia alone kept alive that old Byronic veneration. *Don Juan* still enjoys canonical status in Russia, and the epic's most famous translation was made by one of Stalin's political prisoners, Tatiana Gnedich, entirely from memory. She was held in the cell alone, but with Byron's garrulous narrator for company, her confinement was far from solitary.

Don Juan was not Byron's only tragicomic epic. He wrote a second one, piecemeal, over the duration of his life, a true epic with a plot matching that of his own biography, its hero living a life more interesting than any Lake Poet's and dying a death more interesting than Shelley's. The *Letters and Journals* constitute this incomplete epic, one cut short by the author's death.

2.

Ever since Byron's friend Thomas Moore published the first extracts from Byron's letters in 1830, Byron's epistolary novel of a life has been best savored in a well-chosen selection. (The same holds true of his poetry; writers as prolific as Byron are never consistent.) The Byron biographer Leslie A. Marchand edited the complete letters and journals for Harvard, but over the course of thirteen volumes, even Byron's turbulent company flags. Marchand himself understood this, preparing a selected version as well.

The edition I read and recommend is by Richard Lansdown, who creates self-contained chapters by arranging most of the letters geographically. Byron was a wanderer and exile for most of his later life, which fell neatly into phases: England, the Grand Tour, England again; then a series of Italian cities; and, finally, his fatal sojourn in Greece. Lansdown's selection subdivides only where necessary, according to what Byron was writing, which helps him keep the chapters from getting too long. Each section is prefaced by a keen summary of the narrative background for the ensuing letters. Lansdown picks out the best details, the catnip of gossip and coincidence: how Lady Caroline Lamb's cuckolded husband went on to be Victoria's first prime minister, how the last piece of fan mail Byron received came from none other than Johann Wolfgang von Goethe. Byron's note of thanks was one of the few letters that Lansdown should have included in its entirety. Its irony is exquisite: moments before embarking for Greece, Byron wrote that he considered Goethe's letter a "favourable omen" and promised to visit him in Weimar someday—"if I ever get back."

3.

Are Byron's letters as "good" as those of Keats? It depends on what we are looking for. In the latter, we find great insights into the art of poetry and sighing dreams of poetic fame; in the former, the opposite. Byron *possessed* poetic fame on a scale unimaginable beforehand, but he lived long enough to see that fame reverse its polarity and become infamy. As for insights into the art itself, Byron's letters provide a corrective to Keats's, suggesting that a poet need not have *any* particular insight into what he is doing. Byron, for example, did not know how to improve a poem if it did not come off right the first time: "I am like the tyger (in poesy) if I miss my first spring—I go growling back to my jungle."

Above all, though, Byron tramples on the hothouse-flower notion of The Poet, whether one thinks of the tuberculous nightingale Keats, or Blake and Rilke eavesdropping on angels, or any latter-day botanizing academic. What Byron does is remind us it is possible for poetry to be written in the downtime between pleasure-seeking, politicking, cussing, whoring, and seeing (and saving) the world.

Byron's letters have what you find in those of few other poets: *tumult*. He sought drama, and drama sought him. A future prime minister's wife, jilted, cuts herself for his sake. A few months later, he's sleeping with his half-sister. Whitewater torrents in Switzerland, adultery in Italy. Gonorrhea, malaria, indigestion. We read of him stripping off his coat and boots to keep Shelley, who was unable to swim, from drowning in a storm (in the end, he managed to pull the boat to shore after vigorous bailing). Random gunshots sound a hundred feet from his door, after which he carries a dying policeman into his room to bleed to death. Enough action for one life, perhaps. After all that, he sets off to expel the Turks from Greece ... Byron may well be the Anti-Keats.

This characterization may explain, in part, Byron's animus toward Keats and Wordsworth. I say "in part" because the other part seems to have been envy of elite-critical success; Byron's nastiest remarks about Keats were prompted by the sight of a glowing notice in the *Edinburgh Review*, which had savaged Byron's earliest book. "[Keats's] is the very *Onanism* of poetry," wrote Byron, with the contempt of a man who did not have to resort to onanism much. This sense of Keats as a writer primarily fixated on himself and his feelings, or rather *making* himself feel things, points up the contrast between the introvert and the extrovert. "O for a life of Sensations rather than of Thoughts!" wrote Keats in an 1817 letter to Benjamin Bailey. Byron later wrote to his publisher John Murray, defending the profoundly un-Keatsian *Don Juan*: "Is it not life? Is it not the *thing*?" And earlier, in 1813, Byron had written to Annabella Milbanke, his future wife, that "The great object of life is Sensation—to feel that we exist—even though in pain—it is this 'craving void' which drives us to Gaming—to Battle—to Travel—to intemperate but keenly felt pursuits of every description." Although the two poets agreed about "sensation," it was in two totally different ways: one focused inward, the other focused outward; one wrote odes, the other garrulous satire. One became the poet of sensation. The other became a sensation himself.

With Keats, the letters seem to precede the poetic development, exhibiting a depth of thought and at times a power of expression in advance of the poetry. Much of our sense of what was lost with Keats's death is actually the mind we glimpse in his letters, that paradoxically *metaphysical sensuality*, the poetic expressions of which are those famous odes. With Byron too, this relationship between the letters and the poetry holds, and because his destiny was toward *conversational music* (what else is *Don Juan*?), that is what we get in the letters.

Consider this phrase tossed off to his half-sister, in which he gives us some double alliteration and slips into iambic meter: "… independent as a German Prince who coins his own Cash, or a Cherokee Chief who coins no Cash at all…" It is crucial to recall that this letter was written in 1808, almost coevally with his desultory juvenilia, *Hours of Idleness*. This musical spontaneity would be inaccessible to Byron the versifier for some years; a prodigious amount of deliberate, stylized verse would intervene. Only a decade later, in the ottava rima of *Don Juan*, would the poet catch up to and superimpose on the Byron of the letters. It is in *Don Juan* that the qualities on glorious display in the letters are found from the very start: the dashed-off felicity of phrase, the wild tonal variation, the irreverence, the omnium-gatherum approach to subject matter, the personal voice. These occur naturally in the letters, but Byron had to overcome great obstacles to attain them in his poetry.

4.

What were those obstacles? His audience, for one. From the very beginning, early-nineteenth-century assumptions about what a good poem looked like guided (and misguided) Byron's poetic output. His descriptions of his tour of Albania and Turkey in the letters show his close observation and knack for matching form to content. Consider the crowd of clauses with which he describes the crowded court of Ali Pasha in Tepelena:

The Albanians in their dresses (the most magnificent in the world, consisting of a long white kilt, gold worked cloak, crimson velvet gold laced
jacket and waistcoat, silver mounted pistols and daggers), the Tartars with
their high caps, the Turks in their vast pelisses and turbans, the soldiers
and black slaves with the horses, the former stretched in groups in an
immense open gallery in front of the palace, the latter placed in a kind
of cloister below it, two hundred steeds ready caparisoned to move in
a moment, couriers entering or passing out with dispatches, the kettle
drums beating, boys calling the hour from the minaret of the mosque . . .

Byron uses this raw material when he sets about writing *Childe Harold's
Pilgrimage*, but instead of being heightened or focused, the scene is rendered
diffuse and generic:

> Richly caparisoned, a ready row
> Of armed horse, and many a warlike store,
> Circled the wide-extending court below;
> Above, strange groups adorned the corridor;
> And ofttimes through the area's echoing door,
> Some high-capped Tartar spurred his steed away;
> The Turk, the Greek, the Albanian, and the Moor,
> Here mingled in their many-hued array,
> While the deep war-drum's sound announced the close of day.
>
> The wild Albanian kirtled to his knee,
> With shawl-girt head and ornamented gun,
> And gold-embroidered garments, fair to see:
> The crimson-scarfed men of Macedon;
> The Delhi with his cap of terror on,
> And crooked glaive; the lively, supple Greek;
> And swarthy Nubia's mutilated son;
> The bearded Turk, that rarely deigns to speak,
> Master of all around, too potent to be meek,
>
> Are mixed conspicuous: some recline in groups,
> Scanning the motley scene that varies round;

There some grave Moslem to devotion stoops,
And some that smoke, and some that play are found;
Here the Albanian proudly treads the ground;
Half-whispering there the Greek is heard to prate;
Hark! from the mosque the nightly solemn sound,
The muezzin's call doth shake the minaret,
"There is no god but God!—to prayer—lo! God is great!"

This is early Byron, making all the wrong decisions: syntactical inversions; archaisms; substituting a war-drum for a kettledrum, making the object *harder* to visualize; and making sure a muezzin is minaret-shakingly (!) calling Muslims to prayer (what English readers expected in a poem about the Islamic world), instead of just "boys calling the hour."

By *Don Juan*, the formality would be gone—and the form would be perfected. The familiar and cheeky tone of his letters to college cronies like John Cam Hobhouse would be cast in an ottava rima that swaggered on light feet. Byron's memory of Turkish dress would find a place there, but in *Don Juan* such memories would be focused and quickened:

A Candiote cloak, which to the knee might reach,
    And trousers not so tight that they would burst,
But such as fit an Asiatic breech;
    A shawl, whose folds in Cashmire had been nurst,
Slippers of saffron, dagger rich and handy;
In short, all things which form a Turkish Dandy.

5.

Of course, by the time Byron set out on his various exiles, he was every inch an aristocrat—a class of people who did not fetch their own coats from the closet. Whether exiled, disgraced, or battling the Turks in the name of Hellas, certain things simply did not change. So Byron, even when thousands of pounds in debt, traveled with his share of servants, and wrote home complaining that their coarseness interfered with his raptures over the Alpine scenery.

He much preferred his animals. Byron had kept a bear on a leash while in college, but by the time of his Italian sojourn, the entourage had grown to include a badger, a crow, a monkey, an Egyptian crane, and a fox, not to mention the usual cats and dogs. What with the prolific poetizing, the bisexual vortex of his bed set amid the smells and noises of a small zoo, the international fame, the international infamy, the looks, and the wealth, he must have struck people as a monster of nature, possessing a kind of preternaturally intense life force.

It is hard to put a number on Byron's women, to tally the wives of all classes, serving-girls, and whores who shared his bed. If we are to believe his reports—in one letter he mentions over a hundred liaisons in a single year—a decade in Italy would have seen him surpassing the mille e tre of Don Giovanni himself. The promiscuity at times did wax operatic, if only opéra bouffe, complete with shouting matches between the weeping cuckold and the defiant adulteress as the foreign interloper buttoned his breeches. In 1817, one of Byron's mistresses moved into his house uninvited and refused to leave, even after her husband, her relatives, the police, and Byron himself begged her to go home. (He ended up employing her as a housekeeper-with-benefits, and apparently she performed excellently in both of her duties, reducing his daily expenses by half.) To gauge how sordid Byron got in those years, we need only go to the letters of his neighbor and fellow exile Shelley—who, for all his atheism and his shared contempt for British moral cant, was horrified to hear Byron haggle with an Italian couple over the price of their daughter.

The safest sex Byron had was with other men's wives (except, of course, the wildly unstable Lady Caroline Lamb). Speaking of psychiatric pathology: as Byron's liaisons pile up, his promiscuity comes to seem somewhat diseased or sick—and not just with the clap, which he admittedly contracted. Byron's behavior exceeds that of the usual "handsome rake" at play among the notoriously louche British aristocracy. He had numerous partners of both sexes and all social classes in several countries.

Judging from the letters, Byron's sex life comes across as rather *hectic*. From the perspective of modern psychiatry, he displayed the self-endangering hypersexuality often exhibited by victims of childhood sexual abuse. ("Self-endangering" literally, given that homosexuality was a hanging offense in nineteenth-century Britain; incest, by contrast, got you six months.) It comes as no surprise, then, that Byron was "sexually interfered with" (Lansdown's phrase) by his nurse, May Gray, over the course of several months. He was nine years old when it started. This underemphasized trauma may be why Byron, years later, inverted the Don Juan myth. His Juan remains an innocent youth, not the seducer but the one seduced; women, frequently older and more experienced ones, are the predators.

6.

That preternatural life force was always threatening to turn into its opposite. Over-the-top Byronic promiscuity is never far from the darkest depression. (In our day, for example, porn stars attempt or commit suicide more often than the general population.) In Byron's case, though, the suicidal impulse was matched by an equally powerful joie de vivre. The two reconciled and hybridized into the wish to be *reborn*.

More than once—beginning in 1810 with his *Childe Harold* tourism, actually—Byron sought a way to erase his past and start over in some new, nobler, purer way. His flight to Italy was another attempt to escape his past, or as he tellingly called it, his *"life* in England" (emphasis mine, death wish his). Within a year of his ongoing Italian orgy, he started contemplating ways of annihilating himself. Lansdown gives us a long letter in which Byron tries to make the legal and economic arrangements to settle in Bolivar's South America. The increasingly pudgy aristocrat was many things, but a spade and plow man he was not, and we hear no more about the scheme after that. Nevertheless, this new identity is not so easily dismissed as fantasy, given what we know about his eventual "rebirth" as a commander of Greek rebel forces. He really *was* that eager for a new life—that is, for death. Escaping to occupied Greece was one more way for Byron to kill off Byron while still enjoying boys and hock.

And yet Byron's self-transformation—his *self-overcoming*, in Nietzschean terms—seems genuine, judging from the last section of letters. The jaded, rapidly aging nobleman broke through to actual nobility. These last letters constitute at once the least salacious and most fascinating group. Gone are the petty sniping, the boastful vulgarity, the self-pity (his literary productivity, alas, went with them). In their place, we get instructions to bankers arranging loans for the cause, clear-eyed assessments of Greek mendacity, and accounts of close escapes from capture by the Turkish fleet.

Byron's problems in Missolonghi seem bitterly familiar: mercenary tribes, more interested in foreign money than national independence; endless internal squabbles among half a dozen would-be George Washingtons; questions of equipment and training and trust. Americans would encounter the same intractable factors when trying to "nation-build" in the fractured, fractious areas of Afghanistan and Iraq—and they had the advantage of being the empire. Byron paid for his weapons and soldiers out of his own pocket.

7.

Shelley, whom Yeats would later compare to an angel, drifted decomposing for ten days in the Gulf of La Spezia before his body washed up. The author of *Adonais* could be identified only by the volume of Keats in his pocket (an initial report claimed it was a Bible, perhaps to suggest the wild-eyed atheist had been coming around to Christian belief before the end). The body was cremated on the beach, and Byron reports, with all the deadpan delivery of Gabriel García Márquez, the magical-realist fact that Shelley's heart did not burn "and is now preserved in spirits of wine."

The corpse took four hours to burn completely. Byron, as if to undrown his friend, went for a three-mile swim in the sea while the pyre smoked on the shore. Shirtless in the afternoon sun, Byron too burned. When he emerged—"scorched and drenched," as Lansdown points out—he began the slow process of blistering. For days, he could not lie on his back or flank, and eventually the skin sloughed. Byron described himself to have been "St. Bartholomewed," referring to the patron saint of the Armenian Church, martyred by being flayed alive. (Among Byron's more interesting side projects was a collaboration with Armenian monks to produce a grammar of their language.) That image of death was followed, shortly afterward, by an image of rebirth: "But now I have a new skin, though it is * * * * tender."

Shortly after this self-baptism-cum-sympathetic-cremation, Byron, the most graphomaniacal of the Romantics, stopped producing. He did return to writing for the occasional poem, like the much-anthologized one about reaching his thirty-sixth year. Still, the last year of his life, like Shakespeare's, was mostly one of willed silence, or of the failure to will verse. "Composition," he wrote in 1823, "is a habit of my mind," but it proved to be the first habit he broke to effect his metamorphosis, or his rebirth.

8.

By this time, of course, he had already produced a body of work that, unlike Wordworth's or Keats's, remains too vast and various to describe as a whole. Byron the man can be analyzed and generalized about; Byron the writer, the *whole* writer, defies any single critique.

He was easily the most ambitious of all the European Romantics, and indeed perhaps the most ambitious writer of the nineteenth century—barring Victor Hugo and Goethe, both of whose literary ambitions included nonpoetic forms (and both of whose lives and letters are not nearly as interesting). Zoom out and observe how, within a mere ten years, Byron stormed almost every imaginable type and genre of poetry: the narrative, the lyric, and the dramatic; within narrative and lyric, both Romance and satire, and within drama, both the history play (e.g., *The Two Foscari*) and the religious biblical mystery play.

Dates of composition suggest *Cain* was composed during a lull between cantos of *Don Juan*. This toggling between the worldly-coarse and the mythopoetic would not be seen again until James Joyce, who knew better than to go fully mythic and bring his otherworldly beings onstage, as it were. Joyce kept his mythic material covered with, coded into, his Dublin and his Dubliners. Byron, by contrast, wanted to be everything in full, with no concessions to the spirit of the age because he had *done* the spirit of the age. In his last years, he wanted to become utterly untimely (*unzeitgemäße*, to again invoke Nietzsche). He wanted to be a neoclassical satirist like Pope *and* the Miltonic bard of the Beyond. Granted, he succeeded at his satirical project, but he failed to nail his

Miltonic one—but Milton's biblical blank-verse sublime has escaped everyone, even Milton himself in *Paradise Regain'd*.

This breadth is what makes generalizations about Byron's oeuvre so difficult. What can be said of the satires cannot be said of the blank-verse plays; what can be said of the blank-verse plays cannot be said of the Oriental romances. The haunted Byronic hero of *Manfred* is nowhere to be found in *Don Juan*. The letters alone, which show us Byron's rapid-fire multiplicity, possess a breadth and variety equal to the *Collected Poems*. In fact, his worst poetry seems to be material that has no parallel or context in his life and letters. You can't imagine this letter-writer also writing *Sardanapalus*.

9.

You can, however, imagine the Byron of the letters writing *Don Juan*—so readily, in fact, that it is hard to understand why his closest associates were so turned off by it.

As for the readership at large, it is rather more understandable. Byron's reputation followed typical patterns of fame. Sudden adulation suddenly reversed its polarity. One month he was the embodiment of Poesy complete with a dimple in the chin; the next he was an incestuous devil, complete with a limp. His contemporaries were utterly incapable of balanced appraisals when it came to him. Byron's fame cooled for a typical reason as well: He stayed a bestseller even in disgrace and exile so long as he kept churning out Oriental romances, but when he broke with this pattern, no one wanted this new *risus sardonicus* Byron.

Shelley was one of only a few who saw *Don Juan* for the masterpiece it was (in fact, the boat that capsized in the Gulf of La Spezia was named after it). The letters show us how, just as Byron hit on his true theme and style as a poet, people around him started turning on his masterpiece—even John Murray, who had made a killing off of Byron's earlier works; even Countess Teresa Guiccioli, who was sleeping with him. This happened *while Byron was still writing it*. Each set of two or three cantos weathered leery distaste and recommendations for cuts before it even saw print.

Most poets claim indifference to public reaction, then anguish over a nasty review; Byron claimed indifference too, but as it turns out, he actually meant it. Judging from his own testimony, Byron would have given up on *Don Juan* if so many friends and strangers had not booed it. He knocked out sixteen cantos and the opening part of a seventeenth, admirably self-assured about its worth, perhaps channeling that new kid who had arrived in London years earlier with a Scottish accent and a limp:

> I care nothing for what may be the consequence—critical or otherwise—all the bullies on earth shall not prevent me from writing what I like—& publishing what I like—"coute qui coute" [cost what it may]—if they had let me alone—I probably should not have continued beyond the five first—as it is—there shall be such a poem—as has not been since Ariosto—in length—in satire—in imagery—and in what I please.

Why have the letters, and *Don Juan*, aged so much better than vast tracts of Byron's other poetic work? Like Coleridge, but unlike the other English Romantics, Byron created dramatic scenes and situations that were *separable from their language*. Compare Keats's urn, or Wordsworth's daffodils: there, the beauty of the language is the truth of the poetry; the two cannot be separated. In much of Byron's High Romantic work, imaginative force compensated for a lack of linguistic force. *The Corsair* was written in one hot week, and a reader today can tell. The style and power are in the teller and the tale—not in the telling.

Don Juan, by contrast, has aged so well precisely because of the narrator's leisurely disinterest in his own story. He is far more interested in his rhymes, digressions, and epigrammatic clinchers—in other words, the *words*. Byron's great comic epic was produced just as quickly as his other works, but what makes those seem half-thought-out makes *Don Juan* seem effervescent. Haste and inattention freed up his tongue to do what it does best.

The same principle is at play in the letters, with their incorporation of foreign phrases, associative leaps divided by proto-Dickinsonian dashes, and lucid ludic prowess. Here too we find abrupt riffs and dilations where extemporaneous linguistic delight takes over. Associations tumble out of him. When a review expressed distaste for *Don Juan*'s mode-mixing—"We are never scorched and drenched whilst standing in the same spot"—Byron seizes on the metaphor to accumulate an energetic, profane, chockablock little catalogue:

> Blessings on his experience! Ask him these questions about "scorching and drenching." Did he never play at cricket, or walk a mile in hot weather? Did he never spill a dish of tea over himself in handing the cup to his charmer, to the great shame of his nankeen breeches? Did he never swim in the sea at noonday with the sun in his eyes and on his head, which all the foam of ocean could not cool? Did he never draw his foot out of too hot water, damning his eyes and his valet's? Did he never tumble into a river or lake, fishing, and sit in his wet clothes in the boat, or on the bank, afterwards "scorched and drenched," like a true sportsman?

Shakespeare too suffered the disapproval of later critics for mixing comedy and tragedy. Byron's letters from day to day, like Shakespeare's dramas from scene to scene, vary genres and moods. Byron the letter-writer was not above skipping up into rhymes, just as Shakespeare did not hesitate to dash off a scene in prose. Both writers approximated the alternations of life as it is lived.

That riff I quoted, triggered by a trivial critique, is not the sort of thought, tone, or blithe vulgarity that could be cast in a conventional nineteenth-century English poem—or a poem in *any* tradition, really, save the comic/bawdy tradition (which is not quite the same as "light verse"). This tradition, often linked to satire, can be found in parts of Chaucer, in those bits of Shakespeare most often cut by directors, and in the bawdy doggerel of many an otherwise prim poet's private letters, including T. S. Eliot's. In *Don Juan*, a comic, *inspired* vulgarity surfaced shamelessly. After that, it dove deep to wait out the Victorians, then made a splashing spectacle of itself again in Joyce's *Ulysses*.

Byron had something in his nature that was alien to the ode or the blank-verse meditation or the sighing romance, but it was not something "unpoetic." Only the poetic culture deemed it so (and still does). Though he expressed it immortally in *Don Juan*, he expressed it first in his letters.

As Victorian England became even more prudish and pious, Byron fell into disrepute as a womanizer and a godless type—after all, he had heroized Cain and given British literature its first and, to my knowledge, only sympathetic treatment of incest (Manfred is tormented, yes, but you're still meant to feel for him). The letters don't contradict these impressions. Once, severely ill on his first visit to Greece, Byron scared off the priests and their extreme unction by threatening to "turn Mussalman if they come again." And his half-sister Augusta seems to be one of the few women he truly loved, both as a sibling and as something more.

Byron's anticlericalism is rather commonplace among contemporary intellectuals, and his doomed relationship with his half-sister now seems more tragic than shocking. We can see through to a different Byron in his letters. Take his relationship with Coleridge, for example. In a letter soliciting Byron's help, Coleridge compared Byron to a swan and himself to a cygnet taken under Byron's wing. He wanted Byron to lean on his publisher, John Murray, to give him a contract. Byron's reply was full of generous praise, and sure enough, Murray ended up publishing *Christabel and Other Poems* the next year. Coleridge's new volume was no great score for the publisher of Scott and Austen, but Murray could afford to do Byron this favor: Murray paid Byron well for rights to his poems, but his star author, even when in debt (and he was always in debt), steadfastly refused to accept royalty checks for his bestsellers.

Byron did not stop there. Within a few days, he was urging his friend Thomas Moore, the once bestselling, now forgotten Irish poet, to review Coleridge favorably upon the book's release: "I do think [Coleridge] only wants a Pioneer and a sparkle or two to explode most gloriously." While Byron the satirist made the occasional quip at *Ancient Mariner*'s expense—"I wish he would explain his explanation"—Byron the man proved supportive and generous, and Coleridge remained grateful. Decades later, Coleridge's grandson co-edited Byron's thirteen-volume *Complete Works*.

Coleridge was not the only poet Byron helped. After the *Don Juan* capsized in the Gulf of La Spezia, Byron wrote to Shelley's estranged father, aristocrat to aristocrat, and secured an allowance for the poet's widow.

Byron also seems free of the prejudices typical of his time and class, such as antisemitism. His Scottish ancestry, his clubfoot, and his bisexuality seem to have immunized him. In 1814, at the height of his fame, Byron collaborated with two Jewish musicians, eventually publishing the volume *Hebrew Melodies*. "The Destruction of Sennacherib," a common classroom text, emerged from this collaboration. A few days before Byron—in disgrace, messily separated from his wife, barred from seeing his baby daughter—was driven out of Britain, the composer Isaac Nathan sent him a package of matzos as a gift for his journey.

11.

Byron wanted to be buried in Greece, but his companions brought his body back to England. In a symbolic denouement that would seem terribly heavy-handed in a novel, the sexual sinner was buried at the Church of St. Mary Magdalene.

He had been famous during his lifetime, but "fame" does not sufficiently describe Byron's posthumous legacy. He went from Britain's most famous poet to a pan-European phenomenon, crossing over from the history of literature into history at large, as the countless comparisons between him and Napoleon reveal. How did this come about?

Neither Byron's backstory nor his looks had as much to do with it as one would think. Paradoxically, it was his writing—even some of the worst of it. Notice that many of his most enthusiastic admirers were writers from other languages; only Shakespeare traveled better. Both poets crossed languages and cultures so well because their effects were not limited to nuances of language alone—that is, their poetry derived its effect from elements that were *not* lost in translation. The histrionics of Hamlet leaping into Ophelia's grave or Othello stabbing Desdemona have counterparts in the Byronic hero springing a princess from a Turkish harem or Manfred brooding on a mountaintop. Such scenes and situations, products of Byron's highly dramatic imagination, could be shelled from their original language and still captivate.

So a year after Giuseppe Verdi made a grand opera out of *Macbeth*, he made one out of Byron's *The Corsair* (*Il corsaro*, 1848). So did Berlioz, incidentally. Adolphe Adam, better known as the composer of *Giselle*, made a ballet of it. All three *Corsair*-based productions premiered between 1844 and 1856, defying the usual pattern of a famous writer's reputation declining after their death. 1844 also witnessed the publication of the bestseller by Alexandre Dumas in which Edmond Dantès returns as the Count of Monte Cristo, a rich and haunted nobleman who loves dressing in Turkish clothes and is repeatedly compared to Byron, both by the author himself and by fascinated characters in the book.

As the century progressed, Byron's example hurled forth larger-than-life figures whose lives and careers—consciously or unconsciously—paralleled elements of Byron's. The Byron who fought alongside natives for freedom from the Ottoman Empire had a human echo one hundred years later in T. E. Lawrence, who even shared Byron's philhellenism, translating the *Odyssey* while on campaign. (Lawrence's great difference with Byron, however, was his sexually repressed lifestyle; some of his contemporaries believed him to be asexual.) The seducer in dashing exotic garb rode again as Rudy Valentino as *The Son of the Sheikh*, one Western cultural infatuation echoing the other. Simply compare photographs of Valentino as an Arab with Thomas Phillips's portrait of Byron in Albanian costume, and you will see how Byron settled into the collective memory of the West. And the Byron whose unapologetic sexual deviance flouted British mores and British law, resulting in disgrace and exile, lived and loved again in Oscar Wilde. Both men, neither one an Englishman, died in exile from the London that had toasted their brilliance. Wilde, like Byron, flourished when he pursued art forms that showcased wit and epigrammatic flair and utterly underperformed the moment he attempted a poetic drama on a religious theme (in Wilde's case, *Salomé*).

Among contemporary poets, it is hard to find a single poet whose life or work has anything Byronic about it. This has to do, at least in part, with how poetry in general has turned inward and toward solemnity. We are, in this respect, the descendants of Wordsworth and Keats. The unifying characteristic of Byron's poetry in any of his genres—lyric, narrative romance, satire—is that it's freewheeling. This is why, at its worst, it is slapdash, while at its best, it has spontaneity, serendipity, *sprezzatura*.

We have had no Byronic poet for a few generations now, and we are all the duller for it. Luckily for us, this situation is not without remedy. It is time to talk about—and read—Lord Byron again.

KEPLER'S SNOWFLAKE

Johannes Kepler (1571–1630) wrote some of the foundational works of modern astronomy. He was the first to prove that planets orbit the sun in ellipses, not perfect circles. His curiosity was far-ranging, however, and in 1609 he wrote a brief treatise about, of all things, a snowflake. He presented it to his patron at court as *Strena Seu de Nive Sexangula* (A New Year's Gift of Hexagonal Snow).

Kepler's question—*Why do all snowflakes have six corners?*—wouldn't be answered until the development of X-ray crystallography in the twentieth century. Though it may be inconclusive from a purely scientific perspective, his essay has great historical value. It is full of surprising revelations about the workings of early modern science—above all, its underemphasized relationship to mysticism . . . and poetry.

KEPLER AS POET

Kepler thinks about snowflakes by way of visual metaphor.

Neruda never wrote an ode to a snowflake, but if he were to do so, how readily we can imagine him invoking *la granada* and *la colmena*. Masterfully unexpected juxtapositions, these: two warm-weather comparisons for an ice crystal. Neruda would have done it purely by sensory intuition. It's precisely these poetically charged connections—snowflake, pomegranate, beehive—that Kepler hits on in his found poem.

But there's more than just Neruda here. You can find notes of court poetry, and of Donne's love for paradox. Kepler presents the treatise as a *New Year's Gift*, but then, with a wink, says his gift is a mere snowflake, a nothing, a *nix*—punning on how *nix* means "snowflake" in Latin, but sounds like "nothing" in German (*nicht*). Kepler's snowflake, like Donne's flea, becomes something much bigger than itself by the time he's done talking. (Kepler isn't the only astronomer-mathematician with a poet's instincts; Omar Khayyam, for one, is famous for his *Rubaiyat*, a series of quatrains he jotted down between spells in the observatory.)

Kepler's treatise even eschews easy closure, much like a contemporary avant-garde poem. Spoiler alert: he never actually explains why a snowflake has six corners. In fact, at one point in his speculations, he actually concedes that he may be building his next few ideas on poppycock: "I will pursue... this conjecture as far as possible, and not examine until later whether it is in fact true. Otherwise, the untimely discovery of a mistake could keep me from my undertaking." This is an absolutely Keatsian comfort with uncertainty. I find it poetic too that this booklet about snowflakes (1611) came *after* the *Astronomia Nova* (1609). After, that is, Kepler had calculated the elliptical orbits of the solar system. This *New Year's Gift* marks a turn—a "volta," to use poetry lingo—from the heavenly to the earthly, a poetic transition if ever there was one. Imagine: the tired astronomer, eyes bloodshot, fingers ink-stained (Kepler made all his own calculations), walks along a Prague bridge and notices the snowflakes landing on him, his celestial mind quickened by this symmetry on his sleeve.

THE ONLY POETIC QUESTIONS ARE QUESTIONS OF FORM

The American poet John Frederick Nims, in 1990, wrote a pattern poem about this treatise. "The Six-Cornered Snowflake" is a multipart riff on the text and on Kepler himself. Nims shapes his stanzas as six-cornered snowflakes, an asterisk at every point.

```
                    *
                   But
                  today
                the Royal
             Astronomer's late,
   *    hunched there, his mind aswirl with more    *
        than whimwhams of an emporer—all bemused
         by signatures of something from above:
           the dædal snowflake crystaling in six.
           Old thunders roll: "Hast entered
            into the treasures of the snow?"
            Not yet; but mind is given to know;
           the great world to be known. Why six?
          Perhaps no reason but exuberant joy?
         Pattern's a pleasure; often nature plays
   *     not for rude truth but loveliness of line:    *
                item: this Gothic
                   mandala's
                    set of
                     six
                      *
```

This use of the asterisk is a masterstroke of ingenuity—*asterisk* is Latin for "little star."

Kepler's *snowflake* takes shape very seriously too. The astronomer was also fond of geometry; he is known for discovering two solids, to this day called "Kepler's polyhedra," the faces of which are equilateral triangles. Here, Kepler examines octahedrons, spheres, and hexagons, running "thought experiments" with them, stacking them and squeezing them together in the hope of deriving some insight into the snowflake's structure.

LANGUAGE

Burton, in the *The Anatomie of Melancholie*, thought he was writing a text on medicine. He never imagined the theory of the four humors would evaporate, and only the fantastic mouthfuls of his *prose* would hold future generations' interest. Galileo's books are taught in Italian high schools as masterpieces of style. We know Aristotle only from his students' lecture notes, which is why he's no good for pleasure reading; his finished works, lost to time, were actually dialogues, praised by Cicero for their literary style.

Today, we have far fewer examples of major scientists presenting their own ideas in an entertaining form. Stephen Hawking and Freeman Dyson come to mind. Most scientists only write for each other, with "reporters" and "popularizers" serving as intermediaries for the general reader. Popular science texts avoid literary flourishes. They are after clarity, not beauty—no gratuitous puns on "nothing," no quotes from Virgil's *Georgics*.

Kepler, luckily for the reader, came from an era that antedates the death of literary style in scientific writing. He also came from an era before jargon. You don't have to familiarize yourself with a special vocabulary to understand what he's saying. You do have to pay attention, though; it may be poetry, but it's difficult poetry. (His works of astronomy are harder to follow—too much math.) What works in our favor is that he's writing not to a fellow scientist but to his patron at court: the delightfully named Lord Wacker von Wackenfels.

METAPHOR, MOTHER OF SCIENCE

Late in the treatise, Kepler ponders snowflakes by observing the frosty window above a hot bath. Another visual metaphor, another example of poetic thinking. Metaphor, to a mind like Kepler's, is not a literary device or stylistic frill. The metaphor *is* the thought, not some ornament on that thought's expression: the gift itself, not the bow on top. A law of physics doesn't ornament the universe. It *governs* the universe. Today's scientists may roll their eyes at poetry, but they have kept their love—their *need*—for metaphor. The most useful metaphors of the modern era, after all, have come from scientists.

It's not just that scientists rely on metaphor to describe things and processes they can't directly observe (electron "cloud," quantum "leap," genetic "transcription"). Take it from a radiologist: The discipline of anatomy hides a visual metaphor under every pin. Listen to the music of the spheres, and the ear bones involved are the "stirrup," the "anvil," and the "hammer," which in turn bangs on the ear's "drum." We lose this sense of analogical—that is, poetic—thinking when we memorize "stapes," "incus," "malleus," and "tympanum." Metaphor was present at the very beginning of modern biology—and before the beginning as well. This is why a daisy is the "day's eye," and a *bluebell* is exactly what it says it is.

Scientific Latin is rarely as dry as it seems. A title like *Sidereus Nuncius* becomes a little less forbidding when you find out it means "Starry Messenger" (its author was the same Galileo who exclaimed, with high-poetic anthropomorphism, that Saturn had "ears"). Kepler, a contemporary of Galileo's, played along, writing a response to Galileo's work called *Conversations with the Starry Messenger*. Similarly, there is an interesting touch for the modern reader in the treatise's title with *Nive Sexangula* (Six-Cornered Snow): that juxtaposition of the natural and the Latinate—"the Pedigree of Honey," "an Amethyst remembrance," "Inebriate of air"—is one of Emily Dickinson's most alchemical effects ("inebriate," either the verb or the participle, has never been used powerfully before or since, anywhere in English).

Noticing those six corners, then contemplating, through a series of metaphors, why it should be so and not some other way: this is at once childlike wonder and grown-up investigation. It's a mix that gives us both the best science and the best poetry.

THE "FORMATIVE FACULTY"

Kepler came from an earlier scientific culture when hard science wasn't quite so hard. One more way of marveling at the universe, it hadn't yet disassociated itself from theology or the humanities. Modern-day atheists, in their bestselling polemics, tend to present science and religion as opponents in a centuries-long duel. True, the Church was out to destroy Galileo—but Galileo was never out to destroy Christianity. This tends to be forgotten.

In the history of science, piety is more common than we would expect. The boom years (or rather, boom *centuries*) are full of reverent revolutionaries. Isaac Newton was religious to the point of wackiness; he spent years trying to decode the exact dimensions of Solomon's Temple, which he believed could be found in the Hebrew of the Old Testament. The religious mind of Blaise Pascal has been preserved in his *Pensées*, a glowing book that braids the rational and poetic in an eloquent double helix. Kepler himself studied theology at Tubingen, and he got his start as an astronomer when the university's faculty assigned him to teach astronomy at a provincial high school.

These two things—the era's indistinct boundary between science and religion, and an innate theological streak—lead to some truly unusual visions toward the middle and end of *A New Year's Gift*. Kepler, as it turns out, was not just a poet. He was also a mystic.

"THAT THRICE GREATEST ANIMAL, THE ORB OF THE EARTH"

Let me quote the whole passage where this startling phrase appears:

> From this almost Nothing I have very nearly recreated the entire Universe, which contains everything! And having before shied away from discussing the tiny soul of the most diminutive animal, am I now to present the soul of that thrice greatest animal, the orb of the earth, in a tiny atom of snow?

Or, as another well-known mystical poet phrased it:

> To see a World in a Grain of Sand
> And a Heaven in a Wild Flower,
> Hold Infinity in the palm of your hand
> And Eternity in an hour.[1]

That "thrice greatest," by the way, may be a nod to Hermes Trismegistus ("Thrice Great Hermes"), founder of the "hermetic tradition" of alchemy, astrology, and magic. This connection isn't idle speculation; Kepler's mother was accused of witchcraft.

By calling the earth an "animal," Kepler invokes the Latin word for "soul," *anima*, which implies that the planet has a soul. He sounds like the Western world's first environmentalist. Elsewhere, the treatise speaks of the earth as a living thing—again, metaphorically. This time, though, the metaphor he selects is the human being: "There is thus a formative faculty in the body of the earth, and its vehicle is vapor, just as breath is the vehicle of the human soul. . . . " This vapor condenses into snowflakes when its "constructive heat" meets the winter cold. Snowflakes are the earth's breath on a cold day, rising as fog, falling as ice crystals.

For Kepler, symmetry is divine. A plant has symmetry because it has an *anima*, but this *anima* is dependent on that of the earth. Kepler's analogy is host–parasite: the planet is to its flora as "the human body [is] to lice." Water vapor, the breath, is alive, just like the earth that breathes it. Remember that in Kepler's time people believed in "lifesbreath," the *nishmat chayim* that God breathed into Adam (they thought you could die if you sighed too deeply). The snowflake's sixfold symmetry arose because this seemingly inorganic thing was actually organic. Kepler couldn't figure out why the snowflake had six corners, but he was certain that its symmetry was divine. "I believe that the cause behind the six-cornered snowflake is no other than the one responsible for the regular shapes and the constant numbers that appear in plants," he writes. "I cannot believe that this ordered shape is present by chance." Centuries later, Einstein would famously echo this religious conviction: "God does not play dice with the universe."

FEARSOME MYSTERY, FEARSOME KNOWLEDGE

As Nims writes in his poem, "Today, more knowing, we know less. But know / less more minutely. A schoolboy could / dazzle poor Kepler with his chemistry, / chat of molecular bonds, how HOH / freezes to crystal, the six struts / magnetized by six hydrogen nuclei." X-ray crystallography has resolved the question Kepler so brilliantly failed to answer; physiology and genetics have replaced "the formative faculty" with sodium-potassium ion pumps and deoxyribonucleic acid. Does that mean that we can't partake of Kepler's reverent wonder, now that we know better than he did? Is there any point in reading a seventeenth-century treatise that doesn't accomplish what it set out to do? I say yes. This is a great mind dancing, and there is no such thing as a correct dance.

As for us, our modern wonder is of a different kind. Where mystery has receded, curiosity has flooded in. We revere by knowing, and we find that awe never needed mystery. That has been the story of science for centuries now: the death of awe; the investigation; and, finally, the resurrection of awe, this time unkillable. We experience that awe—not the *mysterium tremendum* but the *scientia tremenda*—when we see the Hubble telescope's pictures of a dumbbell nebula, or an electron microscope's snapshot of a dodecahedral virus. Kepler experienced both kinds of awe too, the large-scale and the small-scale: once when he looked to the heavens and realized the orbits were all ellipses, and again when he looked to the earth and was charmed, as I have been, by the six-cornered snowflake.

VOYAGING WITH CHARLES DARWIN ON THE *BEAGLE*

1.

I did research a long time ago. Not because I wanted to, but because I wanted future residency program directors, years later during interview season, to ask me about CXCR3 expression in multiple sclerosis. I planned to sit back, gaze intellectually into the near distance, and deliver a prepared speech on the promise of immunological markers toward *a treatment, and, we hope, a cure*—a project I had been involved with for maybe four weeks between ten in the morning and two in the afternoon.

During my research summer, I looked through a high-powered micro-scope and counted cells. The cells I needed to count were stained a deep green, simultaneously dark and fluorescent, if you can imagine that. My immediate superiors were two brilliant twenty-somethings, one a Swede named Pia, the other a German named Corinne. I had to count these dark green stars in one field of view, then ease the slide north, until the topmost star was just below the margin, and count again. Eventually I'd make it through a whole slide and jot down a number.

This seemingly tedious task went very quickly once I realized all the slides had counts that fell between twenty-five and forty-five cells, except for the outlier slide that had fewer than five. Soon, I could just kind of sweep back and forth and get a feel. "Thin-slicing," Malcolm Gladwell might call it, though I think you need ten thousand hours of experience before you're supposed to do that.

As you can imagine, I made a serious mistake that first morning: I assumed that box of slides was my morning's work. I made short work of the whole batch so I could read Nabokov. That was a rookie researcher's mistake; the box had been meant to occupy me for a week. Corinne and Pia were so impressed by my efficiency that they held a small conference with much enthusiastic nodding. I realized I had gotten myself assigned a whole new task in exchange for three chapters of *Pale Fire*. Fortunately, the next task was actually pretty cool: I was going to be the "runner," fetching freshly tapped cerebrospinal fluid from the main Cleveland Clinic hospital and transporting it back to the research facility.

I showed up at the main hospital that afternoon and received my package, a light styrofoam box about the size of a toaster oven. I secured it under my arm, took a deep breath, and started running. I ran through the lobby, into the summer traffic, through the line by the hot-dog stall. I hurdled a stroller, punched a kid and stole his bike, ditched the bike and hopscotched over car roofs against the flow of traffic, and eventually burst through the door of the lab, holding the box over my head like Charlton Heston holding the tablets on Sinai.

"I've got it!" I shouted.

Pia turned to me. "How hot is it out there?"

I lowered the box, hiding the sweat blotches under my arms. "Seventy-two, seventy-three?" I felt my left earlobe drip.

Corinne rose and looked closely at me. "Are you okay? What happened?"

"I ran."

"Why?"

"I'm the runner." I regretted the tautological sound of this immediately. "And I, um, didn't want the heat to, uh, denature our cells."

Corinne took the lid off the box. "The CSF is on ice, ja? Look."

A test tube full of clear liquid was nestled in about forty ice cubes.

"In fact," commented Pia, "the only thing that could damage the cells is if they were jarred about."

I walked after that. Once I realized that I had a lot of time before the ice melted, and that they *wanted* me to take my time on the errand, I went to the falafel place for a wrap on every trip. If I'd already had lunch, I'd treat myself to a baklava piece. The CSF would sit on the chair next to me, freshly drained from some unfortunate MS sufferer's spinal canal, and I would stare at it and think about how terrible it would be, on the one hand, to grow old and have health problems, and on the other hand how shitty it would be to die young, having sacrificed your twenties to memorizing the mechanism of insulin and the Krebs cycle. I couldn't even enjoy my summer vacation without tainting it with this mindless research. Well, I thought, maybe I'd get a publication out of this. That would look great on a résumé. A real conversation-starter.

I actually *did* get a paper out of it (the coveted "fifth author" spot), and this is what I/we sounded like:

T-cell accumulation in the central nervous system (CNS) is considered crucial to the pathogenesis of multiple sclerosis (MS). We found that the majority of T cells within the cerebrospinal fluid (CSF) compartment expressed the CXC chemokine receptor 3 (CXCR), independent of CNS inflammation. Quantitative immunohistochemistry revealed continuous accumulation of CXCR3+ T cells during MS lesion formation. The expression of one CXCR3 ligand, interferon (IFN)-γ-inducible protein of 10 kDa (IP-10)/CXC chemokine ligand (CXCL) 10 was elevated in MS CSF, spatially associated with demyelination in CNS tissue sections and correlated tightly with CXCR3 expression. These data suggest a critical role for CXCL10 and CXCR3 in the accumulation of T cells in the CNS of MS patients.[1]

In other words, it was 1) the work of a collective, not an individual; 2) unbeautiful; 3) uninteresting to a layperson; 4) from a verbal perspective, overly Latinate and jargon-laden (see #2); 5) divorced from direct observation (unless counting cells through a microscope qualifies); and 6) really, really "zoomed in" on one specific detail, with no hint of a larger perspective.

You may think number 6 only seemed the case to *me* because I was a medical student with no eagle's eye perspective on MS research. Yet repeated attempts to find out—from Pia, Corinne, and eventually the chief neurologist in charge of the whole lab—exactly *what* our paper meant from the standpoint of treatment, experimental therapies, or even our "understanding" of the still obscure pathogenesis of MS lesions, revealed that there *was* no answer. The distances between act, interpretation, and application were just too great. Our paper was just *another piece of evidence* that the immune system *played a role* in MS. What we were doing was necessary to the furthering of neuroscience, yes, and yet we were focused not on the forest, not on the trees, not on the leaves, but on a single segment of single vein of a single leaf, tracing it back and forth, going nowhere in particular. What did I expect? Research isn't visiting the Galápagos and adumbrating a fundamental secret of biology while chasing bugs over the rocks—or at least, research isn't that *anymore*. That ship has sailed, as they say.

Its name was HMS *Beagle*.

2.

Its most famous destination, as every biologist knows, was the Galápagos Islands. Charles Darwin's research happened in an environment nothing like the stainless-steel basins and glass panes and microscope-slide-nudging quiet of the modern laboratory. We imagine the father of evolutionary science clambering over volcanic landscapes, reeking of sweat, covered in dirt and beetles, like some kind of animistic shaman communing with the wilderness. Darwin arrived at evolutionary theory by traveling very far indeed: deep into the stubbornly prehistoric, pre*human* rockscapes of these islands off the coast of nowhere.

The closest I've come to visiting the Galápagos is through the eponymous BBC One documentary, which happened to be streaming on Netflix the same week I started reading Everyman's Library #104, *The Voyage of the* Beagle. Apparently there are no resorts on these islands, no parasailing Missouri-based insurance agents and their freckled wives and daughters, no islanders offering to braid the wife's hair into dreadlocks, no piña coladas with the little umbrellas; the Galápagos remain as pristine and primordial as they were one hundred and fifty years ago.

As I watched these baroquely decked-out birds and weird insects, I thought about Darwin poking around on these islands, about how he never recorded a single bug bite even though he must have experienced his fair share. I thought about modern-day Darwinists: the slick academics, symposium atheists, and all the self-certain undergraduates who scoff at traditional religion in his name. Darwin's Darwinism feels *earned* in a way these campus Darwinisms don't, as evidenced in this excerpt:

> On the 13th the storm raged with its full fury: our horizon was narrowly limited by the sheets of spray borne by the wind. The sea looked ominous, like a dreary waving plain with patches of drifted snow: whilst the ship laboured heavily, the albatross glided with its expanded wings right up the wind. At noon a great sea broke over us, and filled one of the whale boats, which was obliged to be instantly cut away. The poor *Beagle* trembled at the shock, and for a few minutes would not obey her helm; but soon, like a good ship that she was, she righted and came up to the wind again. Had another sea followed the first, our fate would have been decided soon, and for ever. We had now been twenty-four days trying in vain to get westward; the men were worn out with fatigue, and they had not had for many nights or days a dry thing to put on. Captain Fitz Roy gave up the attempt to get westward by the outside coast. In the evening we ran in behind False Cape Horn, and dropped our anchor in forty-seven fathoms, fire flashing from the windlass as the chain rushed round it.

To go on a sea voyage in the early 1800s was to put yourself at mortal risk, especially if you ventured so far outside the usual trade routes. Darwin accepted danger in a way even today's most dedicated evolutionary biologists don't (and don't have to). Boarding the *Beagle* required a physical fearlessness that mirrored the intellectual fearlessness involved in challenging nearly two millennia of Christian dogma.

3.

Because the *Beagle*, by sailing into the history of science, sailed through the history of religion as well. That is as inextricable a part of Darwin's story as it is of Darwinism's. He chased butterflies directly into the sanctum of theology. This had happened before with astronomy (Galileo) and history (David Strauss's 1835 text *The Life of Jesus, Critically Examined*). In 1859, with *On the Origin of Species*, another investigation into nature would prove an accidental investigation into God.

The traditional interpretation is that evolutionary theory contradicted the parts of Genesis about God creating Adam and the animals, such as 1:25: "And God made the beast of the earth after his kind, and cattle after their kind, and every thing that creepeth upon the earth after his kind: and God saw that *it was* good." But that's just the literal contradiction. Darwinism calls out Brahma and Pangu just as it does the Old Testament God, but it's only in Abrahamic monotheism that this truly bitter resistance to evolutionary theory shows up (every Hindu I know, for example, seems quite at ease with the idea). This is because the source of the revulsion resides in the verse immediately *after* the one in which God creates all the animals: "And God said, 'Let us make man in our image, after our likeness: and let them have dominion over the fish of the sea, and over the fowl of the air, and over the cattle, and over all the earth, and over every creeping thing that creepeth upon the earth.'"

"And let them have dominion." In Abrahamic religions, we human beings are set apart because we are made in God's image. We sit imperviously at the top of a hierarchy. In the Eastern religions that believe in rebirth, the hierarchy exists—it's better to be born a human than to be born a monkey—but humans always risk slippage. The Jataka tales tell of the prior incarnations of the Buddha; it turns out he had appeared in the past as a rabbit, a deer, a mallard, etc. Of the ten incarnations of Vishnu, the first three are animals—a fish, a tortoise, a boar—while the fourth is a man with a lion's head and claws, a transitional form before the human avatars to follow. There is no sharp boundary between the animal world and the human world, and the animal can even reside above humankind: Ganesha has an elephant's head. The Scopes Monkey Trial is unthinkable in a civilization where there are temples and hymns to Hanuman.

This is why *The Voyage of the* Beagle is so crucial a counterpart to Darwin's later scientific work. It shows us the image of this biologist—this biological *philosopher*—seeking out nature at its harshest and most indifferent and most beautiful:

The day was glowing hot, and the scrambling over the rough surface and through the intricate thickets, was very fatiguing; but I was well repaid by the strange Cyclopean scene. As I was walking along I met two large tortoises, each of which must have weighed at least two hundred pounds: one was eating a piece of cactus, and as I approached, it stared at me and slowly walked away; the other gave a deep hiss, and drew in its head. These huge reptiles, surrounded by the black lava, the leafless shrubs, and large cacti, seemed to my fancy like some antediluvian animals. The few dull-coloured birds cared no more for me than they did for the great tortoises.

There is something proud and unconquerable in these tortoises, both the one that hisses and the one that turns away. They can be caged or killed or driven to extinction, but no human being can have dominion over them. Darwin came face to face with nature radically unbowed, and, eventually, he placed himself (and the human species) in a continuum with it. After millennia of Abrahamic hubris, a scientific humbling.

4.

Darwin got where he got intellectually by sailing there and hoofing it, all for the sake of knowledge. The Everyman in my edition's logo was a powerfully striding fellow too. I used to think he looked jaunty, but now I know he looks determined (and if he's going to get through *The Tale of Genji*, he'd better be). If I could pencil in a detail, I'd draw in a headphone cord leading to his ears, since I do most of my "reading" in audiobook form. This allows me to live my other life as a diagnostic radiologist and still blaze through a small library's worth of literature every year.

Diagnostic radiologists, incidentally, are the most hands-off of medical specialists. Never do we venture onto the tectonic and sulfurous Galápagos of patients' social histories. We avoid boarding the *Beagle* and coming face to face with the species we study. I myself "see" about sixteen thousand patients a year without ever actually *seeing* them, except in pixelated form on a set of computer screens. After my summer of research, I ditched neurology and set my sights on radiology instead, precisely because it would keep me from having to see, or smell, or touch patients. I go through whole workdays without meeting a single patient. I spend my time delivering catastrophic diagnoses . . . into a voice-recognition software that asks me no heartrending follow-up questions.

I also chose radiology because I wanted to be a writer and didn't want my day job to bleed into my time outside the hospital. It's easy to leave the CT appearance of Stage IV cancer behind when you go home; the face of the thirty-six-year-old woman to whom you delivered the bad news, not so much. I chose radiology to insulate myself from the realities of medicine—from life and death and human suffering, basically—so that I could create art about . . . life and death and human suffering. It's paradoxical, I know. I chose detachment over compassion, sterile lab work (office work, technically) over the messy surgical "field." I preferred to be Siddhartha in the climate-controlled palace, not Buddha in the mosquito-ridden forest—much less Darwin on Tierra del Fuego.

5.

Dante went *down* to the Inferno. Darwin's descent was latitudinal, but both of them—one below the sea, the other atop it—ended up exploring a "Land of Fire."

The Descent is the one of the oldest narratives in all of literature. Gilgamesh, Odysseus, Aeneas, Dante—and those are just the poetic examples, where it's out there in the open. You see it crop up again, in a masked form, wherever a mythopoetic talent wanders into the novel. Quixote gets lowered into the dreamlike Cave of Montesinos. *Les Miserables* has an extended discussion of the catacombs under Paris, and at one point Jean Valjean is actually fake-buried. Melville, like Hugo, was a poet working the prose beat—and sure enough, the voyage of the *Pequod* around the horn of Africa, mapped out, graphs the descent-and-climb we find in the old poetic epics:

You have to go down to the Underworld in order to rise again, enlightened and ready to save the world. Jesus was said to have visited the Un-

derworld too, during the period between the crucifixion and resurrection: the so-called Harrowing of Hell. This event shook Hell with an earthquake, and Dante (in that journal of his own transformative voyage) documents a collapsed bridge in Hell that dates back to it.

> The ground in many parts was fissured in north and south lines, perhaps caused by the yielding of the parallel and steep sides of this narrow island. Some of the fissures near the cliffs were a yard wide. Many enormous masses had already fallen on the beach; and the inhabitants thought that when the rains commenced far greater slips would happen. The effect of the vibration on the hard primary slate, which composes the foundation of the island, was still more curious: the superficial parts of some narrow ridges were as completely shivered as if they had been blasted by gunpowder.

That's Darwin on Quiriquina Island, off the coast of Chile. He too descended to a Land of Fire and came back up, in his case to England. He wasn't quite the enlightened teacher yet, but in time, he would end up changing human self-conception as profoundly as the founder of any religion—more profoundly, that is, than any poet or fellow scientist.

This is the other reason Darwin still appears in theological discussions, whereas Galileo, who also ran afoul of Christian dogma, no longer does. Galileo, Kepler, and Copernicus all challenged the Church on the organization and mechanics of the heavens. Because they challenged it on astronomy, they challenged the old story about *where* we are. But Darwin was the first scientific teacher to challenge the old story about *what* we are. The two challenges point different ways: one at the sky, the other at your heart. That's why the astronomical challenge was so successful: today, even the most conservative cardinals in the Vatican subscribe to the heliocentric model. Evolution, however, is another story.

6.

Considered as a story, *The Voyage of the* Beagle is one in a genre. Darwin's journal is part of a now-defunct branch of scientific literature: the literature of exploration. Perhaps the greatest practitioner of this tradition, and Darwin's inspiration, was the German explorer-scientist Alexander von Humboldt, who also wrote about visits to South America. Humboldt, the most famous scientist of his day (Darwin made a pilgrimage to him), has enjoyed something of a revival recently with Andrea Wulf's 2015 book *The Invention of Nature: Alexander von Humboldt's New World*. Humboldt didn't accompany Darwin on the *Beagle*, but he was never far from Darwin's thoughts:

> On a point not far from the city, where a rivulet entered the sea, I observed a fact connected with a subject discussed by Humboldt.
> [...]
> Travelling onwards we passed through tracts of pasturage, much injured by the enormous conical ants' nests, which were nearly twelve feet high. They gave to the plain exactly the appearance of the mud volcanos at Jorullo, as figured by Humboldt.
> [...]

The house in which I lived was seated close beneath the well-known mountain of the Corcovado. It has been remarked, with much truth, that abruptly conical hills are characteristic of the formation which Humboldt designates as gneiss-granite.

[...]

During this day I was particularly struck with a remark of Humboldt's, who often alludes to "the thin vapour which, without changing the transparency of the air, renders its tints more harmonious, and softens its effects."

[...]

Humboldt has related the strange accident of a hovel having been erected over a spot where a young crocodile lay buried in the hardened mud. He adds, "The Indians often find enormous boas, which they call Uji or water serpents, in the same lethargic state. To reanimate them, they must be irritated or wetted with water."

I could go on—*The Voyage of the* Beagle converses with Humboldt's work in almost two dozen places.

Today, it's only popular-science writing that uses sustained narrative, descriptive passages, jargon-free language, and the first person. Such writing summarizes the findings of "serious" scientific studies for consumption by laypeople. In Darwin's day, by contrast, important scientific work was still being done by inspired amateurs. You didn't need to get a university degree or use discipline-specific jargon to be taken seriously. The sciences back then were somewhat like poetry and fiction today in that credentials (in those days, from the Royal Geographic Society or what have you) helped, but they weren't *necessary*.

Even better, the scientific disciplines themselves were indistinct. I notice how both Humboldt and Darwin observe rock formations, insects, flora, fauna, weather patterns, tribes, and troubled histories with equal interest. Today, a geologist, an entomologist, a botanist, a zoologist, a meteorologist, an anthropologist, and a historian would each board a hypothetical *Beagle* with a separate agenda. Their eyes would zero in on only what related to their disciplines.

Darwin's bombshell was probably the last *readable* one in scientific history. We've come a long way from the pre-Socratic speculations on the natural world in Heraclitus and Parmenides. Today, the great advances require mathematics, and where they require words, the words require abbreviations; a word like "deoxyribonucleic" uglifies every sentence it is in. Crick and Watson's original 1953 paper positing the structure of DNA may well, over the next hundred years, transfigure us (literally) far more than our intrepid Victorian's speculations on apes and men. But the Everyman Library would be hard pressed to justify, on literary grounds, the inclusion of paragraphs like these:

> If it is assumed that the bases only occur in the structure in the most plausible tautomeric forms (that is, with the keto rather than the enol configurations) it is found that only specific pairs of bases can bond together. These pairs are: adenine (purine) with thymine (pyrimidine), and guanine (pyrine) with cytosine (pyrimidine).

This is why I like Darwin's *journal* so much: It takes me back to an era when the practices of doing good science and writing well—my personal ideals— were one. I write far more pages as a radiologist than I do as a poet or novelist, but when I write that stuff, I am always imitating a computer: *2.3 × 2.1 cm left renal superior pole hypodensity has a Houndsfield unit value of 7 consistent with a simple cyst.* I dictate these sentences into a voice-recognition microphone, and to make sure the software picks up and transcribes the words accurately, I actually flatten my voice into a computer's monotone. I *never* wax poetic; the radiology report is part of the medical record, and using poetic license could get my medical one revoked.

The eye of a scientist and the eye of a poet or novelist are not so different in that observation is all-important, but their voices, in the modern world, have nothing in common. Best to end with a passage from Darwin that hybridizes precision and magic—like this one, where he describes rubbing a zoophyte. It responds by glowing:

> Having kept a large tuft of it in a basin of saltwater, when it was dark I found that as often as I rubbed any part of a branch, the whole became strongly

phosphorescent with a green light: I do not think I ever saw any object more beautifully so. But the remarkable circumstance was, that the flashes of light always proceeded up the branches, from the base towards the extremities.

The natural world responds to his curiosity, growing luminous at his touch, "from the base towards the extremities," his style and his subject welling up, in synchrony, with the color of life.

NOTES ON THE GHAZAL

The ghazal is made up of couplets, each autonomous, thematically and emotionally complete in itself: One couplet may be comic, another tragic, another romantic, another religious, another political.... A couplet may be quoted by itself without in any way violating a context—there is no context, as such.... The opening couplet sets up a scheme of rhyme and refrain by having it occur in both lines—the rhyme immediately preceding the refrain.... Then this scheme occurs only in the second line of each succeeding couplet.... A ghazal has five couplets at least; there is no maximum limit.

—Agha Shahid Ali, introduction to *Ravishing DisUnities: Real Ghazals in English*

THE GHAZAL AS PLINKO

On *The Price Is Right* there was a minigame called Plinko. A huge, slanted board had an array of evenly spaced, uniformly staggered rows of pegs. The contestant stood at the top and let a disc drop. The disc bumped and slid its way through that geometrical forest and ended up in one of several slots at the bottom, each one worth a different amount of money. One of them was the jackpot in glittery numbers.

Just like that of the Plinko disc, a ghazal's slip and stumble to the bottom of the page is impossible to predict, and where it ends up may not be worth much—but it could, of course, also find its way to the jackpot, and that's what keeps us playing. The formal properties of language, those mathematical components of poetry that account for why poets used to

141

call verse "numbers," are the pegs shaping the ghazal's path: regularities that make randomness inevitable, an obstacle course that thwarts aim and will, giving the game all its excitement as the ghazal drops from couplet to couplet. Each end-rhyme and refrain bumps the ghazal off course until its course is determined wholly by deviation—until its movement, unguessable beforehand, seems inevitable in retrospect.

THE GHAZAL AND ISLAM

The ghazal is a refuge of pre-Islamic polytheism. Its ancestry can be traced back to the coda of the *qasida*, a major form in Arabic poetry that predates the Qur'an. The ghazal believes, as it were, in many gods at once; it entertains opposites and elliptical ambiguity, Keats's "negative capability" given formal embodiment.

Randomness marries predetermination. The force of accident acts synergistically with the force of destiny. Its cyclicity, its systematization of repetition, is a profoundly un-Islamic tendency; the Prophet's time on Earth, according to the Qur'an, was a one-time phenomenon. (The expectation of a Mahdi in some circles is not the same as a Second Coming, in which *Christ himself* returns.) Hence the ghazal's appeal in Sufism, the mystical tradition within Islam opposed to the orthodox, doctrinaire *ulema*. The appeal to mystics is inevitable. The ghazal formulates unity using the disjunct, and the perception of unity in disparate things is the goal of mysticism and the basis of metaphor.

Just as the ghazal's polyphonic structure is a refuge of dissent and polytheism, its final couplet, the makhta, is a refuge of individuality. The makhta strives *against* dissolution in the Brotherhood of the Faithful, *against* the collectivism of Islam: It contains the poet's signature.

This insistence on a couplet that names the poet contradicts the mystical desire for unity (another paradox, befitting the ghazal). To counteract this anti-mystical tendency, Rumi signed his ghazals with the name of his friend, Shams, and titled his collection the *Divan-i Shams-i Tabrizi*, attributing his entire oeuvre to someone with whom he had attained a *unio mystica*, someone who was therefore the same as he, their signatures interchangeable.

In the ghazal's cultures of origin, both its phonetic predeterminism and its atomization feel natural. In a poetic culture like our own that has reservations about rhyme, especially exact rhyme, the ghazal advertises its artifice. Readers today tend to pick up a "padded line" or an "unnatural" locution purely for the sake of the rhyme and single it out for scorn. This is a deeply unpoetic practice, the perversity of which may become evident only a few generations from now; most great poetry of the past, after all, from the *Bhagavad-Gita* to Dante's *Commedia* to Shakespeare's plays, contain metrical fillers in some form. The genuine ghazal, whose seed-crystal is sound, sets off every alarm universities have installed in the contemporary reader. Placed in the Western tradition, in which all poetic forms are holistic, the ghazal's disjointed couplets make it read like a showcase of mutually irrelevant rhymes, an exercise in epigrammatic phrasemaking.

We must understand that in its cultures of origin, the ghazal may lack *unity*, but it does not lack *context*. This context is most often love, whether a love for the divine or the love of a woman, or some ambivalent Persian mélange of carnality and mysticism. In English, however, the ghazal has no such background into which its couplets, like tiles from various spots on the same mosaic, can fit. The issue, therefore, is not one of writing a ghazal "in English"—a technical problem that demands, even in our supposedly rhyme-poor language, mere invention. Rather, it is an issue of the ghazal *in the West*.

THE GHAZAL: FORMAL MODELS, FORMAL MODIFICATIONS

The first solution is to write a ghazal consisting of thematically unified couplets. Or we can mute the refrain and employ off-rhymes; refrains in Persian and Urdu ghazals are often monosyllabic and embedded in the ghazal's grammatical makeup.

Muting the refrain: though the refrain follows the rhyme in the Urdu ghazal, it does so naturally, often with no more emphasis than a little sigh. This happens by way of relatively unobtrusive words—"ke," "kiya," "hai"—that appear normally at the end of a sentence, as minor and phonetically negligible as "had" or "did" or "is" (all of these are refrains of Ghalib's). In English, we may place the refrain *before* the rhyme in order to more closely approximate this grammatical incorporation.

The following examples of variants of the ghazal come from my own di-wan—awkward, I know, but this is only because English-language examples, to my knowledge, do not exist elsewhere.

NOTHING DOING NOLENS VOLENS

Was it wrong to look my fill?
What the will won't, the eye will.

For life eternal's sake
I kill, kill, kill, kill, kill.

What I sing. What I choke.
What I scorch. What I till.

Activity soils its cuffs.
The purest of heart are idle.

Desire nothing, Amit.
I won't. Wait. No. I will?

The refrain, in this variant, must become an unobtrusive component of the verse-sentence; the emphasis is consistently on the rhyme word, not the refrain. Except in rare, precision-engineered instances, it does not sound natural to end six lines of Urdu verse on the same noun, and even less so to end them all on the same article and noun in English.

The rhyme-refrain, in a language as consonant-dominated as English (the millennium-long attempt, beginning in 1066, to escape the essentially Anglo-Saxon nature of our language has led to our dullest poetry), may in some iterations be substituted with alliteration-assonance.

1. Rhyme-refrain with independent couplets (classical ghazal):

MINE

Pain trains an undisciplined mind.
I will end yours if you end mine.

Little feet, little feet are playing
Hopscotch among the landmines.

Hope has worked miracles before.
If yours didn't, how can mine?

I could have learned to welcome darkness,
If only you had been mine.

*How dare you put words in God's mouth,
Amit?* Why not. He put ashes in mine.

2. Rhyme-refrain with enjambment of content:

FAKE I.D.

The voice? breath? body?
Not me. Not me. Not me.

Think of me as the lost vowel in God's name,
And as the battered rabbi who forgot me.

I spend my time arranging letters.
All my kabala hasn't caught me.

*Who messed you up
Like this?* God? Me?

*So who are you,
Amit?* You got me.

3. Rhyme-refrain with enjambment of couplets (the enjambment of content is implicit):

THE WORD

Word made flesh? Word
Made fresh. Word

Was stones till one
Made moan. Less words

The better, no
Words best. Word

Makes zealous, word
Gives zeal its zest. Word

Made heme. Word
Laid waste. Word

Made olives and
Expeller-pressed. Word

Made breastbone, word
Made blessed. Word

Made to suffer in
A neural vest. Word

Made man. Man
Made mess. Word

Breathed through a flute
Called death. Word

Emerging on the other
Side as breath.

4. Alliteration-assonance with independent couplets (modified classical ghazal):

THE OUTCAST

What are you? A carnal
Creature, but a cripple.

You're not the first stranger I've hugged the legs of.
Did the others rebuff you too? With cudgels.

What sadness in watching the porcelain horses!
The moms don't like you staring at the carousel.

After pure pasture, a snout-to-rump corral.
We are branded as we pass in, born cattle.

These earrings are made from the bones of my hand.
Did you keep the receipt? I prefer coral.

Hold me. *Don't act as if all*
You want to do is cuddle.

I, who built the Lord a temple,
Staff a booth at the carnival.

Is there an upside to being a hunchback, Amit?
You handle your thirst better, like a camel.

5. Alliteration-assonance with enjambment of content:

THE ALTERCATION

This? When just now you called me your vessel?
That's not what I said. Not vessel. Vassal.

Oh. I see now. My mistake.
The devil's in the vowels.

Like the ones missing from your name?
I'm nothing if not versatile.

Nothing? I thought you were that you were.
That's just a catchphrase that went viral.

Well I believed it, and took a bullet for you.
All it damaged was your heart, Amit. Nothing vital.

6. Alliteration-assonance with enjambment of couplets:

ELLIS ISLAND

What survived of us (mostly just
A mousy susurrus) shushed,

What cohered of us
(Whispery cirrus)

Dispersed, we arrived with mere
Memory to succor us—

Sickly freakshow,
Mirthless circus—

Unsure we still had bodies
Until your arms circled us.

7. Hybridization of sonnet and ghazal ("sonzal"). This variation preserves the sonnet's volta by introducing an antonymic refrain at the sestet (couplets 5–7). The "sonzal" end-rhymes the first lines of each couplet, which is not a requirement of the ghazal; this rhyme sound switches at the volta as well. Multiple variations are possible with the first-line rhyme sounds:

DISCIPLINARY

Get with the times, Amit. Abandon discipline.
How can I, when my sole passion has been discipline?

The universe is endless, and endlessly expanding.
I give chaos the mischievous grin of discipline.

Everywhere I look, it's abandon, abandon.
People look away from my indecent discipline.

I ask of indulgence only that she be demanding.
My fantasy: reckless, hot, abundant discipline.

Sure I'll drink that: I'll do anything on a dare.
My mind walks water with a wind's abandon.

The singers spin, and we outside the circle stare,
Rapture a language we have long since abandoned.

Love is scarce, angels are extinct, but rhyme I find in abundance.
What's your secret, Amit? No secret. Just disciplined abandon.

8. Interdigitated double ghazal ("fugue"). In this variation, two complete and related ghazals are threaded together; one reads top to bottom, the other bottom to top:

The blast crater they were so proud of, Amit,
Hasn't so much as dimpled the empire.

The war had less to do with souls than oil.
Sheikh Shaitan would not let God control the oil.

We feel strong only when the empire's cameras
Record us swearing we will humble the empire.

The devil likes reprocessing temptation:
From wine he made the blood, from coal, the oil.

First they will take our veils, then our faces,
Till we come, over time, to resemble the empire.

Uranium, amphorae, water, bones.
I hope for one thing when I dig a hole: the oil.

From shards of a world much older than theirs,
Children have assembled the empire.

We hold the city, they hold the streets.
In this standoff between shadows, who holds the oil?

They saw your work on the Dome of the Rock
And want you to help them build the empire.

They stole the land, the seeds, the rain, the harvest,
But swear to God they never stole the oil.

The tank and the school are twin symbols of empire.
Is the cause of our squalor as simple as empire?

When the empire comes to burn your village, Amit,
Remember: one of your own sold them the oil.

Just as the sonnet did not "take" in English without Shakespeare's modifications of rhyme scheme and content, the ghazal is also unlikely to do so unless we help it adapt to its new environment. For example, the substitution of a rhyme word that includes both rhyme and refrain ("landmines," see above) or a variant ending ("The Word") would outrage an Urdu-speaking audience; for an English-speaking one, there is more potential delight in variation than in a rhyme-refrain safely stenciled to its magic sixth.

THE GHAZAL AND AGHA SHAHID ALI

SHAHID

I have looked all over. No Shahid.
You're one to grieve. Did you even know Shahid?

A name like a color. A blue.
Violet, indigo, shahid.

The sky he scooped I color in.
Needs more rain. Go borrow Shahid's.

Hold on. This storm is all me. *The clouds,*
Maybe—your lightning you owe Shahid.

Shahid taught you English. I taught you American.
Right. But who taught me to dance, toe to toe? Shahid.

To purists (among whom Agha Shahid Ali counted himself), the formal variants in the preceding section would seem like violations. These English ghazals, however, preserve the ghazal's formal basis in phonetic repetition.

Shahid Ali's role in the history of the ghazal is central. His sometimes ungainly refrains and graceless, chockablock couplets ("God's angels again are—for Satan—forlorn. / Salvation was bought but sin sold in real time") did not always have the felicity and tightness of the best Urdu models, but he insisted on the demanding system of rhymes and refrains, rightly deploring the handful of two-line nonsequiturs that went under the form's name before his arrival. He understood that the ghazal's formal basis was the muscling-out of intellectual logic by musical logic. These adaptations use the form's musical logic to arrive at intellectual conclusions.

A writer of ghazals must become privy to occult musical relationships among the words of the language. Those who merely speak or write the language subjugate it to their desire to express themselves, or to record their surroundings, or to pass on information. A writer of ghazals must set the language free and allow it to speak for itself.

The language engages, then, in a dialogue with the mind. That dialogue is poetry. The mind calls the language, the language answers, and then the mind tries to transcribe that answer as accurately as it can. "Finding your voice" in the ghazal, and perhaps in any poetic form, is really about becoming a more perfectly passive amanuensis: you must broaden and hollow yourself so that the passage to your page lets through as much poetry as possible.

The ghazal loosens the mind's grip on the tongue. It keeps the writer of ghazals susceptible both to the force of accident and the force of destiny. It's as if the rhyme and refrain are destiny, and whatever comes before them is an accident, hopefully a fortunate one.

Two words that snap together do so for a physical reason—a reason of shape. The external shape of a word, what we call its sound, is governed by its internal shape, its meaning. If the human race had trusted the English rhyme pair "round"/"ground," we would have saved Columbus the trouble. The kindred pair "found"/"sound" summarizes the compositional principle of the ghazal.

I believe in rhyme's ability to reveal and seduce. There are whole religions contained in rhyme pairs: "love"/"above" is Christianity; "above"/"love" is Buddhism; "immemorial"/"ephemeral" is the Hinduism of the Upanishads, with its paradoxical emphasis on the extreme age yet essential transience of the material world; "dismember"/"remember" summarizes Judaism after the breaking of the Temple and the Diaspora. That last pair contains an oblique reference to antiquity's cults of the cut-up and regenerated God of the vine, as well as such imagery's subsequent transfer into Catholicism—as if the Chosen People were collectively the body of Dionysus, dismembered but, by a feat of prodigious and deliberate remembering, coming together again. The regenerated Dionysus, of course, is also the resurrected Christ, and so the rhyme pair suggests the Holocaust is the Passion writ large, the crucifixion of an entire people.

If we just trusted the language a little more, it would write us far better poems than we are capable of on our own. And that's another pregnant rhyme: "just"/"trust."

THE GHAZAL AS JAZZ

The ghazal works best as an improvisation, a set of riffs on rhymes and refrains. The Sufis, themselves prodigious writers of ghazals, have a saying: *The Sufi is the child of the moment.* So is the ghazal.

ARS POETICA

Ghah-zall? What's a ghah-zall?
A musical gamble.

You either win
A gorgeous girl

Or one night with
A gargoyle.

Shove it and see how its wings look:
Sometimes angel, sometimes seagull.

Sounds risky. You have to
Be game for a gambol

And able
To gobble

Opposites in a single sitting.
What do I wash them down with? Guzzle

A Sufi wine
By the glassful

After lacing it with
A little gasol-

Ine: a volatile Molotov
Cocktail of godly gabble,

A.k.a.
A ghazal.

THE GHAZAL AS POETRY OF THE FUTURE

It is often observed that the human attention span has shortened. This is a trend across our species, the same way average height and life expectancy have increased.

Because it is visually hyperstimulated from birth, the human mind is altering to more closely approximate the human eye. They are almost a single organ now. The eye, even when it focuses, suffers a microscopic jitter and does not rest on a single point. Imagine a mind that does that, and you have us.

The ghazal composed itself out of soundbites centuries before the soundbite was invented. Though the ghazal dates back further than the sonnet, the human species in the twenty-first century is the ghazal's "ideal reader." The ghazal's cloud-to-cloud leap makes the sonnet's *eight lines forward, turn, six lines back* seem plodding and obsolete. The sonnet is, at best, liquid; the ghazal's couplets are gas molecules under heat and pressure, in agitated ricochet. American society is infatuated with music and sports; there is no song more athletic than the sextuple-rhymed ghazal. It transfigures our shallowest tendencies into art. What Elizabethan tragedy did with its audience's love of violence, the ghazal may do with our love of variation.

THE LUDLUM IDENTITY

Premise is everything. Your opening scene? A man floating on the ocean. Of course—the origins of life. Vishnu sleeps on an ocean. It fits. Now the man is rescued, drawn up from the preexistent state into existence. After he's revived (that is, reborn), it's revealed he has amnesia. He was someone else before his immersion and emergence. But now he has no memory of that life.

Perfect. Your little scenario is coming along. Set up the action: he was a bad person in that past life. He was an assassin. Powers that know about his past life are out to get him. Gunfire and explosions, terror, confusion, and general suffering ensue, and he doesn't know why (but *you* know why, wink wink: it's his bad karma). He struggles to recall his past life. One crucial thing he learns is his name. Here's the kicker: His name is Born. Wait, that's too on the nose. Switch up the spelling. *Bourne.* It has a high-literary aspect too: "The undiscovered country, from whose bourn / No traveler returns"... at least not with his memory. Yes, "Bourne" is perfect. The book will write itself after that. And what will you call this clever allegory of rebirth, the Self, the expiation of karma? *The Bourne Amnesiac?* No, that's no good. How about... *The Bourne Identity*?

In *The Matrix*, the theological structuring is obvious and deliberate. It shows every sign of an aging civilization's spiritual eclecticism. The digital unreality of the Matrix is analogous to maya, the illusion of materiality that the unenlightened believe to be the "true" reality. Neo (oNe) is *the* One, the Messiah—he actually dies and comes back to life at the end of the first movie. The Matrix itself has, according to the third movie, been created and destroyed several times: another Indian idea, that of the *kalpa*, the periodic destruction and creation of the cosmos. Books have been written on the religious elements in the *Matrix* franchise; I myself think it's the most successful example of that kind of thing in the history of film. Hollywood attempts it all too often, sometimes so hamfistedly it makes a heathen like me a bit uncomfortable, as in the case of 2006's *Superman Returns*. Just as in that movie, the *Matrix* trilogy's religious echoes aren't accidental.

What about Ludlum's?

Bourne's *real* real name, by the way, is Webb, which brings to mind spiderwebs: the insect trapped, paralyzed, and bound; the sinister invisibility of design. Don't get me started on the significance of Bourne's archenemy, Carlos the Jackal, the jackal being traditionally associated with Kali....

Did Robert Ludlum set out to do this, or is his theologically spot-on premise just an accident that happened in the course of churning out thriller after three-word-titled thriller? He knocked them out at the rate of one a year during the '70s: *The Gemini Contenders, The Chancellor Manuscript, The Holcroft Covenant, The Matarese Circle*. And then, in 1980, came the one that has lasted, *The Bourne Identity*. If you look at the math, he was writing *Identity* in 1979, the year *I* was born. I'm not solipsistic enough to think such a coincidence is significant, but if I *did* believe the universe exists solely in my perception, it would click in place nicely.

In more than one daydream-sequence, I have encountered Robert Ludlum. He is clad in the somewhat pretentious trench coat that he wore for his dust-jacket photographs, as if he himself were a spy in a movie, some Cold War runner who had agreed to meet me on a side street in Berlin, or Zurich, or whatever European locale we choose for our scene. For atmosphere's sake, let's make it nighttime. Rain. A siren in the distance. We engage in a predetermined exchange, the precursor to those authentication questions so crucial in internet security. He challenges: *Woe to that man who betrays the Son of Man.* My passphrase: *It would be better for him if he had not been Bourne.*

He nods. *I don't have much time.*

And so, in a hushed, pressured voice, I lay out the secret I've discovered. That he, Ludlum, wrote an esoteric Hindu parable in the guise of a popular spy thriller. He tapped into some Jungian archive in the collective mind deeper than the Kremlin's sub-basement, totally went above his Eyes-Only clearance, accessed some *Third-Eye-Only*-level material, and hid it, as they say, in plain sight: a 544-page doorstop published by Random House (a nice touch, going through Random House, flaunting the—seemingly—random nature of the parallels). I tell him that I am onto him. I haven't been fooled by the distractions he surrounded it with, those formulaic cat-and-mouse genre novels. I show him a chronological list of his novels between 1971 and 2001; between *The Scarlatti Inheritance* and *The Sigma Protocol*, there are exactly eleven novels before and after *The Bourne Identity*. He buried it a little too neatly. Even the most brilliant covert operatives will make the occasional mistake.

Because I know what he is. The perfection of his premise is beyond chance. If I concede the operation of chance in the novel, I must admit the *possibility* of chance in the theology it mirrors—which would be sacrilege. It might cause the collapse of the entire Eastern bloc. Widespread unrest, revolution, a mutually assured destruction between myself and my faith. This secret is too dangerous to keep. I have to go public with it, send it to all the papers. I have to expose Ludlum as the supreme Hindu novelist he is, the one Greater Maker who has translated ancient Indian metaphysical concepts, until then locked in Sanskrit terminology and cross-eyed guru-speak, into language indistinguishable from middling popular prose. For this has been the most staggering feat of all: sublimity of idea descending and taking on the form of a crude genre novel, like a god taking on human flesh—in Sanskrit, "avatar." I have decrypted Bourne's *Identity*, and now I'm going to expose Ludlum's.

But I give him a choice: He can confess to me now, privately, whether he designed this premise or hit on it by accident. Whatever he says, even if it's not what I want to hear, I'll accept it and keep this matter hush-hush, deal with the fallout on my own. Langley won't find out, and neither will MI6, Interpol, the Mossad, or the Russians. He can go on living his double life. But he has to tell me.

Ludlum stares off at a blinking neon sign across the street. The water runs off our umbrellas. He is holding a cigar. He flicks the ash from it and speaks smoke. *Your books don't sell very well, do they?*

Then he turns and disappears into the night, headed for the safest of safe houses, where I will never find him again.

THE MASTER
AND EMILY

1.

The daguerreotype we have is not of her.

People always experience recordings of their voices as somehow not their own. But it wasn't just the sixteen-year-old Emily who didn't recognize this stranger. Her own family thought it looked nothing like her. They didn't keep it on display at the Homestead because guests kept asking, in her presence, whose it was.

The head—full of a lighter-than-air, lighter-than-ecstasy gas, like helium or Shakespeare—tried to float away. That is why the neck looks so long. It's under strain; it's getting stretched.

The eyes were overlarge and not that dark in real life. The stranger's pupils had blown on some interior tincture of laudanum.

The skin too had an otherworldly pallor, even though the real Emily loved to amble every summer out among the Indian pipes and clover.

And who is *this*, Miss Emily?

You?

Beautiful—as Pictures—
No Man drew.[1]

157

2.

A daguerreotype exposed silverplated copper to light. The plate had to be polished to a mirror finish. The image on it, still latent, was reversed. Developing the image required exposure to mercury vapor.

The high priestess at Delphi used to set up her tripod over a chasm in a cave. This chasm emitted ethylene gas, which caused her to experience a prophetic euphoria. Out of her came riddling poems. The future alone could understand her. To the future, her supposedly cryptic, oracular verse made sense.

Emily's latent image, on the daguerreotype plate, breathed in that mercury vapor and altered into this other face, this face that we, the future, would one day recognize on sight.

> . . . a Face of Steel—
> That suddenly looks into ours
> With a metallic grin—[2]

Mercury delivers messages. In the nineteenth century, he would have spoken in telegrams, curt, clipped, elliptical. He was also the patron God of travelers. "There is no Frigate like a Book."

From Mercury's Greek name comes our own word for someone or something sealed off from external influences.

> How powerful the Stimulus
> Of an Hermetic Mind—[3]

The latent image, once it swam up to the surface of the daguerreotype mirror, was not Emily. The latent image developed into an image of the latent Emily.

This was the Emily whose lips were never that voluptuously full in real life. This was the Emily who would seclude herself in Amherst—Homestead, herbarium, hermitage—for the next fifty years.

The seal was not hermetic, of course. "The Soul selects her own Society." She had crushes on a married preacher, on a widower judge. Maybe she had lovers, though it is impossible to know for sure how wild her nights actually were.

A narrow Fellow in the Grass—
Occasionally rides.

There was one companion who never left her.

It might be lonelier
Without the Loneliness—[4]

3.

The ancient Greeks used a resin from the scent glands of the beaver.
  The medieval Europeans threw the whole herb garden at it: valerian, mistletoe, peony, gathered in lovely dactylic profusion.
  Belladonna ("beautiful woman"). Bitter orange. Foxglove, the nightshade, well known as a hallucinogen.
  "The little Tippler— / Leaning against the Sun"[5]
  could drink mugwort-laced absinthe against the Falling Sickness and, hopefully, never fall.
  Medieval surgeons slit the scalp and scraped the skull and spooned the patient their own pale flakes.

It will not stir for Doctors—
This Pendulum of Snow—[6]

Thornapple. Common henbane. Peruvian bark. Amulets made of adder's vertebrae. Prayers offered at the shrines of saints.
  Epilepsy, for all its stigma, was an affliction believed to be divine.
  In 1860, Emily went to Boston. Then, as now, the city was a tertiary referral center, where those who could afford it went to see the experts of last resort. She went to be seen for her eyes. Or at least, that's what the Dickinson family told the Amherst gossips.

A woman with epilepsy wasn't marriageable. There was something improperly sexual in the physical abandon of the seizure. Under their bustles, the gossips recognized, perhaps with envy, the seizure's orgasmic enlivening of the whole body "in the hand of God."

Or of some less forgiving Master.

4.

Aura: the preliminary sensations, sometimes musical, that precede a seizure.

She would awaken without warning at three in the morning. At a square table seventeen inches by seventeen inches, prime number by prime number, she began to transmit. On stray envelopes, on chocolate wrappers, on the backs of recipes. One thousand seven hundred and seventy-five linguistic seizures. And those are just the ones that made it through her fingers.

Who was seizing her?

Her brother and sister would not have recognized her if they had seen her at that hour, her candlelit face ghosting the window. They would have seen the stranger in the daguerreotype, slightly older, her eyes bigger and wilder, rolled back in her head, her red hair loose over her white dress. They would have seen the Master.

The Master always wore white because the Master swore to dress in purity, like a vestal virgin. A vestal virgin, if she broke her vow of chastity, had to die by live burial.

Emily always wore white because doctors thought dust and dirt might be a seizure trigger. The white made sure she could see every trace of the world's contact with her.

Fabrics—of Cashmere—
Never a Gown of Dun—more—
Raiment instead—of Pompadour—
For Me—My soul—to wear—[7]

There are the lost poems too. The ones that sparked, cooked, blackened the neuroelectric circuits.

Those who saw one of those poems happen saw Emily pause in place and follow her own gaze into the distance. Medicine called the phenomenon, even then, an "absence seizure."

Where Presence—is denied them.
They fling their Speech—[8]

To be seized by an absence. To be ravished away by awayness.
Whenever her sister Lavinia heard a shattering, she knew that Em had dropped another dish. The hands were there. The hold had vanished.

5.

Ictus: the violent surge of brain activity corresponding to the seizure.

In the original manuscripts, individual words have asterisks beside them, with alternates in the margins. The words of the poems remain volatile. They flicker among possibilities.

Maybe Emily sought to publish so few of her poems because she had never settled them into a single, final form. They might yet be detonated into a rearrangement at the slightest jostle. They might yet *explode*.

Could those dashes and erratic capitalizations be the typographical correlate of a seizure? The capital letters—A, M, P—rise above the run of lowercase letters in brainwave spikes; the dashes dramatize the synaptic leap of current from cathode to anode. She could write no other way.

I could not live without the love of my friends—I would jump down Aetna for any great Public good—but I hate a Mawkish Popularity.—I cannot be subdued before them—My glory would be to daunt and dazzle the thousand jabberers about Pictures and Books—I see swarms of Porcupines with their Quills erect "like lime-twigs set to catch my Winged Book" and I would fright [th]em away with a torch—[9]

Maybe, maybe not. There may be a simpler explanation, hiding in plain sight. The passage above was not typographically erratic Emily justifying her reluctance to publish, but typographically erratic John Keats, in a private letter dated 1818.

The formatting of Dickinson's poems may simply derive from the epistolary tradition of the nineteenth century. She sent her poems in or as letters all her life. Except for the few poems published in her lifetime (some without her consent, some "corrected" into more conventional formatting), she sent them only to an intimate inner circle. No wonder the poems would read, in the future, as breathlessly private communications, addressed beyond us, overheard.

6.

In a later 1818 letter, Keats wrote about one of history's most influential epileptics. What triggered the reference was a fall—appropriately enough, given that epilepsy was the "falling sickness."

> Tom tells me that you called on Mr. Haslam, with a Newspaper giving an account of a Gentleman in a Fur cap falling over a precipice in Kirkcudbrightshire. If it was me, I did it in a dream, or in some magic interval between the first & second cup of tea; which is nothing extraordinary, when we hear that Mahomet, in getting out of Bed, upset a jug of water, & whilst it was falling, took a fortnight's trip, as it seemed, to Heaven: yet was back in time to save one drop of water being spilt.[10]

Keats is referencing the Mi'raj, the Night Journey of the Prophet to Jerusalem and Paradise.

> Into this Port, if I might come,
> Rebecca, to Jerusalem,
> Would not so ravished turn—[11]

The first encounter of the Prophet with the Archangel Jibril came after a long period of seclusion in a cave of Hira the size of a small Amherst bedroom. The Archangel embraced him. "He touched me, so I live to know."[12]

The Prophet too ("Called to my Full—The Crescent—dropped"[13]) was an epileptic.

Dickinson and Dostoevsky were the last few writers to write through epilepsy. In the late 1800s—too late for them, fortunately for us—barbiturates became a therapeutic mainstay. This new class of drugs worked by blunting and flattening the sharp, choppy spikes of the epileptic's brainwaves.

It's possible that Dickinson's poems and Dostoevsky's novels might have been quelled along with their seizures, if not killed off entirely. "The Nerves sit ceremonious—like Tombs—"[14]

Barbiturates, barbaric, would have sacked the temple, silenced the oracle, placed the high priestess in chains.

7.

Aura.

Most of Emily's poems were written over a hot decade and a half, beginning a little before the Civil War.

At three in the morning—just before the years-long neuroelectric lightning storm that would set her scribbling poems on stray envelopes, chocolate wrappers, and the backs of recipes—Emily awoke to the stranger from her own daguerreotype straddling her body.

She recognized the face immediately. It was her own, only with bigger, darker eyes; a longer neck; fuller lips. Emily asked who she was anyway.

I, said Emily staring down at Emily, *am the Master.*

Two Bodies—therefore be—
Bind One—The Other Fly—[15]

Master and apprentice. Master and slave. Master poet. Master of all she surveyed with her poet's eye in a fine epileptic frenzy rolling. Before she could be any kind of master at all, Emily would have to be her own master.

The Master, ruthless, knew this.

But I want to love, pled Emily the young woman. *I want to marry.*

She wanted too to have a man's weight on top of hers instead of this weightless waif's. She would not mind having her wrists pinned this way, the rise of her chest suppressed this way, if the one doing it were a man of her choice. Representative Edward Dickinson's daughter was a living woman, after all.

But the Master would have none of it. For the Master, marriage was a live burial. Being buried alive under the laundry of three kids still meant being buried alive.

The Master, her funhouse-mirror face aligned with Emily's, made her demands. Emily must not marry. Emily must not have children. Emily must wear white from now on, like a Vestal Virgin. Emily must not leave this house.

If you betray me, said the Master, *remember, we will both be buried alive.*

Nor ever turn to tell me why—
Oh, Master, This is misery—[16]

Now get up, said the Master, *and write.*

8.

Ictus.

She wrote so many of her poems at three in the morning, by candlelight, because that was when wakefulness weakened and couldn't hold down the poems bucking and jerking beneath her consciousness.

Sleep deprivation is known to increase the likelihood of epileptic events. This was originally observed in epileptic horses. Even as foals, they announced their diagnosis with a thunderous collapse in the stables. Neurologists sedated the horses and shaved their heads—buzzing the manes first, then lathering the skulls for the straight razor. To this strikingly pale horse skin, they pasted EEG leads.

The spikes the neurologists waited for, like seismologists studying the swinging needle, were known as Interictal Epileptiform Discharge. Later, the same three letter acronym would find a use in military parlance: Improvised Explosive Device.

A Dickinson poem is an IED.

Her visit to the doctor for a "complaint of the eye" had nothing to do with her eyes.

The telltale medication prescribed to her in Boston was glycerin, believed by the medical community of her time to be an antiepileptic. When dispensed in higher amounts, it was used in hand lotion. Emily was prescribed a far lower dose—implying she took it by mouth. "I taste a liquor never brewed—"[17]

Add the element of fleshly decay to glycerin, and you get nitroglycerin: a compound so volatile the slightest jostle can set it off.

A partial list of documented seizure triggers: flashing lights, alternating patterns of light and dark, wasabi, sushi made with raw eel, high fevers, hangovers, stress (deaths in the family, visits from archangels), cuckoo clocks, coyote howls, peppermint essence, microphone reverb, inversions of circadian rhythm, church bells, Bach fugues, dubstep.

9.

Emily was born in the Homestead, but the Dickinsons moved to a different house when she was a child, then moved back when she was twenty-five.

In that intervening house, the house of her girlhood, Emily's bedroom overlooked a cemetery. The Master never came inside that other house. The Master played outside all night among the graves—"I watched the Moon around the House"—and bounded on all fours, feral, into the woods come day.

After they moved back to the Homestead, the landscape outside Emily's bedroom regressed, in the darkness, to that dwarf forest of tombstones. While she sat at the square table, the Master stood behind her, a second shadow bobbing and snapping in the candlelight, observing the spasms of her hand.

The archangel commanded the epileptic Prophet: *Recite!*

I am older—tonight, Master—but the love is the same—so are the moon and the crescent.[17]

Sometimes, when she longed for a *narrow fellow* in the grass to ride, the Master took the form of an archangel.

The slow archangel's syllables
Must awaken her.[19]

The first time this happened was in 1858, the year of the first "Master Letter," one of three that would be addressed to an unknown recipient referred to by no other term.

The Master addressed in those letters was male, but the archangel hid the daguerreotype's face under the beard. When Emily beckoned the Master to "come to New England, come to Amherst," she was beckoning her own poems home from the beyond.

Amputate my freckled Bosom!
Make me bearded like a man![20]

10.

Aura.

The archangelic alter-Emily straddled Emily, the flowing white robes draping the white calico dress with its mother-of-pearl buttons.

Emily experienced the queasy feeling familiar to her as the aura that preceded her seizures.

The moment the Master sank into her body, disappearing into her, the neuroelectricity surged. She bowed and shuddered like those inspirited Quakers and Shakers who had sailed their fine physical frenzies to New England a century earlier.

Ictus.

Emily was entered, possessed, penetrated completely. The seizure lasted until the Master decided to let up, and the Master let up only when Emily was on the verge of lethal exhaustion. As she wrote in her 1861 letter: "Like the little mother—with the big child—I got tired holding him."

Together, the Master and Emily visited the locales invoked in her poems. Buenos Ayre, India, Golconda.

Sister of Ophir—
Ah Peru.[21]

In the dizzy, disoriented aftermath of the seizure, Emily rose from her passion-damp and swirled-wild sheets onto the listing, tilting frigate deck of her bedroom floor in Amherst.

Everything around her and in her was volatile and flickering—like her brainwaves, like the flame on the wick, like nitroglycerin, like diction.

Reality had not briefly altered in Emily's perception; Emily, altered, could see reality, briefly, for what it was.

The clock said three o'clock in the morning, but it struck eternity.

Where had the Master gone?

To come nearer than presbyteries—and nearer than the new Coat—that the tailor made—[22]

Emily's face, reflected in the window, matched her daguerreotype's at last. The Master was inside her now.

She *was* the Master. The Master and Emily commanded each other exclusively; and they commanded each other to do one thing.

Write!

INTÈRLUDE
ESSAY ON IRON

THE ARGUMENT

In January 1813, Goethe wrote to a friend that as a poet and artist, he was a polytheist; as a natural scientist, he was a pantheist; and as a moral man, he was a Christian. No wonder, then, that in his shorter poems, as in *Faust*, he could not devote himself to a single style or tone. The "Olympian" remained a pagan in this regard and never accepted a One True Form. Wordsworth, in his last decades, seemed to believe there was no poem but the sonnet; Dante spent much of his career proliferating tercets; Spenser established his stanza and stuck to it; Rumi's *Masnavi* is couplets all the way down ... some poets get excellent results repeating themselves. Others get restless.

I am very much in Goethe's camp, but part of my compulsion to mix things up is the compulsion to make exceptions to my own rules. It is in my poetic nature to (on occasion) go against my poetic nature. The verse essay I wrote immediately before this one was Essay on Repetition. In most cases, that would have been a one-off. But the poem's theme challenged me to essay a repetition. This is it: another verse essay on repetition—repetition of a kind not mentioned in the first verse essay, though one I perform almost daily.

The heroic couplet has the bipartite structure of a weight-room repetition. The second rhyme sets down what the first rhyme lifts; the tension in the line is the tension in the tendon. This essay on (pumping) iron, like its twin on repetition, has a personal trainer in Alexander Pope, who stood only four feet six inches, wore a canvas back brace for scoliosis, but maxed out at a positively beastly six hundred thirty-four couplets in his "Essay on Man." I lift way less than Coach Alex, as you will see—but as the essay itself explains, in lifting as in writing as in life, it's best not to compare.

*

No manhood ceremonies now, no rite
Of passage that exiled a boy all night
In piss-dank woods until he trudged home with
A steaming kill, no transformation myth—
Only the intractable fact of weight,
The non-negotiability of plate
And plate. That is the door boys push against,
Grimacing through to the other side as men.

I walked my twin sons downstairs to the rack
Of twinned dumbbells in waiting rows, the stack
Of plates, the trap bar, wrist straps, lifting gloves,
The pullup bar I swore they'd learn to love.
You would have thought I was a grand inquisitor
Giving a guided tour to scare my visitors
With iron implements of coming torture
The way they looked at me. This was the border
At boyhood's end, where brotherhood began.
They muttered—*Dad's whole "time to be a man"*
Thing—feigned a headache, shuffled, slouched their shoulders,
Recalled assignments in their homework folders....
When ruses and excuses failed to get them
Out of it, to my shock, they *cried*. I let them;

Then made them start. Can't curl fives? Try threes.
Can't do a pushup? Do one on your knees.
I didn't have them deadlift. But an air squat?

So long as you can stand up, you can bear that.
I preached no coach's sermon, though I could
Have given them a *Gita* on the good
That lifting does the mind. You think you train
Your body, but what you train is your brain
To see reality for what it is.
The weights make no exceptions. They persist
In stubborn, Himalayan immobility.
The only thing that changes: your ability
To lift them. There's no special pleading with them,
No way to game the system. It's the system—
More weight, more sets—that is your only shot.
You bring this up, you set this down. Or not.

That's what I might have told them, if I thought
It helped. But talking deadlifts never got
A bar to jump up off the floor. You fold
The hinges nature fit you with to hold
That weight like an idea in your mind.
I made them start. We are three of a kind:
I was a skinny brown boy too, my upper
Lip fuzzy, *rotli daal bhaat shaak* for supper,
Gujarati name with an Ohio accent,
My music Black, my best friends Anglo-Saxon:
A khichdi kid. (It shows in my aesthetics
To this day.) Good at math but not athletics,
I ate no chicken, but had chicken legs.
I wasn't someone anyone would peg
As future meathead, daily at the gym.
I've shown my twins the photographs—I'm *them*.
It's way back then the fanatic was born:
Religion, literature, and fitness. Scorn
Is healthy in a modest, tonic dose.
If I had been well-liked, and if my nose
Had been a little shorter, I'd have written prose

And sold my debut thriller for a stellar sum
And sunbathed ever after in bestsellerdom.

That first year out of high school, I escaped
My body, or I tried to. I reshaped
What wasn't there to start with, potter's hands
Encircling empty space. So I began
To *eat*. The herbivore grew new, sharp teeth.
This Hindu savaged tuna, deli meat,
The Brahma bulls forbidden my forebears,
Those Texas Roadhouse steaks I asked for rare
And, to be honest, didn't even care for.
The workouts worked—now I had something there for
My will to harden into muscle. I got bigger,

But diligence can tweak, it can't transfigure,
Revising, re-envisioning a form,
My lines imperfect from twiggy forearm
To sprain-prone ankle, slender but not svelte . . .
No bookshelf abs, no teardrop-tapered delts
With body fat at less than ten percent,
No calves with brickbats sewn beneath the skin,
No gymnast's thighs, no varsity swimmer's back
Hairless as Hellenistic marble, waxed
And flaring upside-down-triangle lats:
My lineage denied me lines like that.
I saw it in the photorealist mirror
Behind the power cage: some sculptures here
Had started out at twice my strength and size.
I'll never be half as built as half these guys!
No matter how much sweat the treadmill cost me,
I never would escape the shape that boxed me.
Though one guy's warmup benched my one-rep max,
I worked out anyway, at peace with facts.

The weight room taught me never to compare:
We're *not* created equal, nothing's fair,
And protein-crazed, ascetic antics don't
Outweigh genetics in who will or won't
Deadlift eight hundred pounds and, trembling, stand,
Then drop and step clear, hand unwrapping hand.

A daydream works out in the world once you
Redream it as a list of things to do:
These many sets, these many repetitions.
In poetry alone, I keep ambitions
Properly foolish. You can see how daft
In these impromptu lines—dashed off, one draft—
I jot them as Erato whispers them to me,
Each couplet's music using muscle memory.
Ink's a libation poured before a God, the
Idealized, imaginary body
Of work, but so is sweat, that pours from me
Into my body heat like Vedic ghee.

My agony is Agni. I'm a rishi
As ancient as my ancestors could wish me,
My sacred mandala the power cage,
And ink—*svāhā*—an offering to the page.

I fast, I test my joints with yogic stress,
I seek, through verse, a higher consciousness,
My poems, chants—divinely ordered words
Not meant for men—I hope, divinely heard.
Which is to say, I knew at age nineteen
The torso I worked on would stay unseen
Save by the one (now wife) I love. The same
Is true of every book that bears my name.
I don't work out or write for a stranger's eyes;

Ami's, and Saraswati's—*theirs*, I prize.
Just as I strive to outwrite my last work
(I don't write, now, with one eye on the Master)
The poem's "I" is someone to compete with.
I strive to beat the man I share my seat with
When living, lifting, writing. Self-revision,
Each rhyme a rep, more weight and more ambition
Will grow my karma as I grow my work,
From strength to strength, each birth a clean and jerk.

As Dante wandered, Rumi strummed and whirled:
Soul in the poet, poet in the world,
The Secret anchors all in mystic movement.
To *be*, you have to *do*. There is no proving
Your axiomatic maximum except—
Rep after rep after self-transcending rep—
By reaching for your inner asymptote.
You're lifted, higher than you ever hoped.
The weight of Being pushes through you.
You serve a sheikh. Your body is your guru.

There's one right way with any ritual action:
Strict form is everything. *Don't round your back, son!*
Slow down, look out for any sudden pains,
Don't overdo it, son, don't rush your gains.
I give pointers, not philosophical points
Because philosophy won't keep their joints
From twinges, aches, or one conclusive pop that
Means I caught flawed form too late to stop it.
Now breathe out slowly as you push, I say,
As if I'm coaching at a birth. And they
Are birthing, in a way, themselves. Each strains
A chrysalis that is what it contains—
A teen, a man. *Feet shoulder width apart,*
I say. *Get on that air bike, work your heart!*

I made them start, and that was all it took
To bait the line and get them on the hook.
Within a week, I found them both downstairs in
The thick of leg day. Nubbins of keratin
Studded their palms, proud calluses they showed
Each other, battle scars. They upped their loads,
Riding the upsweep of an S-shaped graph,
That bright exhilaration of the grasp
And heave, their newfound superpower
Pushing the workout to a second hour.
Now it was *their* thing, something that they loved.
They fit their hands into my workout gloves.

I saw them pausing at the mirror, flexing,
Turning their torsos in the light and checking
Which angles flattered. Egg-sized biceps, taut
And small, that cordlike vein-bulge—*Shit*, I thought,
I've got to keep from preaching at the boys.
But out my sermon came. I had no choice.

"The incline press, dead lift, bent-over row—
In time, my boys, you're certain to plateau.
Lifting rewards you most when you're beginning.
The gains spill in your lap like jackpot winnings
Out of a slot machine—you pull the lever
And figure you will win like this forever.
Sure, check yourself out, vanity comes first to the
Appraising gaze—but next comes insecurity,
And either one's a sickness of the psyche
That outweighs any good from lifting, hiking,
Lap swimming, yoga. Boys, it's *all* unhealthy
If you're just doing it to stage a selfie.
Never compare yourself to anybody,
Not Daddy, not your twin. You let your body
One month ago be what you juxtapose

The mirror with, and whether progress shows
Or slows or goes the opposite direction,
Look with detachment at your own reflection.
Just cells! Short-lived as pixels on a screen.
Your being is distinct from being seen."

And yes, in case you're wondering, at the time
I said exactly those words, rhyme for rhyme.
A bit of moralizing, yes, but I'm their father;
If I didn't care, I wouldn't bother.
A little self-aggrandizement, ego-
Dilation, drove me too to grow, to go
Heavy, to make myself get bigger. Vanity's
One engine; old age subs it out with sanity.
You'll never read it in a fitness book,
But what begins with *I want girls to look*
Here ends with *I want Time to look away.*
I live that shift in motive nowadays.
In college, schools of tuna found a grave in
My belly. Now, I fast. I feel no craving
For meat. For twelve years now and counting, I
Have werewolfed down no creature with an eye.
These hours on the air bike, dripping sweat,
I flee in place, as in a nightmare, death.

Death, disease, age, pain: the Buddha's list
Holds true, and bare palms iron-crosshatch-kissed
Can't push that deathweight off the chest, can't power
Through failure to a single extra hour.
With death, there's no negotiating. Age,
Disease, and pain are willing to engage.
You cut a deal with pain, court soreness, risk
The agony of herniated disc
Or torn rotator cuff, and pain delays

Disease and age. There aren't any stays
Of execution. Every body blinks
And sees again through different eyes, and thinks
Again with ganglia, or denser neural thickets,
Our bodies like so many shredded tickets
Dropped as we go one station to the next,
The fingerprint an overwritten text
That says the same thing in a changeling tongue,
Lifesbreath translated, selfsame, to new lungs.

You build a body, oeuvre, tower, culture
Aware that each one is an ice sculpture
That melts to steam beneath the chisel's futile
Pursuit of a beautiful, brief, inutile
Perfection. Time is relative. The soreness
After a workout makes us lighter, soars us
Outside the body's atmosphere. Up there,
The clocks are lazier. Your floating hair
Stops going white, the way the astronaut
Rocketing at light speed in Einstein's thought
Experiment returns to find the earth
Has gotten older. Each clockwork rebirth
Hisses and deadlifts karma off the floor.
Death is a rest before we load up more

Because there is a peak, and that peak past,
The muscle bellies shrink. It happens fast—
Before-and-after photos always show
The gains, but no one takes them of their slow
Shrivel—the turkey-wattle triceps-dangle,
Sandpaper neck skin, ortho-booted ankle,
Small-scale humiliation of the pin
Slid out, moved up two plates, then slid back in.
I know this strength was never meant to last—

Who curls the same dumbbells at eighty as
He does at eighteen? This adrenaline
That I'm addicted to, this game I win
Against myself, it starts up when it ends,

And true, I've got now, in my twins, two friends
I get to work out with, advise, and spot,
But what perplexes me is how they got
So tall so soon. I mean, I wanted this—
This manhood rite, the Wrapping of the Wrists—
But I've uncorked some tricksy timelapse voodoo.
They've shot up, broadened, baritones now . . . who knew
They'd step into the hex bar like flyweights
Into the ring and step out nine, no, eight
Bells later in a whole new weight class? Giggling
Thumb wars leave my spry stub wriggling
Below a hairy bludgeon. Pinned—in seconds!
Now I am Time but God I never reckoned
On this acceleration of their boyhood
Destroying worlds like cradles made of plywood,
Sandboxes full of ashes, ancient phones.
Our hands align—they just have bigger bones.
But (one twin tucked in either armpit) I
Could keep their hands from poking their own eyes,
Threading their tiny wrists among my fingers;
They'd drift off right away. I should have lingered
When setting down that weight. A lullaby—
I never wrote them one—why didn't I?
Those topsy-turvy hours parents keep . . . .
I felt so grateful they had gone to sleep
I slept, I sleepwalked past them year by year,

And now they're men, and only visit here,
My basement setup quaint, with a low ceiling,
Their college fitness-palace more appealing,

Two darkhaired giants standing at the head
Of Daddy's flat bench, nodding, *Go ahead,*
Just breathe out, Dad, you've got this, so I push
The weight, stall; grimace; feel my whole head flush—
Until two fingers cradling the bar
Remind me who I am, and who they are,
My body doubles, in whom I live again,
My dumbbell nebula, my babies, men.

SPECIFIC THEORY OF UNITY

>> CONTEMPORARIES

OUR HIDDEN CONTÈMPORARIES

1.

Consider this poem from Matthew Arnold's sequence addressed to Arthur Hugh Clough:

THE RUSHLIGHT

      I love gossip
and the small-wood of humanity generally
among these raw mammoth-
belched half-delightful objects
the Swiss Alps.
                    The limestone is terribly
gingerbready: the pines terribly
larchy...
            and the curse of the dirty water—

I have seen clean water in parts of the lake of Geneva
whose whole locality
is spoiled by the omnipresence there
of that furiously flaring bethiefed rushlight,
the vulgar Byron.

These lines, in the opinion of almost any contemporary poet, read as vastly superior to almost any of Arnold's other poetry, like the benumbing first stanza of "Courage":

> True, we must tame our rebel will:
> True, we must bow to Nature's law:
> Must bear in silence many an ill;
> Must learn to wait, renounce, withdraw.

But "The Rushlight"—a rushlight, Wikipedia reports, is "a type of candle or miniature torch formed by soaking the dried pith of the rush plant in fat or grease"—doesn't appear in any anthology of Arnold's poems. Its fullness of phrase ("furiously flaring bethiefed rushlight") and delightfully contrarian irascibility (a vacation to Lake Geneva provokes a crack at Lord Byron) has escaped anthologists fixated on the classicizing dean.

Of course, another reason this gem hasn't found its due is that it's not actually a poem. Arnold never deployed those late-twentieth-century, Charles Wright–esque line breaks—I added them. Arnold wrote that passage as prose in a letter to Arthur Hugh Clough, failing to recognize it as poetry that would be far more appealing, less than a hundred years later, than his bland iambs. Here's another Arnold gem, a tender gay love poem excavated from the same unrecognized sequence:

THE POURQUOI

> Perhaps you don't see the pourquoi:
> but I think my love
> does
>
> and the paper draws to an end....
>
> My feeling with regard to (I hate
> the word) women.
>
> We know beforehand
> all they can teach us: yet
> we are obliged to learn it
> directly from them....

Farewell, my love,
to meet I hope
in Oxford:
not

    alas

        in heaven.

Some traits that we value in poetry—irregularity of rhythm, unpredict-ability of language, a highly personal bent—were things that the Victori-ans allowed themselves only in their letters. The letter also lent itself to a structural characteristic so ubiquitous in contemporary poems it is almost unrecognized: the first-person anecdote.

Matthew Arnold is terribly out of favor among contemporary poets; I myself find much of his *poetry* unreadable. But what a shock in his letters! Nineteenth-century English lyric conventions strictly limited how much detritus of life was allowed in verse, much like French neoclassical tragedy. This is why the Victorians were so far from Shakespeare even when they set out to imitate him (just read the blank-verse plays of Tennyson, or rather do yourself a favor and *don't*). Today we have different conventions, different preferences—we treasure that detritus, and we try to charge the disjecta membra of daily life with poetic power. Poets like Arnold, milquetoast and stiff when they're writing poesy, are at their most engaging and contem-porary in their letters. Here, from the same sequence—let's call it *My Dear Clough*—is a poem in which Arnold dwells on a long journey home:

ITINERARY

Tomorrow I repass the Gemmi
and get to Thun:
linger one day
at the Hotel Bellevue for the sake
of the blue eyes of one of its inmates:
and then proceed by slow stages
down the Rhine to Cologne,
thence to Amiens
and Boulogne
and England.

2.

In Arnold's "vulgar Byron," we have another example of a poet whose most contemporary poems are buried in plain sight. In his letters, Byron has leave to show us just how delightfully vulgar he is:

THE PERTINACIOUS PORTUGUESE

When the Portuguese are pertinacious,
I say "Carracho!"—the great oath
of the grandees, that very well
supplies the place of "Damme"—

and, when dissatisfied with my neighbour,
I pronounce him "Ambra
di merdo." With these two phrases,
and a third, "Avra louro,"
which signifieth
                    "Get an ass,"
I am universally understood

to be a person of degree
and a master of languages.

How merrily we lives that travellers be!—
if we had food and raiment.

But, in sober sadness,
any thing is better

than England . . . .

The shifts of mood and register, that wryly pseudobiblical "signifieth," the Scottish Lord's self-reflexive sarcasm ("a person of degree")—this is a poetry over a century ahead of its time. We even catch the half-poignant, half-bitter end note of "England," which Arnold, in spite of himself, would echo decades later.

Byron's travels in Greece and Asia occasioned some of his best poems, and I don't mean the so-called Oriental romances.

Know ye the land where the cypress and myrtle
Are emblems of deeds that are done in their clime?
Where the rage of the vulture, the love of the turtle,
Now melt into sorrow, now madden to crime?
Know ye the land of the cedar and vine,
Where the flowers ever blossom, the beams ever shine;
Where the light wings of Zephyr, oppressed with perfume,
Wax faint o'er the gardens of Gúl in her bloom;
Where the citron and olive are fairest of fruit,
And the voice of the nightingale never is mute;
Where the tints of the earth, and the hues of the sky,
In colour though varied, in beauty may vie,
And the purple of Ocean is deepest in dye;
Where the virgins are soft as the roses they twine,
And all, save the spirit of man, is divine—
Tis the clime of the East—'tis the land of the Sun—
Can he smile on such deeds as his children have done?[1]

Edward Said couldn't bear this stuff, and neither can we (but Byron's contemporaries, mind you, *loved* it). The poet's vision blurs the harder he tries
to set a scene; here, Byron decides against his own memory and reaches
for Goethe's 1795 poem "Mignon." "Kennst du das Land, wo die Zitronen
bluhn?" Yes, we *do* know the land, both by the opening question and by the
telltale "citron."

To understand what Byron was really capable of, both as a poet and a
witness, we must turn to another of his embedded masterpieces, "The Arrival." Here we find a clear, Homeric eye delighting in the accoutrements of
war; here we find the poet focused on things as they are. The opening lines
belong not in a romance but in an epic:

THE ARRIVAL

The Albanians, in their dresses (the most magnificent
in the world, consisting of a long *white kilt*, gold-
worked cloak, crimson velvet gold-
laced jacket and waistcoat, silver-

mounted pistols and daggers), the Tartars
with their high caps, the Turks in their vast
pelisses and turbans,

              the soldiers
and black slaves with the horses, the former
in groups in an immense large open gallery
in front of the palace, the latter
placed in a kind of cloister below it,

two hundred steeds ready caparisoned to move in a moment,
couriers entering or passing out
with the despatches, the kettledrums beating,
boys calling the hour from the minaret of the mosque ....

Today I saw the remains of the town of Actium,
near which Antony lost the world, in a small bay,
where two frigates could hardly manoeuvre.

An elaborate description of Ottoman grandeur followed by a three-line vignette of vanished imperial might: It is a brilliant juxtaposition, presented in the letter just as it is here, without commentary or transition (or line breaks, of course). "Immense large open" ... the same could be said of Byron's poetic style here.

Besides the off-the-cuff epic snippet, Byron at this point was also throwing down charming poems in the confessional mode. When else have we heard a nineteenth-century poet talking about his waistline and his workout routine? A familial tendency to obesity troubled Byron throughout his life, and he dilated and shrank cyclically, like a dying sun. Here the young Byron kvetches about money, but he still finds an upside to the situation:

WEIGHTS & MEASURES

Wine and *Women* have *dished* your *humble Servant*,
not a *Sou* to be *had*; all *over*; condemned
to exist (I cannot say live) at this *Crater* of Dullness
till my *Lease* of *Infancy* expires. To appear
at Cambridge is impossible; no money

even to pay my College expences.
You will be surprized to hear I am grown
very thin; however it is the *Fact*, so much so,
that the people here think I am *going*.

I have lost 18 LB in my weight, that is one Stone
& 4 pounds since January, this was ascertained
last Wednesday, on account of a *Bet* with an acquaintance.

However don't be alarmed; I have taken
every means to accomplish the end,
by violent exercise and Fasting, as I found myself
too plump. I shall continue my Exertions,
having no other amusement; I wear *seven* Waistcoats
and a great Coat, run, and play at cricket
in this Dress, till quite exhausted by excessive
perspiration, use the Hip Bath daily; eat
only a quarter of a pound of Butcher's Meat
in 24 hours, no Suppers or Breakfast,
only one Meal a Day; drink no malt liquor,
but a little Wine, and take Physic occasionally.
By these means my *Ribs* display Skin
of no great Thickness, & my Clothes
have been taken in nearly *half a yard*.

Erratic italics and capital letters give Byron's "verse" a typographical idio-syncrasy, much as Dickinson's dashes do hers. This very twenty-first-century obsession with weight is presented in an equally twenty-first-century con-versational tone, reminiscent at times of Frank O'Hara's "I do this, I do that" poems. But here's the kicker: The prose I adapted into "Weights & Measures" was dashed off on April 2, 1807, when Byron was still half a decade away from publishing the single longest purple passage in English literature, *Childe Harold's Pilgrimage*. That was the work of poetry that would make him famous, but it is tough going today in a way that "Weights & Measures" isn't.

In fact, all of the Byron "poems" in this essay come from before 1812, the year the first part of *Childe Harold* was published. The one below comes from

1810, and it's a love poem with a surprise ending. Yet its final line reveals the pedophilic tendency that was as unforgivable then as it is now, and it shows us why Byron was, for so long, considered disreputable.

POSTSCRIPT
I almost forgot to tell you
that I am dying

for love of three Greek
girls at Athens,

sisters.

I lived in the same house.

Teresa,
Mariana,
and Katinka,

are the names of these divinities—
all of them

under fifteen.

3.

Byron did get some of his outrageous, capacious, wry approach to life into his verse—hence the enduring appeal of *Don Juan*. Others were not so fortunate. Algernon Charles Swinburne, for example:

I hid my heart in a nest of roses,
Out of the sun's way, hidden apart;
In a softer bed than the soft white snow's is,
Under the roses I hid my heart.[2]

Compare that typical snippet of Swinburnese to the kinetic, chockablock language and scatological superflux of his 1874 flyting of Ralph Waldo Emerson. In this little-known transatlantic literary showdown, Emerson called Swinburne "a perfect leper, and a mere sodomite" in an interview. In response, Swinburne wrote a "poem" in letter form to the *New-York Tribune* that described the transcendental sage as, among other things,

> … a gap-toothed and hoary-
> headed ape, carried first
> into notice on the shoulder
> of Carlyle, and who now,
> in his dotage, spits and chatters
> from a dirtier perch
> of his own finding and fouling;
> Coryphaeus or choragus
> of his Bulgarian tribe
> of autocoprophagous
> baboons who make
> the filth they feed on.

Now that puts the "burn" in "Swinburne."

Tennyson is another nineteenth-century poet who wrote twenty-first-century letters. In 1853, the poet laureate described a seaside stroll:

> … forth they came and paced the shore,
> Ran in and out the long sea-framing caves,
> Drank the large air, and saw, but scarce believed
> (The sootflake of so many a summer still
> Clung to their fancies) that they saw, the sea.
> So now on sand they walk'd, and now on cliff,
> Lingering about the thymy promontories,
> Till all the sails were darken'd in the west,
> And rosed in the east.

Just a year before, he had described something similar in this hidden masterpiece of natural description, the keenness and immediacy of which prefigure Bishop and Montale:

ST. HILDA'S SNAKES

for Emily Sellwood Tennyson

You see beautiful little ammonites
which you stoop to pick up but find them part
of the solid rock.

                        These are the snakes St. Hilda drove over
the cliff and falling they lost their heads, and she changed them
into stone.

                 I found a strange fish on the shore
with rainbows about its wild staring eyes,

                              enclosed
in a sort of sack with long tentacula beautifully colored,
quite dead,

               but when I took it up by the tail
spotted all the sand underneath with great drops
of ink,

         so I suppose a kind of cuttlefish.

                            I found too
a pale pink orchis on the sea bank

                      and a pink vetch,
a low sort of shrub

              with here
       and there

               a thorn.

HER SEVEN INGENIOUS MASKS

1. INFINITUDE DISGUISED AS THE SOUNDBITE

Each of Kay Ryan's poems runs no longer than a commercial. Brevity is the first mask. It fits over the other masks and makes what they hide seem smaller, more containable—much like the poem as it looks on the page, taken in whole at a single glance. Traditionally, poems that occupy this much space will reward you, at best, with either a memorable image or a witticism. Even that would come after padding, a little setup before the spike. You're unlikely to get so much infinity out of it.

This is why the similarity with Dickinson keeps coming up, even though the two poets' natures are so totally different, ecstasy and watchfulness. They are both metals (strangely marked indeed) of the same atomic weight and density. But they exist at totally different temperatures: Dickinson close to the melting point; Ryan cool to the touch, a surprise like steel.

And yet how perfectly her soundbites subvert the nature of the sound-bite. They don't reduce complexity to simplicity. However short and at times epigrammatic, they are surprisingly difficult to quote, and especially to quote *from*; no part is detachable. Rather, their brevity and irreducible simplicity are pinpoint apertures that focus on vastness: the viewfinder on a handheld camera fitted with a panoramic lens.

2. IRRATIONALITY DISGUISED AS LOGIC

What applies to Ryan's poetry applies to metaphor generally, and to (the best) poetry by extension. Metaphor is the meaningful irrationality that distinguishes poetic language, and it's a testament to the power of poetry that the higher orders of physics and biology have required metaphor to make sense of their own ideas. Even the basic, near universal association of, say, "desire" with "burning," a feeling and an element, is too sophisticated an operation for syllogism. At some point, someone made that connection, and it *stuck*. It stuck because it was *right*. Not because it could be proven, but because it was *right*. The same applies to clichés. Ryan herself has professed an affection for clichés and uses them in her poetry; she is not afraid to recognize them for their rightness. To originate that kind of rightness, to be the first to announce the connection of intention and an edible cotyledon (as she does in "Intention"); that is metaphorical power, as good a way as any of ranking poets.

To me, Ryan has the greatest metaphorical power of any living poet. Her connections stick because, again, they are *right*. But the finest touch is the rather unexcited way in which the sublime madness is conveyed. This is the second mask: the tone. It's the tone of detached observation, of a perfectly sane companion pointing out something interesting. But then you listen to the words, and there turns out to be a quite revelatory madness at play.

3. INDIVIDUALITY DISGUISED AS THE IMPERSONAL

For decades now, poets have been trying to set themselves apart by talking about themselves. In Ryan's poems you will find no childhood traumas, no fond memories of growing up, no messy breakups, no anecdotes about the students, no elegies for the dog. Late-twentieth-century memoirists, whether they wrote poems, novels, or autobiographies, are beginning to blend together. Their oppressive fathers are the same oppressive father; their drinking problems are the same drinking problem. Suddenly, by some trick of harmonics, of peaks canceling troughs and wavelengths overlapping just so, that chorus has canceled itself out. (Because they *were* a chorus, weren't they? For all their "individuality.") One voice is still audible. It sounds distinctive, but it's coming from a face curiously devoid of any memorable mole. Actually that's not a face at all; it's a mask, impersonality. It covers this totally individual voice—and, like the mask in a Greek drama, amplifies it. That voice, incidentally, is talking about a flamingo....

4. SUBJECTIVITY DISGUISED AS DISSOLUTION

Description is not always futile. But it *is* always a waste of time. We are living through the heyday of the physical image. "Thousand words"-ing birds, landscapes, cities, flowers, or any other choice picture of reality is the least profitable thing one can do in our situation. Any muggle with a digital camera can show you up, literally. There is only one way a poet can make an anglerfish more real than a marine photographer's: by getting *inside* the anglerfish and looking out ("To an Anglerfish"). The camera can get no deeper than the surface. This jump into other minds is the supreme form of subjectivity, yet it comes across as a kind of free-floating detachment.

Poets who accomplish this feat are only loosely tethered to their own ego. Or maybe it's the ego that isn't tethered, that can move in and start perceiving anywhere it's sent. This kind of subjectivity requires the self-abnegation that is so often praised in Shakespeare, the ability to identify with anything at will ("Turtle"). Mystical religious traditions ascribe a similar polyvalence to the enlightened.

This is the mask of dissolution. Ryan's air of detachment, her refusal to get worked up over her own observations, keeps the mask snug. Dissolving the self has freed her to indulge a subjective, lyrical delight in the smallest things of the world. And she does it without the behold-me-beholding-this, self-important "selflessness" of Rilke in his *Dinggedichte*.

5. DESIGN DISGUISED AS ACCIDENT

Or, formality disguised as informality. She takes care to eschew the clinching couplet and to have it too. The extra syllables and internal rhymes are often intentionally put there, according to her interviews, to obscure a fundamentally regular structure, the set/spike of introduction and finishing rhyme familiar to any reader of epigrams or Shakespearean sonnets. In English, "epigram" inaccurately connotes minor poetry, the "barb," light verse. Her verse is often funny, sometimes slight—but it is never light.

About that verse. Our great-grandfathers probably would have called it "doggerel." They would have used that term pejoratively, but our ancestors never had their doggerel so good. Ryan herself calls it "recombinant rhyme," a rare slip for her; she is so nimble with metaphor, you would think she would spot and evade another easy, misleading analogy between science and art. "Recombinant" implies some sort of *advance* in rhyme, analogous to those in genetic engineering. But the discovery here doesn't strike me as genuinely musical. I have always thought it a *typographical* masterstroke, not a musical one (but a masterstroke nonetheless, her spoonful of irregularity helping the chime go down). Consider, for example:

> One advantage
> of the advancing
> years: They do
> something to
> your ears. A touch
> of deafness lightens
> one of life's heaviest
> chores: Listening
> to bores.[1]

These lines were written by Ogden Nash, albeit with different lineation. You can see how it comes off a lot like Ryan on the outside if scissored up with line breaks, but it's empty of Ryan on the inside (I say this not to fault Nash, who was pursuing a different kind of poetry).

Wouldn't it have been wonderful if her style had succeeded Ashbery's as the next "period style"? I suspect it had as good a chance as any of doing so; like Ashbery's, hers is easy to imitate, allowing weaker poets to produce an echo stronger than their own voices. Personally, I would rather read her minor contemporary imitators than original Ashbery. She would probably be horrified to imagine thousands of tiny writing-program goslings swimming in her wake, but I have had quite enough of the flippant, pop-cultural, and disjointed; I would *have loved* it if she became the coming generation's primary model. She would have forced them to listen to what they were saying and, most radically of all, to *say something*—that is, like Frost and Dickinson before her, to arrive at ambiguities in the course of assertion.

6. INCLUSIVENESS DISGUISED AS EXCLUSION

I have already mentioned (with delight, mind you) what Ryan's poems exclude. That was actually a description of her sixth mask. Exclusion, like all her other masks, hides its opposite; this mask too allows her to have it both ways. Style is defined as much by what it chooses to hide as what it chooses to present. An illuminating comparison is with Albert Goldbarth, born less than three years after Ryan, though publication and recognition came much earlier to one than to the other. On paper, they seem totally different. Yet her connections are as strangely appropriate, and pull together from as far apart as any of Goldbarth's; you can find Ryanesque gems buried in the messier stretches of Goldbarth. He has buried them a little too effectively, I suspect, having paid too much attention to voice and not enough to sound. She, by contrast, has streamlined herself, and just as her poems—physically lighter, verbally tighter—travel faster, they may also travel farther into the future.

A poet achieves substantiality by laying mask over mask, filter over filter, veil over veil, discipline over discipline, as many as possible. I call it Goldbarth's Folly: seeking inclusiveness through . . . *inclusion*.

7. VISION DISGUISED AS OBSERVATIONS

Every pair of eyes is unique; retinal scans are even more reliable than fingerprinting. But it's a rare pair of eyes that *sees* differently. Corrective lenses can sharpen your vision, but they can't focus your gaze in the right place—they can't help you see *under*, or *through*. I could discuss how Ryan is the first human being to see what a zebra drinking water looks like *to the zebra* (and vividly enough to be justly terrified), but what good would that do? It's the old problem of how to explain color to the blind. Her irreducibility extends to the discussion of her irreducibility. *Insert illustrative quotation*, which is to say, *insert full text*. You have to see the world through her observations of it to understand her vision. That vision is singular, in both senses: "unusual or striking" and "composed of one member, set, or kind." It is also multifarious, picking up any little thing and knowing it all the way through.

This last mask is the one that is all her own, as flush as the wetness of the eye. Everything else—the tone, the slant rhymes and enjambment, the identification with things, the brevity—can be taught and learned. Lift this mask, and you find nothing behind it . . . or, more accurately, you find the universe again, all things in Heaven and Earth, unfiltered and therefore unknowable. And so, one by one, you lay her masks back on. You never saw the universe so clearly as you heard about it through her masks. What we want, after all, is not the whole universe. What we want is *The Best of It*.

APPENDIX: COMPACT AND DANGEROUS

SHARKS' TEETH

Everything contains some
silence. Noise gets
its zest from the
small shark's-tooth
shaped fragments
of rest angled
in it. An hour
of city holds maybe
a minute of these
remnants of a time
when silence reigned,
compact and dangerous
as a shark. Sometimes
a bit of a tail
or fin can still
be sensed in parks.[2]

Kay Ryan's poetry embeds its rhymes like sharks' teeth. Her rhymes are sounds that draw attention to themselves, but not too much attention, so that all the ear senses is "a bit of a tail / or fin."

The first internal rhyme, *zest*, sets the theme of the rest of the poem, but obliquely. The buried metaphor relates to the second, culinary meaning of zest, a shred of lemon or orange rind that adds flavor to a dish. Noise may seem to have "enthusiasm or energy," the other meaning of *zest*, but the poem upends our understanding of noise. The enthusiasm or energy really derives from silence—or, as *zest*'s other embedded rhyme would have it, *rest*. Rest's many meanings echo by the end of the poem, as well. Besides musical rests—those silences that structure music—the "rest" of something is the "remnant" of something, just as the teeth are what remain of the shark. Sharks' teeth served as raw materials for some of the earliest weapons in North America—the weapons themselves remains of bygone indigenous civilizations, long since laid to rest by noisy modernity, but never—in our genes, in American place names—completely gone.

The sharks are vanished dangers at the start of the poem, only their teeth left behind. Yet by the end of the poem, they are circling a bench in a city park: solitude's quiet, fragile raft. The sharks are silence. Why is the silence dangerous? Everyone will have a different answer to that question, but they only have to answer it when they are alone, or alone with silence. Safer to return to the noise of the city, that cacophony created to distract from the fin that awaits us, the appetite that lurks beneath the surface of everything.

Silences, Ryan tells us, have teeth, and sharp ones. Silences swim silently up to us. Silences can tear us open and tear us apart. Conscience-haunted memory quickens its pace through Ryan's silence-infested park. The unease is not the poet's; it is the reader's. Her poem is not confessional. It is a confessional, coaxing the reader to fill in lived context . . . to fill the awkward silence after its "resonant" image of sharks' teeth, all the more personal for not being about a person at all, neither the poet's subject nor the poet herself.

This reveals one of the central strategies of Ryan's versecraft in general. Notice the absence of specific context in Ryan's poems: The reader rarely learns *of a* personal story behind the utterance. The poet does not share details about the unhappy marriages, messy divorces, dead siblings, abusive fathers, social injustices, or childhood traumas that fuel so much of contemporary poetry. A Ryan poem cannot be quoted out of context because it has no context, other than the observed world it is a part of—embedded at an angle, like a shark's tooth. Each poem is small enough that it must be recited entire if at all; the hidden rhymes and rapid-fire enjambments refuse to cooperate with anyone who would make an excerpt.

An absence of grounding detail does not impoverish the poem; rather it allows the poem, like all Ryan poems, to travel anywhere. This trait is shared by the most famous poetry in our language. "To be or not to be" has long since floated free of its dramatic moment in *Hamlet* to become a general, existential meditation. Notice that Hamlet, in that passage, does not refer to his mother, his father, his uncle, Ophelia, or Denmark. That lack of signifiers became an advantage. Kipling's "If," because it's Kipling who wrote it, may evoke historical images of pith-helmeted British officers keeping their heads under fire, like the outnumbered soldiers at Rorke's Drift. The poem itself lacks any such references; Kipling kept "If" all-purpose so the reader or listener could imagine the context.

Paradoxically, even though Ryan manages to keep the poem contextless, she also manages to encode a back story entirely through metaphor. The back story of the poem is the antediluvian back story of all civilization. By the time "Sharks' Teeth" opens, silence has retreated like flood waters from Ryan's nameless, placeless city. Mountaintop seashells (and sharks' teeth) hint at a world before the world. Imagine that bygone environment, the ambient noise muffled, the emptied sky an original and liquid womb. The mind, embedded in meditative silence, rests like a shark's tooth in an underwater city. Ryan's suggestive phrasing drowns this city. Shadowy hammerheads thread its skyscrapers and parking decks. A deluge of some kind antedated the sunlight and chirp. It is a city like any other, with a park and a fountain whose shallow waters run impossibly deep. No Swimming.

Poems are not always about themselves, but every poem is a commentary on poetry, if only at the level of style. Ryan's efficiently unending poems are "compact and dangerous." Each poem resembles, with its "small shark's-tooth shaped" form, silence itself. It angles strangely in the memory. A minute of one contains an hour.

RAY BRADBURY, WORD-WIZARD

Mention Ray Bradbury, I've found, and faces light up. Strangers reach out to you on Twitter with testimonials. A voice on the phone changes as if you just mentioned a childhood best friend. This is something beyond fondness, beyond admiration. The name conjures up poignant wonder, exhilarates the imagination. No one seems to be just "familiar with his work." You've either never read him, or you love him.

One place to read his best work (his stories are as innumerable, and as luminous, as the stars) is in the Library of America's omnibus, which contains *The Martian Chronicles, Fahrenheit 451, Dandelion Wine,* and *Something Wicked This Way Comes.* It's illuminating to have them all in one place. You can see, in the early work, the later work in embryo. "Usher II," a story from *The Martian Chronicles,* speaks of an exterminationist campaign against fantasy literature, dovetailing with *Fahrenheit 451.* An ethereally robed Martian, shot dead, dies "like a small circus tent pulling up its stakes and dropping soft fold on fold"—an image that flows into the carnival memories of *Dandelion Wine,* and from there into the sinister beauty of *Something Wicked This Way Comes.*

You can also see Bradbury's most wrenching theme in all its iterations: the past. The men of the doomed third expedition to Mars encounter long-dead loved ones, who welcome them and then slaughter them. The "dark carnival" promises a return to youth in exchange for eternal captivity. The firemen of his totalitarian dystopia go the other way and incinerate the past wholesale. Trying to live in the past is tempting but fatal; trying to forget the past entirely is a different kind of death. The wisest, sanest approach to the past is to turn it into dandelion wine, the treasured distillate of nostalgia that Bradbury has bottled for us in his books.

His body of work is at home in the past and the future at once. Visions of the far reaches of space are "grounded" in the early-twentieth-century Midwest. The emblematic image comes early in this volume, when that third expedition hears "Beautiful Ohio" playing uncannily across the alien landscape of Mars. This is one secret of his charm and timelessness: Bradbury, the prophetic visionary, never stops being Ray, your next-door neighbor.

Those visions can break your heart in the ways they contrast with—and match—the present. Bradbury's Martian stories have explicit dates: In the 2005 of the book, Americans walk the surface of another planet; in the 2005 that Bradbury lived to see, Americans were walking the alien, ancient landscapes of Iraq and Afghanistan. In both the book and the reality, they leave behind an imperial desolation. Our aggressively ignorant contemporaries do not use fire to destroy physical books as those in Guy Montag's world do, but social media, with its faux-moral crusades against writers alive and dead, stinks of kerosene. I am unaware of any attempts to attack Bradbury's legacy so far, but if they ever try, they are going to have a war on their hands.

Bradbury has all three qualities by which T. S. Eliot defined the greatest poets: "abundance, variety, and complete competence."[1] It feels right to speak of Bradbury as a master poet. Whenever he unleashed his natural lyricism, he created Baroque sentences best understood, and appreciated, as a poetry far more kinetic, intense, and, well, *poetic* than what goes by the name of poetry, whether in academia or on Instagram:

> And while the wave of applause came in, crashed, and went back down the shore, he looked again to the maze, where the sensed but unseen shadow-shapes of Will and Jim were filed among the titanic razor blades of revelation and illusion, then back to the Medusa gaze of Mr. Dark, swiftly reckoned with, and on to the stitched and jittering sightless nun of midnight, sidling back still more.[2]

Go ahead and marvel at the metaphors, the classical allusions, the paradoxes, the synoptic syntax that sees and shows the reader everyone in the scene (Bradbury wrote screenplays too). How rare this is! Especially in the twentieth century, the time of Raymond Carver–esque, "well-crafted" literary fiction. ("Usher II" features a dig at Hemingway and realism; Bradbury knew his antithesis early on.) Listen to how nothings multiply in

> the Mirror Maze, the empty oblivion which beckoned with ten times a thousand million light years of reflections, counter-reflections, reversed and double-reversed, plunging deep to nothing, face-falling to nothing, stomach-dropping away to yet more sickening plummets of nothing.

The meta-miracle is how Bradbury's supercharged writing can go unnoticed. You can race right past his beautiful complexity to find out what happens next. I know I did, when I was younger. My revisiting of Bradbury has been a re-envisioning. As early as high school, when I read "All Summer in a Day" and *Fahrenheit 451*, I knew he was a great storyteller. Now I recognize him as a total word-wizard, capable, like Shakespeare, of using language in ways that combine poetic magic, emotional weight, and dramatic tension. This writer sacrifices nothing.

Which is why this volume is going straight from my desk to my thirteen-year-old son's. He wants to be a writer, and this is the only teaching text he needs. One day, he too will smile reflexively at the mere mention of this writer's name. He too will become a member of what may well be one of the biggest fan clubs in American letters. Best to join early and let Bradbury influence him into the best possible writer he can be—warmed, brightened, flowering under the rocket summer of his work.

WHY LOGUE
WORKS

No one, aside from the occasional one-star Goodreads churl, has ever re-viewed Christopher Logue's *War Music* unfavorably. No surprise there—it's a masterpiece. In fact, its masterpiece status is so obvious to me that I do not wish to waste words convincing anyone of it, listing virtues and bedaz-zlements and the like. The fact of Logue's triumph resembles, for me, the roundness of the Earth: A case can be made, but why? Instead, I would like to do something related to, but different than, merely heaping more praise on this book. Taking Logue's success as a given, I want to discuss *why* Logue's *War Music* works. How exactly did he pull this off?

First, of course, we must decide what *War Music* actually is. "Translation," clearly, is inaccurate, seeing as Logue retains very little of the original text (not even "Sing, Muse"). The title page's term, "account," is far too modest. What Logue did was *re-create*. In the Western tradition, continuations and translations are far more common than re-creations. In classical Greek, there's an entire epic cycle that tells the rest of Ilium's story, featuring now unknown poets like Arctinus of Miletas and Stasinus, who today are buried deep in the Loeb Classical Library. The history of English Homer translations is illustrious; George Steiner edited an entire anthology of them for Penguin in 1996. He included an excerpt from Logue, but he probably shouldn't have.

Logue's re-creation is something uncommon in the Homeric tradition but very common in India's *Ramayana* tradition—that is, he remade the same epic in another language, more or less sticking to the story but dispensing with the words and formal characteristics. With the Indian epic, the "original" was Valmiki's *Rama's Travels* (the literal meaning of *Ramayana*). As centuries passed, it kept getting rewritten in other languages, as in the case of Kamban's Tamil *The Avatar Rama* or Tulsidasa's Hindi-dialect *The Lake of Rama's Deeds* (the two most famous of countless re-creations in the regional dialects of India, both written and oral, over about two and a half millennia). In the West, what Logue did with the *Iliad*—a full-scale re-creation—is usually only done using other art forms, like the Hollywood movie *Troy* or that high-literary mirror-novel *Ulysses*.

Logue's was not an easy task. What were his strategies, other than deploying language so vivid and violent it makes all of his contemporaries (save Ted Hughes) seem milquetoast by comparison? First and foremost: anachronism. In any art museum, you will find elaborate eighteenth-century biblical canvases in which a burgher or knight in ceremonial armor has been inserted in the crowd at the foot of the cross. The painted phenotypes of the main Gospel cast—Mary's golden hair and milky skin—commandeer a story about Jewish Middle Easterners and insert Western Europeans (that is, the intended audience) into the story. Compare this to the casting of the Broadway blockbuster *Hamilton* with people of color who speak with the delivery style and vocabulary of contemporary hip-hop. Even in closely researched historical fiction like Hilary Mantel's *Wolf Hall*, anachronism adds immediacy; in Mantel's novel, it takes the form of speech patterns, both of the narrator's voice and the dialogue. Anachronism hides, as it were, in plain sight, diffused over the linguistic texture of the writing.

Logue's use of anachronism is more aggressive than that. He doesn't just render Homer in today's colloquial language. Formally, he reworks the classical epic narrative into a verbally charged variation of the contemporary American screenplay. A more fitting title for *War Music* might have been *War Movie*. Sometimes he bids the reader "see," sometimes he bids an imaginary cinematographer "go close." At other times, he simply uses a screenwriter's notations:

Troy.
The Acropolis.
The morning light behind the Temple's colonnade.

Then through that colonnade, Hector of Troy,
Towards his mass of plate-faced warriors.

This partial genre shift is how Logue updated the very nature of the *Iliad*. The ancient Mediterranean world's most hallowed text, quoted as commonly as the Bible would be in Christian Europe, was also its *Star Wars* and its *Apocalypse Now*—popular fantastic epic and gritty classic historical war film—in one.

Reading Logue, you experience this lowbrow/highbrow duality, but it doesn't come off as the conscious inclusion of contemporary life's detritus for its own sake. Nor does a reader, or at least *this* reader, experience the juxtapositions as jarring. His recruitment of contemporary tropes and images feels subordinate to Homer's sense and, in some ways, subordinate to Homer's original text. And they are irresistibly stylish and *right*. Two fighting warriors stand with "Dust like dry ice around their feet." The Greek camp has a "bodyshop" for war chariots.

As Paul Fussell showed in *The Great War and Modern Memory*, a shift occurred after World War I in how British poets thought, remembered, and wrote about war, a shift away from the stirring martial poem or the portrayal of martial violence as exhilarating or beautiful. Though Logue, a noted pacifist, certainly does not present war as a good in itself (and neither does Homer), *War Music* manages to leap, on occasion, into a perspective that antedates the shift described by Fussell. It becomes Homeric enough to take as its birthright the broad-spectrum Homeric perspective on warmaking: the beauty and gore, the envy and triumph, the swagger and tantrum, the thrill and anguish all together. It is the one of the few poems in English written after World War I that includes both what Wilfred Owen called the "pity of war" *and* the exhilaration of it. Exhilaration is what many soldiers feel on the battlefield, if only because there's a great deal of adrenaline involved, but it has become indecent to transcribe in literature the cheering of fighters who, say, just vaporized a hostile with a shoulder-mounted RPG. To hear that side of warmaking, you have to go to USMC helmet-cam footage on YouTube ... or to *War Music*:

And here it comes:
That unpremeditated joy as you

— The Uzi shuddering warm against your hip
Happy in danger in a dangerous place
Yourself another self you found at Troy —
Squeeze nickel through that rush of Greekoid scum!

This holistic approach to war writing is truly Homeric. Warriors rejoice when they kill the other guys and anguish when the other guys kill one of theirs. The emotions are raw. The eye flinches from nothing. Logue the poet does not fixate exclusively on the elegiac bits, as Alice Oswald did in *Memorial*; Logue the storyteller indulges in no campus moralizing about how no one should be fighting anyone else. Conflict is not some collective human error made by fallible politicians; conflict is human.

This lyricism also leaps so far back in stylistic terms that Logue feels positively futuristic. He pulls this off with a partial modal shift: *War Music* is so effectively lyrical because it is so effective as a narrative. He stays free of the pressure implicit—and sometimes explicit—in several contemporary poetry cliques (Language poetry, say, or the New York School) not to make *too* much sense. Like Homer, Logue pretty much always makes sense because his imperative is to be rapid, plain, direct, and noble, just as Matthew Arnold advised in "On Translating Homer."

Logue couples anachronisms of reference and outlook with a technique of deliberate alienation. This is a counterintuitive strategy, ostensibly at odds with the project of modernizing Homer, but it works to the same end because it distances *War Music* from the *Iliad*. Logue does this mostly through his choice of names. He picks ones that sound somewhat Hittite or Assyrian ("Chylabborak," "Thakta"), vaguely London-underworld ("Quist," "Lutie"), or like they came from poor Tom's ravings about demons in *King Lear* ("Pipko," "Bluefisher," "Chuckerbutty," "Lox"). It's an ingenious way of cultivating incongruity, of making the new work less classically Greek and keeping readers from settling into familiarity. The setting is always in flux, and the text is always picking up interference from modern warfare.

But throwing in a reference to Iwo Jima is easy enough, technically. Far more impressive is Logue's ability to create evocative similes that could have been written three thousand years ago but still sound fresh:

Try to recall the pause, thock, pause,
Made by axe blades as they pace
Each other through a valuable wood.
Though the work takes place on the far
Side of a valley, and the axe strokes are
Muted by depths of warm, still standing, air,
They throb, throb, closely in your ear;
And now and then you catch a phrase
Exchanged between the men who work
More than a mile away, with perfect clarity.
Likewise the sound of spear on spear,
Shield against shield, shield against spear
Around Sarpedon's body.

The difficulty level in that passage is considerably higher, and the use of the pastoral to describe the martial is echt-Homeric. At one point, Logue even renews the "lion descending on the fold" extended simile, which already appears in Homer more than forty times. There have been research papers devoted to the specific subject of lion similes in Homer; it takes ambition to try one's own.

See an East African lion
Nose tip to tail tuft ten, eleven feet
Slouching towards you
Swaying its head from side to side
Doubling its pace, its gold-black mane
That stretches down its belly to its groin
Catching the sunlight as it hits
Twice its own length a beat, then leaps
Great forepaws high great claws disclosed
The scarlet insides of its mouth
Parting a roar as loud as sail-sized flames
And lands, slam-scattering the herd.

"That is how Hector came on us."

Moxie (among other things) sets Logue apart from most twentieth-century Anglophone poets. Notice that many a laureled poet set out to *translate* the big epics of the past, whether it was Heaney and *Beowulf* or Merwin and *The Poem of the Cid*. Logue went several steps and a quantum leap beyond that, writing a *new* ancient poem in his living voice. I suspect that Ted Hughes owes a debt to Logue; his project had been famous for decades by the time Hughes published *Tales from Ovid*, which uses many of Logue's techniques to weaker effect.

Logue died before he could finish *War Music*. No matter; *The Canterbury Tales*, *The Faerie Queene*, and *Don Juan* are also unfinished. Introducing the collected fragments of the last section, "Big Men Falling a Long Way," Christopher Reid includes Logue's outline for the remainder of the project. "It remains to be seen how this works out," Logue noted at the end of his list of unwritten episodes: "It is rather a lot."

I, for one, don't mind that Logue didn't mirror the entire *Iliad*, episode for episode. As it stands, with its huge ellipses, *War Music* gains an even more ancient mystique. The greatest classical statues are missing limbs and heads. *War Music* feels less like a self-consciously fragmented Modernist poem and more like an actual epic that has reached us only in fragments. The current text preserves lacunae for our imaginations to fill. The reading experience is more compact this way too; I read the entire text in two days. As for Arnold's criterion of "swiftness," I can testify that Logue has achieved it, and that his poetry reads more swiftly than prose. The poetic effect stays tight and impressionistic, and the poem avoids a programmatic feel.

Still, his death denied us his reimagining of Achilles's shield. Would it have surpassed Auden's? Of the missing episodes, the shield is the loss I feel the most. Logue's note on it indicates he would have carried the depictions into our own time. In other missing episodes—e.g., "Trojans driven back across the ditch to the Scamander"—he would have stylistically duplicated passages that already exist. Logue nailed the modernized verse narration of ancient battle; I know he could have done it, and I can imagine very clearly what these other battle passages would sound like. But that unwritten shield! We will never get to hear Logue send Austerlitz and Okinawa through the smithy of Hephaestus. We can only hope that a missing draft emerges from a drawer someday.

There is plenty to admire, though, in what Calliope gave him. The parts we possess are magnificent, rare, and uncanny. Reader beware, though—after you finish, all other poets are going to seem mild-mannered and blood-less. Almost all, I should say, because I know the one poet who will pass muster. The best part about reading Logue's Homer is going back to Homer afterward. You meet Logue there a second time.

GEORGE STEINER, LAST OF THE EUROPEANS

1.

We don't have many examples of writers embarking on a fresh enterprise very late in life. Sophocles was said to have written tragedies into his ninetieth year; in our own time, we have the examples of Richard Wilbur, Stanley Kunitz, and Samuel Menashe. But these writers, for the most part, replicated their earlier successes. It is much rarer for a writer to set out in a truly new direction in their seventh or eighth decade. Goethe, the exception in this as in so many other things, was an octogenarian when he published the second part of *Faust* in 1831, which is still probably the closest thing we will ever have to a poem written for the screen.

A person of letters usually grows quiescent or retrospective in old age. This is the time for interviews with the reverent young, an autobiography, stray writings collected and bound, the occasional introduction to a retranslated classic. In the worst case, the wizened elder can become merely repetitive, stating one or two fixed ideas until they sound truer and truer to them. Harold Bloom, who himself published a memoir in 2019, had been settled on the absolute primacy of Shakespeare for some time. It is no surprise that Bloom's introduction to Edith Grossman's translation of *Don Quixote* is actually about—you guessed it—Shakespeare.

We had every reason to believe George Steiner had entered this phase of his career. His autobiography, *Errata* (1997), was followed by a volume describing various books he would have liked to have written. This book in particular had a distinctly valedictory, if-I-had-world-enough-and-time air. Finally, New Directions issued a collection of essays Steiner wrote for *The New Yorker*. The process of getting the papers in order seemed complete. The big investigations, it seemed, were over. The older works, fortunately, all rewarded rereading, from the earlier, purer literary criticism like *Tolstoy or Dostoevsky* (1959) to the frankly theological riffs of *Grammars of Creation* (2001). We could follow the progression as Steiner gradually left off writing as a "critic" and began writing as what he was: a polyglot polymath, sucking everything into the discussion. He asked the best questions, and his best guesses were as good as non-answers got. But a new question, we assumed, was not going to be asked.

This is one reason why *The Poetry of Thought* (New Directions, 2012) is so fascinating. This fascination is quite apart from the content of the book itself. The startling thing is the Goethean persistence of Steiner's energy and interest in the universe—and, as a result, this book's air of *youth*. Steiner, synapses firing as fast as ever, had set out on a new Steiner voyage, this time "from Hellenism to Celan." It reminds me of Tennyson's "Ulysses," taking to the sea again. Which is only appropriate: To read Steiner is, above all, to be reminded of everything you have ever read or meant to read.

2.

Steiner, in spite of his reputation as a mandarin, came across in his writing as a brilliant *student*, the kind who raises a hand and asks the question no one else has thought of, much less can answer. A Steiner Question is not a question with a specific answer. He simply wonders aloud and starts speculating. The speculations are insights. The questions themselves are insights. How could the country that produced Handel and Goethe go on to produce Hitler and Göring? Whatever happened to capital-T Tragedy? Or, as in this book: How are thought and style related?

In other books, Steiner had traced a single idea through all of literature: the idea of "beginnings" (*Grammars of Creation*) or the Antigone legend (*An-*

tigones). These are works in which he served as an intellectual tour guide, taking us from Greece or Genesis to the present, pointing out the sights along the way.

The Poetry of Thought combines these two approaches. It is, formally, a synthesis. The Steiner Questions are there. The book begins with such questions about music: "What are the philosophic concepts of the deaf-mute? What are his or her metaphysical imaginings?" It ends with similar answerless questions, this time about the meeting between Martin Heidegger and Paul Celan at Todtnauberg: "What could, what would Heidegger have said in extenuation, in remorse for his own role and omissions in the time of the inhuman? . . . Was *anything* said during that long walk on the sodden uplands?"

The larger question that gives rise to the book is very Steinerian in its intelligent, interdisciplinary wonderment (perhaps "interdisciplinary," in this specific case, is inexact: Steiner is making a case for the oneness, or at least the inextricability, of literature and philosophy). Steiner does not conclusively "answer" this Steiner Question. Such a book would exhaust its utility after the first reading. Instead, he speculates aloud about the relationship between linguistic expression and philosophical thought.

This kind of inquiry is better off treated unsystematically. Steiner constructed *The Poetry of Thought* by searching Western culture for examples and connections, but he derived no larger principles or easily summarized "key concepts." Steiner always distrusted the simplifications of bullet-point thought. He offers us none here.

So, broad in scope though it is, the book does not diminish itself by generalizing. Instead of offering one answer to its Steiner Question, *The Poetry of Thought* answers in the only way a Steiner Question can be sort-of-answered: by offering dozens of smaller insights. For the purposes of this book, Steiner arranged his insights in more or less chronological order, structured, as the subtitle has it, *From Hellenism to Celan*. Steiner was always well equipped to embark on these journeys from the source to the delta. *The Poetry of Thought* combines the questioning, speculative thinker and the tour guide through literary history—the best of both Steiners.

3.

Usually, a review is supposed to paraphrase or summarize the content of a book. While Steiner's *argument* submits to paraphrase, his prose, like good poetry, resists it.

The structure can be laid out easily enough. Consider the first hundred or so pages. Steiner begins with an overture on philosophical writing itself—how abstract philosophical thought aspires to music or mathematics, but has to make do with language. This segues to a chapter on the pre-Socratics—the earliest Western philosophers, and the last ones to cast their ideas in verse. Philosophers after Plato have written primarily in prose, so Steiner skips ahead, in this chapter, to some other philosophical poets, including Lucretius and Dante. (This chapter is best read alongside Santayana's *Three Philosophical Poets: Lucretius, Dante, and Goethe.* You will see the difference between a literary critic and a George Steiner.) After Dante, the "full-scale philosophical poem, the use of verse to express a metaphysical *doxa*, becomes rare." Poets do figure in the later chapters, but the book starts afresh with Plato and progresses chronologically after that. The next chapter discusses the dramaturgical finesse of Plato's Dialogues; the chapter after that follows the dialogue form in general, as practiced by writers from Abelard and Galileo to Paul Valéry.

The problem with such a summary is that it misses the best part: the poetry of Steiner's own thought, the observations that made him so precious as a thinker. The discussion on Plato, for example, dwells on Plato's insistence on exiling poets from his ideal *polis*. Steiner, with his characteristic blend of deep memory and historical conscience, juxtaposes a passage from the *Laws* with an excerpt from a 1933 speech by Joseph Goebbels. This takes place in the space of a paragraph and a half. The parallel is exact, and the fast-forward effect is chilling.

Connections like this are why Steiner the thinker must be read, like a poet, in his own words. In the course of discussing literature, he can make lightning arc between philosophy and history. "Literary" has become a term suggesting ornament, detached aestheticism, and irrelevance even among writers. In Steiner's vocabulary, "literary" is all-encompassing; a truly "literary" investigation should extend to every department in the university.

Steiner showed this knack for illuminating connections as early as *Tolstoy or Dostoevsky*. Consider the passage that reveals Dostoevsky's origins in nineteenth-century melodrama: writing it required an understanding of the now disregarded tradition of melodrama (superseded on the stage by Ibsen, but given a second life in Hollywood) *and* a willingness to dissolve the psychological boundary between fiction and drama. Other critics had searched for Dostoevsky in the biographical details, the diaries, the work of previous Russian novelists. Steiner went to nineteenth-century melodrama and found him.

Such interdisciplinary moments continued to distinguish Steiner's work. The leaps only got more daring. They crop up throughout *The Poetry of Thought*, moments when literary discussion penetrates theology and mathematics:

> In mathematical papers, there is often only one generative word: an initial "let" which authorizes and launches the chain of symbols and diagrams. Comparable to that imperative "let" which initiates the axioms of creation in *Genesis*.

Neither pure theologians nor pure mathematicians (nor pure critics) are capable of thinking like this. Steiner's own thought exemplifies its subject. His consistently unexpected connections possess all the power of poetic metaphor. You stroll with Steiner through the walls in your own mind.

4.

Steiner, often praised as a polymath, understood that the polymath is all too often a curiosity.

As Steiner says of Valéry: "He had no interest in the polymath, but rather in the unifier, the maker of unifying metaphor." Mere ability or knowledge-ability in a variety of fields makes a polymath's contribution to any *one* field fall short of significance. The polymath, in that case, is a glorified dilettante, a dabbler in expertise. Their value is a function of their ability to cross-refer and synthesize. Steiner's comment on Valéry plays on the ety-mological import of "metaphor": to *"carry over,"* to *"transfer."* Carrying over religious understanding into the art of fiction, or musical talent into poetry, or scientific keenness into criticism, the polymath serves as a new synapse in the collective mind. The unifying intellect is to be treasured above the many-minded one.

Steiner, the maker of connections, had that unifying intellect. His discus-sions of philosophical thought and literary form are beyond the ken of the finest critics in the generations after his. These minds are far more comfort-able doing shorter reviews of their contemporaries and longer retrospectives on a few twentieth-century, English-language favorites. The analytical sweep of an Auerbach—from *Gilgamesh* to Flaubert in eleven chapters—is beyond our day-traders in literary reputation. The religious engagement of a Frye, the long literary memory of an Eliot—these too are selected against by the compartment-learning of a university education. And so we are left with critics whose idea of a widely read writer is David Foster Wallace. Whether we find it in Steiner (the French-speaking Jew of Austrian parentage who lived in England), Auerbach (the German Jew who wrote *Mimesis* while in exile in Turkey), Kermode (who was born an Englishman), or Eliot (who died one), this kind of long-memory, wide-lens criticism is, alas, European.

Since Western education gave up Greek and Latin—both major elements of Steiner's education in the *lycée* system—literary memory has gotten shorter and shorter. Teachers of poetry use living contemporaries as teach-ing texts with no sense of how unusual that is in the history of poetic edu-cation. Keats studied, took apart, and wrote his way out from under Spenser and Milton; we would have sent him to school to study Wordsworth. Even our focus on English-language writing (with an inordinate emphasis on the past two hundred years) constituted, in Steiner's world, a myopia verging on blindness. He treated English as *e pluribus unum* with other languages.

Both his methods and his ends are different. A Steiner Question gener-ates the insights that flesh out its own elusiveness. Details and quotations are called up because they advance the investigation, not because they sup-port an assertion of taste. Steiner gathers evidence; he does not make points.

Not only did Steiner come from another continent, he came from another time. Not Europe—*Old* Europe. About this he was unapologetic. He wondered aloud whether the ownership of slaves and a male-dominated society helped abstract thought flourish in ancient Greece. And he was not afraid to marvel at Hellas for the "miracle" it was. "Out of Africa, what theorem?" No other writer except for V. S. Naipaul was so frank in 2012. Like Naipaul (born just three years after him), Steiner felt free to point out things that are politically but not factually incorrect.

Steiner's most Old European trait was his approach to literature itself. Consider his casual manipulation of massive writers in the course of working out his ideas. He lifted them, handled them, turned them about, fit them together. Proust, Tolstoy, Sophocles—these were all building blocks in the playroom of his mind, and he stacked them into impossible Babels. Steiner had a very Old European will to global mastery. In the fallen world, that will expressed itself in empire. The same expansive confidence once contemplated the fates of peoples and nations behind closed doors: how to rule the Indians, how to open China, what to do about the Sudan. Europe doesn't do this kind of thing anymore, neither in its parliaments nor its academies. Europe's politics are (mostly) local now, and so are its critics and writers. Culture is a confidence game for the conquerors and the conquered alike. Before you lose your empire, you produce a Hugo; after, a Houellebecq.

5.

After *The Poetry of Thought*, Steiner could no longer be classified as a literary "critic." He was, rather, a literary "thinker." He did not criticize or comment on literature. He articulated larger ideas, philosophical or theological, *through* literature. Literature was to him what logic is to the logician, what mathematics is to the physicist. The illuminating comparison is with Harold Bloom.

Bloom was a true literary critic. This is why Bloom comes off sounding like a teacher, while Steiner comes off sounding like a student. Even Steiner's most expansive pronouncements read, in context, like a seeker sharing his discoveries. Bloom, by contrast, displayed the critical obsession with ranking writers. The incessant urge to declare Shakespeare, for some reason or another, the supreme writer; the habitual selection of "great" or "greatest" poems or, in one absurd case, "minds" (as in *Genius: A Mosaic of One Hun-*

dred Exemplary Creative Minds); the intense satisfaction in declaring some pet poet the best of all at this or that; the presentation of personal tastes as objective truth (and, indeed, the confusion of the two)—these are all telltale signs of the critic. Many other mere critics, like William Logan, take pleasure in belittling writers; this is actually the same tendency.

Compare Steiner, the literary thinker. He was uninterested in the word-by-word, listen-to-the-*o*-sounds-in-this-passage analysis on which so many critics pride themselves. He was far more interested in following the "hermeneutic motion" of literary translation in 1975's *After Babel* or doing an autopsy on the tragic drama.

Both the literary critic and the literary thinker stand in opposition to the literary *polemicist*. The literary polemicist is interested in using literature to make a political or sociological point. We have all seen this kind of thing: Milton is a misogynist, Shakespeare is an anti-Semite, the Western Canon is a form of imperial oppression, etc. Minds like Steiner's and Bloom's used to dominate university literature departments; now these departments produce Marxist, postcolonial, and feminist "critiques" of literature that antedates Marx, Said, and Steinem by centuries. The practice is as meaningless as the early Church Fathers condemning Plato for not being Christian enough (or, contrarily, exalting Virgil for writing that faux-messianic *Fourth Eclogue*). You can find swipes at political correctness and ideologically motivated readings in Steiner and Bloom alike. They represented the old guard of literary critics and literary thinkers. The *very* old guard. It's not that they were apolitical. They simply understood that some things transcend politics, and that literature is one of them.

6.

Which brings us to the ultimate Steiner Question: What is the place of George Steiner in the first decades of the twenty-first century? How should we frame the story of his career?

There are two stories that can be told about George Steiner. One story goes like this: There once was a brilliant man who outlived his time and outstayed his welcome. One day he was the master of all knowledge, and then knowledge itself expanded. Suddenly it wasn't enough to know everything from Hellenism to Celan. What about Lao Tzu and Li Po? What about the *Bhagavad Gita*? Surely, when he wrote about the poetry of thought, he should have included a chapter about a philosophical poem central to the lives of millions. What about the Sufi poet-philosopher Ibn al-Arabi? If Steiner knew Greek and Hebrew, was it too much trouble to learn Arabic?

This multilingual literary cosmopolitan woke up in the twenty-first century and found himself a provincial. His intellectual domain was nothing more than Europe and a few of its colonies. You'd think it would be tough to ignore Asia, Africa, and the Middle East, but he succeeded. The names he dropped in his supposedly "far-reaching" books were mostly those of Caucasian men. In one of his late books, *The Poetry of Thought*, he actually came out and asked, with an imperial air, "Out of Africa, what theorem?" He was the last of the Eurocentric blowhards: George Steiner.

That is the story a literary polemicist might tell. And Steiner *was* Eurocentric, or at least focused on the West. He *did* focus on the writing of men more than that of women, probably because his view included the vast swath of history before women entered literature in full force. He was, according to his *Paris Review* interview, a big Jane Austen fan, but had not singled out "women's writing" for specific discussion. I see no point in defending George Steiner against either of those charges. I am simply going to tell a different story—a story that places him, I believe, in his rightful context.

That story would present George Steiner as the last European. By "European," I refer to a very specific Europe: the strange hybrid culture which arose from a cross of mostly incompatible traditions and tendencies. I refer to the post-medieval, peculiarly European enterprise that began with Dante Alighieri. It sought to hold the Judeo-Christian tradition, the classical pagan tradition, and contemporary events in one mind. It took a monotheistic tradition and crossed it with a polytheistic one. Its dominant religious book, the Bible, remains the only scripture written in languages from two entirely different language families: the Semitic language, Hebrew, and the Indo-European language, Greek. It split its attention between Heaven and Earth; it developed the calculus at roughly the same time its art was proliferating

Madonnas and Christ-children. Considered as a whole, Europe's most representative mind was probably that of Blaise Pascal: at once scientific and religious, mathematical and verbal.

Steiner embodied this hybrid Europe too, just like its founding father, Dante. In Dante, we find Judas, Minos, and Boniface; in Steiner, we find Babel, Antigone, and Birkenau. We must not forget what a bizarre mix the *Commedia* is, with its demons borrowed from Ovid, its Paradisal eagle borrowed from the Roman legions, and its intermittent polemics against bad popes. Steiner showed the same engagement with contradictory pasts and the ignominious present. Steiner the polymath, interested equally in chess, Chomsky, and Celan, showed the Western world's "infinity-seeking" tendency. He would have learned everything if he could. Oswald Spengler called this tendency "Faustian," and indeed Goethe is another Western mind quite akin to Steiner's: universally interested, and tireless into old age, tireless to the end.

Western culture achieved what it achieved as a result of *hybrid vigor*—the genetic principle that makes the mongrel stronger than the purebred. This particular recipe—Greece and Rome, plus the Bible, plus worldliness—resulted in six centuries of progressive Western inquiry, accomplishment, and dominance. It ended with a half-century-long European catastrophe. That this catastrophe went global, twice, only illustrates how central this appendage to Asia made itself. With Christianity declining fastest in Europe and the loss of classical education, two of the three Dantean ingredients have evaporated, leaving the residuum we call Europe today.

History has a sense of irony, a sense of timing, even a sense of humor (the only thing it lacks is a sense of justice). How perfectly ironic, then, that the last European should have come from the people that suffered Europe's worst. The French lose interest in Racine, thinking him a schoolroom text, a musty classic—while a Paris-born son of Jewish émigrés treasures him, making an eloquent case (*Antigones*, chapter 14) for his lasting power. Steiner's life (he was born in 1929) coincided with the decline of European Christianity and European power, but he contained in his memory the best of Europe, that part of Europe worth preserving.

I may seem to inflate Steiner's worth by drawing this line from him back to Dante, but I am not equating their accomplishments. I consider them, rather, as the first and last chapters of the same book. That is the larger story we should tell of Steiner, a story that places him in the largest possible context. Dante was the beginning of something, and that something—the Europe of the thinkers and novelists and poets—ended with the man who contained it whole: the last European, George Steiner.

STOP LOOKING
AT YOURSELF
ON THE DANGERS OF MIRRORS AND SELFIES

We were not meant to look at ourselves too closely or too often. By *not meant* I mean *not designed*, psychologically, spiritually. We are not meant to endure an abundance of sugar, either... but sugar doesn't stop tasting good. It keeps tasting good even after it's started killing you.

An image of yourself, seen for what it is, should be regarded with alarm. "I have been horrified before all mirrors," wrote Jorge Luis Borges:

> I look on them as infinite, elemental
> fulfillers of a very ancient pact
> to multiply the world, as in the act
> of generation, sleepless and dangerous.[1]

In the *Book of Imaginary Beings*, he wrote of a kingdom ravaged by people who invaded it through its mirrors. In the short story "Covered Mirrors," he wrote of meeting a woman—"first by telephone," in an uncanny premonition of modernity—with whom he shared his horror of mirrors. The horror, contagious, intensified upon transmission; she covered all the mirrors in her home and went insane.

222

That same Borges story begins with a reference to Islam's injunction against the making of images. In the Hadith that Borges references, the Prophet declares that anyone who creates an image of a living thing will be challenged, on the Day of Judgement, to make it come to life. If the sculpture or portrait—or selfie—does not quicken (and it won't, because there is only one Power than can quicken it), the maker of the image will be damned forever.

Notice that Borges combines two different objects: the reflective surface and the artistic image. (The original warning, in the Hadith, is prompted by a glimpse of Aisha's embroidered pillow.) Yet his insight here is sound; both objects duplicate reality, and that duplication is duplicitous. Both are, in effect, one and the same. The portrait is a mirror image, frozen in time, for all time. It may be idealized, of course. But so might a selfie, that freeze-frame of the phone's mirroring screen, retouched or passed through a filter.

According to the Hadith, whose injunction echoes the Second Commandment, the unreal, nonliving, generated image—"graven," or pixelated—offends the creator of living things. The image possesses the form but not the soul of the subject. That deceptiveness places it, like the "false idols" that prompted centuries of iconoclasm, on the side of the Deceiver. That is why the making of images, including images of oneself, is a spiritual danger.

But it is not the only spiritual danger. Later in his poem about mirrors, decades before people flipped their smartphone cameras to inspect and capture their own faces, Borges wrote, "The glass is watching us." The constant sense of being observed by others, and constant self-observation *as if one were another*, is a still greater danger inherent in our proliferation of images of ourselves. The locus of your selfhood ceases to be in the mind, *behind* your eyes. Instead, it rises to the surface of your body as it is pictured there on the screen. And then, after altering your sense of self to conform to your body, the image alienates you from yourself. You analyze it as strangers would. You become, instantly, and again and again with every effortless snapshot, self-estranged. The fixation on the body's appearance becomes, paradoxically, an out-of-body experience. On the Day of Judgement, you might be asked by a stern Judge, swiping through your selfies, *Can you bring these images to life?* Of course not; the act of taking them deadened you a little more each time.

Shakespeare adumbrated that connection. In fact, he links the mirror and death overtly on more than one occasion. As Hamlet enjoins the grave-diggers, "Now get you to my lady's chamber, and tell her, let her paint an inch thick, to this favor she must come." He is holding a skull as he says it. Elsewhere, the connection is made more explicitly: "For death remembered should be like a mirror," says Pericles, "who tells us life's but breath, to trust it error." The couplet also refers to the use of pocket mirrors to check whether someone was still breathing. *Pericles* was one of Shakespeare's last plays, but he carried over the mirror–death connection from his earliest narrative poems. These lines come from someone about to commit suicide:

Poor broken glass, I often did behold
In thy sweet semblance my old age new born;
But now that fair fresh mirror, dim and old,
Shows me a bareboned death by time outworn.
O, from thy cheeks my image thou hast torn,
    And shivered all the beauty of my glass
    That I no more can be what once I was![2]

There was a vogue among European aristocrats of the "memento mori": any object that featured foreboding warnings, either visual or verbal, to "remember death." One of these was the memento mori mirror, to which Shakespeare's image might relate. A Swiss example online, dated circa 1670, has a skull occupying the bottom half. It was sure to prevent vanity, the "deadly sin" of pride: yet another reason to fear mirrors.

A similar dread emerged, independently and through a different way of thinking, on the other side of the world. After European contact introduced them to the camera, many indigenous people of the Americas refused to sit for photographs, believing that anyone who possessed your image gained power over you. Your image was not devoid of your self, as in the Abrahamic religious traditions; rather, it snatched and entrapped the self, or at least a portion of it.

Cormac McCarthy's *Blood Meridian* expresses that horror in literary form. At one point, Judge Holden, sketching some ancient artifacts in his notebook, offers to draw a portrait of one of his fellow murderous adventurers. The judge honors the man's refusal and tells a story of how "he'd once drawn an old Hueco's portrait and unwittingly chained the man to his own likeness":

> ... he could not sleep for fear an enemy might take it and deface it and so like was the portrait that he would not suffer it creased nor anything to touch it and he made a journey across the desert with it to where he'd heard the judge was to be found and he begged his counsel as to how he might preserve the thing and the judge took him deep into the mountain and they buried the portrait in the floor of a cave where it lies yet for aught the judge knew.

A pin in the voodoo doll causes a pang in the person it represents. To control the image is to control the person.

"All is vanity," wrote Ecclesiastes, centuries before the Prophet Mohammed, Borges, or McCarthy. There are few better images of vanity than the ones we have today. Instagram influencers performing take after take in front of screens that display their own images. Selfies taken at crash sites and house fires. Selfies taken crouching next to murder victims.

Ecclesiastes also pointed out that there is nothing new under the sun. Our vanity is no exception. The terror of images may well have been a minority opinion in all ages. We are no more or less in love with our own forms than were people in the past. The earliest known mirrors are convex pieces of obsidian dating back eight thousand years. Today, we proliferate images of ourselves because we *can*.

And yet the historical and literary record complicates that notion. A museum's portrait gallery may make it *seem* that people have been in love with their own images forever. But those portraits were commissioned by the wealthiest elites of their day: aristocrats in wigs and ruffs, queens and duchesses in sweeping dresses and their best jewelry. People "in the public eye," already warped by both constant self-regard and constantly *being* regarded. An artist had to be hired at great expense, and the process took several hours-long sessions.

For centuries, commoners—that is, the vast majority of human beings—never saw images of themselves as often or in as much detail as we do.

Certainly not as externalized paintings or images; sometimes not even in mirrors. While their kings were being painted by Francisco Goya or Hans Holbein the Younger, did regular Europeans, by our standards, *see themselves* at all?

> In nineteenth-century [European] villages the barber was the only person who possessed a full-length mirror, whose use was limited to men.... full-length mirrors were all but unknown in the countryside, where peasants still discovered their physical identities through the eyes of others and relied on intuition to control their facial expressions.... It is not hard to understand the taboos on the use of mirrors that existed in rural communities, where people believed that a child's growth could be stunted if it saw its face in a mirror and that leaving a mirror uncovered on the day after a death was an invitation to misfortune.[3]

The taboo on self-regard extended deep into people's lives. Women clouded their bathwater with special powders to avoid seeing their own nakedness. In high-class bordellos, by contrast, mirrors were on every wall.

Jane Austen's fiction reveals the disapproval of mirrors and the vanity a love of one's mirror-image implies. When the family in *Persuasion* takes possession of a house, they make only a few changes. The main one concerns the former owner's wall mirrors, which they find unbearable.

> Such a number of looking-glasses! oh Lord! there was no getting away from one's self. So I got Sophy to lend me a hand, and we soon shifted their quarters; and now I am quite snug, with my little shaving glass in one corner, and another great thing that I never go near.

This is in the early 1800s, on the eve of the invention of the daguerreotype.

Today we live on the other side of a technological transformation that has overwhelmed the past's moral and spiritual reservations about making images of ourselves—reservations that were already often dismissed. The proliferation of images took off in the nineteenth century, shortly after Austen published her novels, when technology democratized portraiture. In 1839, Louis Daguerre brought the exposure time for his "daguerreotype" technique down from fifteen minutes to less than one. That same year, the first documented "selfie" was taken by an American named Robert Cornelius. The "tintype," invented in the very next decade, served as a cheap, quick way for newly enlisted Civil War soldiers to memorialize themselves on the eve of deployment (hundreds of examples from that era still exist). By the end of the nineteenth century, all kinds of portraits, often with props, became commonplace. Friedrich Nietzsche and his friend Paul Ree posed as horses pulling a cart; Lou-Andreas Salome, behind them, pretended to drive them on with a horsewhip. Charles Dickens posed on a reversed wicker chair, reading a book beside two adoring daughters. (The portrait, like many a social media post, concealed the sordidness of his personal life; one of those daughters was the same age as the actress for whom he abandoned their mother.)

The second such technological advance has taken place in our lifetimes: almost everyone has an instant self-portrait device in hand. People have backed off cliffs, waterfalls, dams, balconies, and the rims of active volcanoes, falling to their deaths on the Grail-quest for the ultimate selfie. A remarkable number of people have climbed atop trains and gotten electrocuted by an unexpected wire. Others have tried to pose with a train and gotten hit by it. Drownings and accidental gun discharges abound. An entire Wikipedia page has been devoted to the macabre deaths of selfie-takers. A walrus drowned a Chinese businessman; a helicopter decapitated an Indian bureaucrat. The dangers are no longer just spiritual.

The proliferation of images of ourselves implies the proliferation of images of other people. Offering up your own image grants other people power over you, but so does exposing yourself to their images. There is no such thing as a "local beauty" anymore. That is a quaint artifact of the past, of village life. Today, with the instant dissemination of images, all bodies are compared to the most beautiful bodies in the world. The bombardment creates a false impression of the ubiquity of beauty. Dating apps and hookup apps accustom the eyes to endless variety: Keep swiping, a better-looking face might be up next. The apple that compromised Eden came from the Tree of Knowledge, but the devil could have accomplished the same end by handing Adam and Eve each a handheld screen that scrolled with endless images of alternative mates.

Just as the past could not imagine the capabilities we have, it could not imagine the entirely new dangers that come with them. In 2023, Hollywood actors went on strike because they didn't want any studio using artificial intelligence to make their images act for free. They were protesting *eternal onscreen enslavement*. Whoever owns your image owns you, and they can command you to do anything. Your likeness, a spellbound doppelgänger, will obey. The technology that will command you already exists. AI programs can now use preexisting photographs from Facebook, Instagram, or anywhere else to insert anyone at all into a pornographic scene.

The making of images never seemed so *haram* until the advent of the deepfake. Every image of yourself that's out there is a hostage handed over to the father of lies. There is no cave in which you can bury your images, no way to gather and burn those vanities in a single bonfire. A falsifiable self, a falsifiable *world*, are truly new things under the sun—but presaged, perhaps, in the taboos and restrictions of the past, in Borges's fear of mirrors and indigenous peoples' anxiety about photography.

This new vulnerability has developed rapidly, over less than two decades. Most of us are already thoroughly compromised. Rigorously guarding your image would require drastic and probably unfeasible changes to your way of life. It wouldn't be enough to avoid posting images of yourself and your family, or to lock your social-media accounts. Only veiling in public can prevent "capture" by a stranger's camera, and even then, just a momentary slip would be enough to make all that meticulous concealment a waste.

In any case, the trend is likely to continue in the opposite direction. Facebook and OnlyFans are so successful because given the chance, countless people will eagerly capture and surrender their own images. All is vanity. Glance at the back cover of this book. There it is—unaware of the irony, smiling blandly out at you, desperate for your approval: the author photograph.

The Ten Commandments of Reading

It's an irony I don't really register anymore, but when we radiologists interpret a scan, we call it *reading*. As in: *I read a hundred cases. Is the new hire a fast reader? The patient kept moving, so this one is hard to read. I stayed late and read more.*

The poet in me, always playing with meter, doesn't really register how the cases I "read" are "scans," either. Or how, when a nuclear stress test comes through, I say I *read a heart.*

I write a lot. I started early and just kept at it. Yet the vast majority of my written work, no matter how much longer I live to write, will consist of radiology reports.

I love writing those radiology reports because they earn me the money to take care of my family. I worry about losing my day job sometimes. I worry artificial intelligence will supersede me; I worry I will make a mistake and get fired. But if the family finances could be assured into the future, I would be overjoyed to ditch this job for good. My writing doesn't cover any bills; I have made more money in the past six months practicing radiology part-time than I have made in a quarter-century of writing. And yet if I lost everything someday, and I had to choose one kind of writing to keep and one kind to let go...

Another reason I love radiological writing is how it spawns market-indifferent literary writing. Like this essay, for example: I'm writing it at white heat because I have to work the eight p.m. to two a.m. shift in a few hours. I worked the same shift last night and got about four of five hours of sleep, yet here I am again, tapping away. If driving while sleep-deprived is drunk driving, I am drunk writing. But this is always how I write literary stuff, even the poems that take on complicated forms, even the poems that rhyme and scan in ways that make it seem like I toiled over each line. In front of my radiology screens, writing for patients I will never see or smell or hear the voices of, I am precise, hyperalert, systematic. Here, writing for you, dear reader, whom I love as a sibling, I am helter-skelter, operating on Michelob diphthong and vodka vocative. Goethe's description of how he wrote: "Without haste, but without rest." Mine: with insufficient sleep and with an eye on the clock. Euphoric off the metaphor, game for etymological allusions, metrically meticulous, out of control.

I love writing, but I worry I love it too much, because it keeps me from reading as much as I want. Sometimes, when I am researching a novel, it hijacks my prose reading entirely. But what it really poisoned, for a long stretch of my thirties, was contemporary poetry, especially the praised and Pulitzered kind. I could not read, let alone love, any contemporary poem without a pang of resentment. The writer in me would read a bad book and think, This poet got famous for *this*? But the writer in me interfered with my experience of good poems too. If the poem was good and resembled things I wrote, I thought, I could do this. I *have* done this, only better, and no one cared. If it was good but didn't resemble things I wrote, I thought, I could do this. Track these moves. Incorporate them next time. Get up and try them out. The laptop's right there. You can read the rest later. See if you can do this. Or *out*do this. Go write. Go.

Soon writer-me tormented reader-me even in the safe space of ancient poetry. That increasingly embittered voice wouldn't let up. Back then, I would mutter to myself, there were about six hundred men who could read, and they all resembled each other racially and religiously, more or less. Think about how easy it was for them. They helped each other out, both during their time and across generations, and that's how we ended up with a "tradition." I could write this stuff. How did this middling talent end up staying in print two hundred years later? Two *thousand* years later? And he even has scholars writing about him? It's a scam. It's reputation inflation thanks to the English language's imperial reach. It's ethnic nepotism and ideological favoritism all the way back to *Gilgamesh*. Fame is fake. All is maya.

Eventually, I jabbed an elbow into that dissatisfied, sniveling killjoy's stomach. I shut him out and focused on the books and poems before me, and for some years now, I haven't heard his voice at all. Disappointment has stopped snarling and muttering, and ambition has stopped dismantling the writing in real time to learn what worked. The top of my head feels like a stadium's retractable dome sliding clear, letting the sun shine through onto the turf of me.

Now, because I had that long period of doing the *wrong* thing as a reader (reading as an embittered and power-hungry writer, basically), I have done some thinking about the *right* way to read. The absolute best way to read, of course, is the way children read: total imaginative immersion. The happy springtime of our literary lives! But for me, and probably for you, there is no reverting to that state. Instead, I stand next to the black recliner in my study and observe my own healthiest attitudes while I read. I sit on my own shoulder and, like a reading-light-haloed good angel for once (instead of the red devil poking with a pitchfork-sized pen), I whisper these readerly commandments to myself. Or rather, not commandments, not rules—that feels too regimented for the free play of the mind that reading ought to be. Consider them goals. But they must be phrased in the imperative. For example:

OPPOSE YOUR EGO.

I don't just want to get my ego out of the encounter with the book; I want to completely break down my self-centeredness. Today, I have little interest in realistic novels about the Indian-American diaspora even though I wrote one myself over a decade ago. "Identity" comes from the Latin word for "same," and the reader in me cringes every time I hear someone say *I see myself in this character*, or how a work of art or film or literature makes them *feel seen*. "Representation": not the first aesthetic term to have begun its life in politics.

What were the first books I loved? Books about animals, mostly—not even the same species as me. And then, later, series like *Encyclopedia Brown* and *Pippi Longstocking* in elementary school, featuring a white American sleuth and a white Scandinavian horse-lifting girl, neither of whose ethnicities had anything to do with how much they appealed to me. Probably the novel that made the biggest impression on me in high school was Richard

Wright's *Native Son*, even though I'm not Black. Some of my earliest extant fiction is fake James Bond novels—again, a character whose race and religion created no divide (I have never wished the movies were cast with a "South Asian" Bond or a Black Bond, either). My earliest poems aren't lyric poems at all; they are epic poems in which I imitate an ancient Greek poet who likely flourished in Asia Minor and wrote in a language I have never spoken, about gods and epic heroes who are not my gods and epic heroes (or rather who *are* while I am reading him), in a place I have never visited.

Even at my most selfish as a reader, I rarely sought out sameness of the racial or religious sort. To engage with the Western tradition at all, I had to learn the myth-hoard and spiritual language of the Bible and the Mediterranean world. I have studied the Sanskrit literary tradition and Hinduism as well, but never exclusively. Aesthetic restlessness protected me against parochialism of that kind.

Fitting that the aesthetic imperative should be the same as the spiritual one (unless it's merely a sign of my own lifelong conflation of the two). The inner revolution that books bring about should resemble astronomy's: reading should decenter the self as Copernicus decentered Earth. Why would I want literature to be a hall of mirrors? Do I love my face or race enough to want to see it every time I open a book? Page after page of paper-thin mirrors, false depth and a false other world, with the self-image foregrounded? What the iconoclasts say of idols, I say of mirrors. I want adventures into *other* heads.

For a writer, particularly for a realist writer, it's natural to look around and take notes, to self-examine, to write autofictional novels featuring an author-protagonist who shares your name and anxieties. But I am only interested in proportion to your distance from me, and as a result my taste in reading sometimes takes on an archaeological flavor. Chatty, vulgar, closely observed, satirical poetry set in a modern American city interests me much less than Juvenal writing the exact same way about ancient Rome. Dissolve yourself while entertaining yourself, forget yourself while enlightening yourself . . . maybe those first experiences of childhood reading aren't so far away after all.

I suspect I have attained that dissolution in Brahman, that dissolution in reading, only a few times in the past decades. The out-of-body feeling I got when reading *The Voyages of Doctor Doolittle* or *Around the World in 80 Days* as a boy, I got again as a man while reading Henri Charriere's *Papillon*, or Conan Doyle's underrecognized *Brigadier Girard* stories. Reading anything must be a high adventure, or it isn't worth it. And that adventure must take me far, far from home.

It is easy, natural almost, to "find your tribe" at the level of temperament or style. I try to disrupt that tendency in myself. Within reason, of course; I don't actively seek out poorly written prose or Instapoetry. Diversifying a healthy diet doesn't mean including junk food. The more you read, and the more open-mindedly you read it, the more your definition of the good expands. A big part of broadening my receptivity has involved *not* seeking out poets and novelists who write the way I write or want to write, *not* seeking out only those writers whose interests tend toward the religious or historical, or whose styles make heavy use of metaphors and word-music. For example: I am so averse to substance abuse that I get finicky around caffeine (forget about alcohol or cigarettes or weed), but last month I sought out Hunter S. Thompson.

My poetic tendencies push me toward poets who rhyme and scan and make sense, or at least pay attention to the musical aspects of language. It's easy to find contemporary poets who don't focus on those things. I make a point of reading them, or at least giving them a try.

Which brings me to the second, diametrically opposite directive:

BE SELFISH.

The number of books I start far exceeds the number of books I finish. It's not a sign of lack of dedication. It's a sign that I read "immortal literature" with one eye on my own mortality.

It wasn't always this way. When I was a teenager, first getting into reading, I was a completist. Though I never decided this explicitly, I read as if I intended to swallow the entire Western tradition *and* the entire Indian tradition, with some of the Islamic tradition mixed in for good measure. I had no sense that some books might be too advanced or complex for me, no sense of my right to like or dislike this or that. I read archaeologically. I wanted to *know* what had been written in the past, and that discovery was just as real a pleasure as the writing itself. I remember getting the complete works of Byron and Keats and Shelley and working through them poem by poem, my mind wandering, understanding very little, often just listening to how the words themselves sounded. I still turned every double-columned page and read every poem, even the minor ones.

I broke that habit when I encountered the logorrhea of Robert Browning and the unrewarding later works of William Wordsworth. Distaste asserted itself for the first time. I didn't like this rambling. I set those poets aside and stopped being a completist. I love Shakespeare more than any other English poet, but I still haven't finished *King John* or *Henry VIII*. There are much better texts to read, many of them by Shakespeare himself.

I think if a fortune-teller ever gave me the exact quantity of books I had left to read or listen to between now and the moment of my death, I would break down weeping. My hands would shake and my lips would quiver every time I picked up a book. "Stay, thou art so fair," Faust said to the passing moment. How unbearably poignant to decrease that number by one!

I keep that imaginary tally in the forefront of my mind when I read. I think I was injudicious in my teens because I had that typically teenage unawareness of my own limited time on Earth. No more! The path to what erudition I currently possess is strewn with abandoned books. I am always willing to start a book, classic or bestseller, and demand of it, *Impress me.* Filter feeders in the ocean let infinitude pass through them, taking only what nourishes them. Literature is that ocean for me, and I have not come to scoop up my share of it with a teaspoon. My readerly gaze is a circular hollow, its radius half as long as the ocean is deep, and I welcome as much through it as possible, while I have time. If I love it, I make it mine—no, I make it *me*, part of my body, the literal meaning of "incorporate." If I don't love it, there are plenty of other books in the library, plenty of other fish in the sea.

I also have a problem with this attitude. When it comes to reading, almost every piece of advice pairs instantly with its own contradiction. Opposing muscle groups: adductor, abductor; flexor, extensor. So *being selfish*—guarding your time, not reading anything unless it grabs you immediately—has to be tempered by its opposite:

I used to leave books all over the house. My parents weren't used to that. Ours was not a literary or religious family. The only books in the house were textbooks and medical journals (both my parents were physicians; it's why they made it to America in the first place). There was also a Gujarati translation of the *Gita* at the customary bedroom shrine; it rested there as a decoration, a family heirloom, tattered and well-thumbed by my paternal grandfather, but not by my parents, nor by me.

I did not have a book-buying budget. All my books came from the local library, an uphill mile I biked every weekend. Because we had not a single bookshelf in the house, I ended up leaving the random assortment all over the place. In the beginning it was mostly spy thrillers: Ian Fleming and the novelists authorized by his estate to continue the Bond series, Robert Ludlum, countless others. My parents never registered my abrupt change in taste around age fourteen or fifteen: The plays of Christopher Marlowe ended up on an arm of the downstairs loveseat, *The Decameron* and several more obscure works of Boccaccio scattered around the upstairs recliner, Goethe's plays on the coffee table, the Upanishads next to the TV remote. My mother used to get frustrated and tell me to gather my books in one place. I was making a mess. But all construction sites look like a mess at first.

Did I read all of those books? Yes, but only because I loved them. There were other books, other poems that I rejected. Browning and Wordsworth were just the first, or at least the first I remember. *Paradise Lost* was my biggest howler. I would never have believed you if you had told me in high school that I would circle back to Milton and devour his complete works, much less that my first published poem as an adult would be a blank-verse poem about Adam and Eve titled "Subtle Anatomy." Perhaps I would have been less skeptical that I would one day write a blank-verse epic diffracting *Paradise Lost* through the work of the Sufi mystic al-Hallaj, rewrite it in prose, and then actually get that weird epic serialized in a major literary journal (*The Kenyon Review* had a wonderfully open-minded editor in David Lynn).

But I didn't just get bored with Milton the first time I read him, as I got bored with Browning. I *despised* Milton. Everything about his epic seemed stilted, artificial, and pompous rather than intricate, idiosyncratic, or sublime. How had Shakespeare's speak-the-speech blank verse superflux degenerated, within a single generation, into this? I still don't love Milton as much as I love Shakespeare. But Milton's religious tendency eventually dovetailed with my own and quickened me into creating my best early work. What if I had written him off and never returned to him?

Ulysses is another one. Much like Milton, Joyce is deeply allusive, nearly inscrutable until you have read deeply for a few decades. You prepare to read these writers by reading everything that came before them. Luckily, however, they are also obsessed with sound. At an early age, before you have the background, you can turn off the meaning-seeking part of your brain and experience their work as music. I never got into Joyce until I heard him in audiobook form, read in Jim Norton's lilting, hypnotic voice. Then I loved him. As Eliot, another writer to whom this idea applies, once said, "Great poetry can communicate before it is understood." Great prose too. Now, thirty years after I abandoned Ulysses for the first time, I am reading each chapter, then relistening to it. And I'm getting it. I think.

But *Ulysses* is not the only book I am reading right now. The recliner in my study has a pile of books beside it. The lectern with its book stand too has a couple more at its base. Between the two is a bookshelf holding a few more. This doesn't even account for the three packed bookshelves of books that I own and plan to get to, waiting on the far wall.

Is this scatterbrained of me? Maybe. But I like having books compete for my attention, and I like keeping my options open. I want several to hand at all times. Am I in a poetry mood? New poetry or old? A history mood? What era? How about prose fiction? What genre, what era? Each book is a time machine, a mind-altering drug, at once entertainment and a meditation aid. One imperative has never changed during my life as a reader:

KEEP A LOT OF BOOKS GOING.

Though my religious tradition focuses on controlling the mind and senses, and though I translated a whole poem (the *Bhagavad Gita*) that fixates on this concept, I remain blithely monkey-minded as a reader. Only some readers are omnivores. Many others—perhaps *most* others, judging from the publishing industry's classification compulsion, its fixation on "similar titles"—adore one kind of book and seek out more examples of it, endlessly. "What do you like to read?" "Mysteries."

Writers are guilty of that tendency too. Being a one-trick pony is a market advantage—you build a brand, and the brand builds a following. The most successful genre writers have gone on to create the equivalent of painterly "studios," where they map out a story and delegate to unknowns the drudgery of typing "suddenly, he heard a gunshot" and all that. The book goes out with the familiar author's name in marquis-magnificent font on the cover—Clive Cussler, Tom Clancy, James Patterson—with the actual author's name in small print below it.

I avoid such books not out of highbrow contempt (okay, not *just* out of highbrow contempt) but because I suspect the *replaceability* of such work. The kind of books and poems I look for are ones even the writers themselves cannot reproduce. Joseph Heller never wrote another *Catch-22*, and neither has anyone else. Bulgakov's *The Master and Margarita* stands apart from his other excellent work in its nature, in its *feel*, in the way it moves. I am always in search of the one-off, the anomalous work that defines the criteria of its perfection, the best of its kind because it is one of a kind. The great mystery is how often such incomparable books emerge from a genre, from a crowded field of books that resemble it: *Moby-Dick* from novels about seafaring, *Hamlet* from revenge tragedies, the *Commedia* from mystical vision poems, and so on. Don't the people you love most distinguish themselves, in a similar manner, from the larger and desultory genre of "people"? Over 99 percent of any art form or any genre, the wisdom goes, is trash. My beloved is to the human species what *Orlando Furioso* is to chivalric romances.

I keep a lot of books going because I am always on the lookout for a book that will lodge itself as a seed-crystal in my mind and send sensations and emotions fractalling outward. Because I believe that the number of books—from the perspective of a single reader with finite receptivity, finite attention, and finite time—is infinite, the number of such seed-crystal books must be infinite as well. I want to search for and treasure as many as I possibly can between now and my mind's end. Until I am reborn and equipped with a new mind, that is, at which point I will read them all again for the first time.

Which is not to say I won't read them again in *this* life, for the second, or third, or fourth time. So I urge you:

REREAD WHAT YOU LOVE.

And *whom* you love. A book is a person, and when you truly fall in love, it takes on an infinite lovability. The first date is an opening onto immensity, and that's why you want the second date, and the third, and the marriage, and the meeting in your next lives.

Of course, that second date may not reinforce the match. I sensed, or maybe imagined, something in Wolfram von Eschenbach's *Parzival* at age eighteen that eluded me when I revisited it at age forty-two. I am still trying to figure that estrangement out. I blame the fact that the second time, I listened to the audiobook, which I tried because I figured oral recitation was how the Bavarian bard presented his epic to its original audience. I didn't dwell as long on the details I should have. I am tempted to ask *Parzival* out on a third date, this time in print, where I first fell in love with it.

Most rereading, though, deepens the love. That is the second kind of infinity that you find on bookshelves. The first is the lateral infinitude of Borges's infinite library, bookshelves stretching to the vanishing point to your left and right. But an individual book can also serve as an aperture onto an infinite world, as inexhaustible as a human mind. You peek inside and see that infinitude: the first read. You step through and dwell there a while, and next time, once the bedazzlement of unfamiliarity has waned, you can focus on the dozens of other bedazzlements you missed: the second read. This can go on infinitely. You have other books to get to, but this *n*th reading of *Hamlet* is the one where the detail about Ophelia's dress ballooning out in the river tattoos itself on your memory, how there's a pause before she drowns, and you had forgotten that she sang during that pause, didn't struggle while the water soaked her dress and made it heavy. It's a memory of the book that is as vivid a flash as anything from your own childhood now. Reading didn't give you that; rereading did. When dementia degrades your memory in old age, that passage will linger longer than many things you have experienced "in real life," pausing there, soaking in the Lethe and getting heavier, reciting itself over and over until it too goes under.

That library where I found my first literary loves is long gone. Or rather, it's *worse* than long gone; the building remains, but it's been gutted and refurbished for "technical education" classrooms. It was a little strangely (but for me, serendipitously) situated to begin with, a standalone building on the same campus as my high school. I passed it twice each day on the bus. I could see it through the windows of some of my classrooms, right there across the parking lot. The school ended up subsuming it, degrading it. After that, my heart could not bear setting foot inside, but I understand there are a lot of computer screens in there. I don't want to see. I want the layout to stay as it is in my memory, nothing overwritten. It was always a little dim in there. I imagine garish tube lights have dispelled its cathedral gloom.

The quiet, ill-lit shelves that towered over me used to intimidate me in a good way. I got butterflies in my stomach. I still do, whenever I walk into the stacks at a university library. Why have libraries always done that to me? (That library on my high-school campus used to be the whole county system's repository for the classics—more luck, unless designing deities had set that up for me.) I realize I am excited-nervous, not scared-nervous. I suspect I might be transformed. I am approaching life-changing wisdom. My identity, my mind, my outlook may be annihilated and remade based on what I encounter in these books.

It sounds like I'm overstating things, but for me, this is a literal description. I really do believe that books trigger inner revolutions. The Sikhs call their holy book the Guru Granth Sahib;—"guru" meaning "spiritual teacher" and "granth" meaning "book." I don't extend that to all books, since there is no mechanism to prevent a fool or bigot from making it into print; but I do extend it to all the good and great books out there. A good library is full of books that I can make my guru, either as a writer or a person.

And that is less a commandment or directive than a simple article of faith you have to treasure up against all disappointment:

Believe that truth lives on those shelves, as well as sharp, pointedly phrased insights into human nature, some unexpected fact that upends your sense of a given era's history, themes and techniques that will shape your own literary practice, foreign cultures waiting to welcome a new native … all of this lives in the library. Not on television, which flattens brain waves. Not in music, either, which (sorry, Keats) can be beautiful but never truthful because it cannot do to the intellect what it does to the ear and heart.

Come to think of it, maybe I *am* scared-nervous when I step into a library. The new self-awareness that comes from the disruption feels like a reproach to the prior self. I see how little I saw, I learn how little I knew—I, who thought myself well-read and well-thought. It's the ego again, sensing it will be humbled by the vastness of all there is to read. Consider: Just as a writer, upon seeing another writer do what they want to do but doing it better in a way that they did not know was possible, scrolls through their own suddenly lusterless language, and maybe even glances over at their own shelf of published books, thinking for the first time that they didn't sell because they didn't deserve to sell, thinking, *No, no, no, I've been writing poetry wrong all this time*—someone made a smidgen wiser by the grace of a book can look back and blush at their own life and ideas and self-satisfaction, thinking, *No, no, no, I've been living life wrong all this time*.

It doesn't have to be that way, of course. That attitude is itself unwise, in literature or in life. It's as silly as looking back at the place you were a footstep back and anguishing that you weren't then where you are now, when movement is the whole point. You're walking, and that's what walking (or writing, or living) is about.

That extended simile about the writer glancing at his books, by the way, was a Homeric simile, the first technique I remember registering, if only because it commands several lines' worth of attention every time it appears. I was fascinated by how the world of the *Iliad* contained this *other* world: the world of Homer's own analogies, called upon to describe occurrences in the *Iliad*'s world. I get the sense that the analogy's world is domestic and settled—beekeeping, farming—while the *Iliad*'s is primitive and violent. Homer, in his extended similes, draws from that second everyday world behind the epic world. But he doesn't just reach over, grab a reference, and embed it. He strolls through the fourth wall and dwells in his contemporary world, showing us a later, agricultural Anatolia, long after the age of heroes became the age of husbandmen. That more familiar world always fascinated me because I felt it gave me a glimpse into Homer's life and times (or at least the life and times of the bards whose work someone synthesized into Homer; he is otherwise completely obscure, with seven cities claiming to be his birthplace even in antiquity).

The contrast heartens me. It reminds me that even the West's original epic poet lived far removed from his narrative world. That world was located in the misty past, but it might as well have been imaginary. I recall reading how Homeric warriors combine elements of different phases of warfare, some modern, some ancient. Homer is as artificial and anachronistic as those Renaissance biblical paintings where the three wise men are dressed like Italian nobles.

Observations about contemporary society, verisimilitude (which news stories and nonfiction routinely render irrelevant), dialogue or even a poetic or narrative voice that captures "how people really talk," transcriptions of personal experience—these aren't the locus of "reality" in literature. How characters feel, think, respond, interact, choose, suffer, choose to suffer, or to transform, or to transcend—*this* endows writing with the feel of the real. That "reality" can set its drama on a battlefield in the misty past or on a far-future space colony. Embrace artificiality;

EMBRACE IRRELEVANCE.

Spurn the faddish, the modish. Trends contain their ends.

I don't make this point to insist, in the face of those who pooh-pooh "book learning," that reading will improve your understanding of human psychology. Wisdom waits on the bookshelves, yes—*but don't go looking for it*. I do believe that wisdom, enlightenment, and maturation of mind all await the omnivorous reader. But the idea of someone becoming a reader in pursuit of utilitarian self-improvement revolts me. I do not want to read in order to become wise; I do not want to read in order to become a better person; I do not want to read to derive succor for my worldly problems. In my personal life, I am self-disciplined, under constant self-surveillance, a teetotaler, a one-woman man, a perpetually unimpressed taskmaster in the basement gym. In my literary life, I am a hedonist. I am promiscuous, my middle finger rising at any attempt to edify me. My eyes scan every poem for the usual (that is, progressive) political messaging, then roll. The moral of every story is only whether it held my attention or didn't. Is this relevant? Relevant to what? I know what kind of relevance literary types mean: relevance to whatever the news is on about this cycle. If I want relevance, I'll scroll through my social-media feed. Literature is where I seek pleasure and attain wisdom by accident. What is medicine to some is candy to me. I eat it as candy. Any salubrious effect is a side effect.

Though I claim to embrace irrelevance, I cannot shake the feel of revelation when I read. Cabals of zealots rising to power in Gibbon's declining empire, a wealthy landowner seized with guilt about his privilege in *Anna Karenina* ... I read these things and think immediately of my own times, my own society. Historical analogies never quite match up, and sometimes they mislead us entirely—that is, you fret about an impending Kristallnacht when you should be worrying about an October 1917. I might as well codify what we all do anyway:

READ THE PRESENT AND FUTURE INTO THE PAST.

It doesn't matter how far away in time or geography the writing was written. Even the earliest cuneiform ledgers of Sumeria, the inventories and transactions, tell me something recognizably perennial: many-minded mankind is money-minded most of all.

Can reading history provide analogies to our own moment, or hints of things to come? Do fiction and poetry, with their interior portraiture, crack open the people around us like books? Dubious claims, says the scientific side of me, the side of me that shares something with the shopkeepers of Ur. If historians could suss out the future, I would like history to show me even one who made predictions accurate enough to make money on the stock market. And even if you could prove to me that people who read are more psychologically acute than people who don't (and I'd be curious as to your measurement methods), I'd still find a way to object. How do you know that psychological acuity isn't what drew them to reading, rather than reading that made them psychologically acute?

Nonetheless, I read with these goals in mind, these hopes for myself. Hoffer's *The True Believer* helped me understand contemporary politics by teaching me about the minds of zealots. I read it in 2016, that *annus horribilis* of American politics (though any year spent paying more attention to politics than to literature is a horrible year), but it was published all the way back in 1951. I grasped the Trump era with a book from the Truman era. Emma and Anna taught me to see adultery as sad, not evil, though they lived—live—only in nineteenth-century fiction, and I met them only in prose. To this day, when I hear about a marriage done in by someone cheating on their spouse, my first reaction is pity, not condemnation.

In medieval Europe, the *sortes Virgilianae* served as a form of divination: You asked a question about the future, opened your volume of Virgil to a random page, put your finger down, and the line contained a prophecy, if you interpreted it right. Others have done this with the Bible. I suspect Emily Dickinson's poems too could serve as an appropriately cryptic divination aid. No book can tell you the future, not even one that sets out to do so, like Nostradamus. But that doesn't keep our anxious minds from trying. Everything from avian flight patterns to the night sky has been used to scry the future. It's only natural that we should recruit, in the perennial cause, something midway between the birds and the stars, between the shifting and the fixed: letters on a page.

The only thing about the future that literature reveals with certainty, in my opinion, is that people will behave like people, no matter what. Human nature seems strikingly consistent across centuries and civilizations. Love and fear, wonderment and violence, adventure and grief, gullibility and greed—the themes are consistent, the motives recognizable. Poems from ancient China and ancient Greece, civilizations whose love poets almost certainly never consulted each other, describe the same old bog-standard feeling that feels every time like the first time ever. Sometimes, in fact, poems two thousand years old in a foreign language make more sense to me than poems written by a professor at a university thirty minutes from my house.

But now for the corollary, the contradiction to what came before:

READ THE PAST ON THE PAST'S OWN TERMS.

Because there are, inevitably, places in books where the past's alien nature hits hard, or hits home.

America, at this point in its history, sensitizes its citizens to detect and despise any hint of racial bias. The taboos and shibboleths we adopt in our civil society extend, inevitably, to the books we read too—books written by societies that had other taboos and other shibboleths, and who never imagined the "n-word" might one day provoke gasps of outrage. Everyone knows it shows up in *The Adventures of Huckleberry Finn*, but let's not forget how Joseph Conrad put it in the title of a novel, plastering those six letters on the cover and spine of every copy of the print run. Different times indeed! Characters like Shylock and Gunga Din are points where a given era's commonplace bigotries are interwoven with the West's literary tradition. But even there, in Shakespeare's work and Kipling's, I sense a touch of compassion. Even the sublime and mystical poets are not immune to this; Dante and Rumi too are creatures of their cultures, members of their tribes, partaking alike in group faith and group hate. The *Inferno*'s ninth canto shows us the Prophet Muhammad in hell, hacked down the middle by a giant sword; elsewhere Dante asserts that God used Rome to destroy the Temple of Solomon in 70 AD to punish the Jews for crucifying Christ. Rumi makes casually contemptuous references to Hindus, whose dark skin he associates with the darkness of their *kafir* ignorance. Modern translations, which often float free of the original Persian, edit out the Mevlana's more meanspirited references.

We have seen Roald Dahl bowdlerized for daring to call a character fat, and scholars wax indignant over the private letters of Philip Larkin. But I assure you the past is far, far worse than a few Brits behaving badly. The revered ancient Greeks used to toss unwanted babies on a hill outside the city, leaving them there to either die or be snatched up by man, woman, or wolf. Oedipus was not the only ancient infant to be "exposed." Arab intellectuals under the "rightly guided" caliphate, so often praised for preserving Aristotle, had no problem with a slave trade that harvested and castrated males from Africa, Europe, and India. Harem maintenance required a steady supply of eunuchs. Many sublime Vedantic theologians likely practiced untouchability, conveniently forgetting their grand notion on the unity of all beings. Even among famous British writers, Dahl and Larkin are hardly the worst offenders. Lord Byron never shook rumors of incest, and there is even stronger evidence that he was a pedophile. Shakespeare's contemporary, Ben Jonson, murdered a man but escaped punishment by reciting the "neck verse" that proved his literacy. If you believe adultery to be a cardinal sin, there is no shortage of that among great writers, past or present. Charles Dickens, having penned the woes of orphans like Pip and Oliver, walked out on the mother of his ten children for an actress.

Even when it doesn't violate our ideas of what can be said and how different groups should be portrayed, the literature of the past, wherever you look, skews toward male writers and male perspectives. To my knowledge, every literary tradition exhibits that asymmetry. "Humanism" and "the humanities" left out half of humanity until very recently. Literacy rates were far lower before mass education too. A closed book to most humans for most of history, literature excludes the illiterate, almost by definition. Even works that began as accessible mass entertainment, like Shakespeare's plays or Robert Burns's ballads, require a fair bit of education to follow today. Footnotes encrust the hulls of books as they sail through time. I remember the first footnote I got distracted by, in eighth grade English class. It had to do with carrying coals to Newcastle. I was grateful for the knowledge, but I knew that it was going to kill my experience; today my personal Shakespeare is an old edition with no footnotes. I miss some stuff, but the footnote-free experience keeps me from being pulled out of the book and into the present. That is the final, irreversible estrangement: the past excludes the present simply by being the past.

But seeing a visionary's blind spot can help us see ourselves anew. When it comes to literature, wisdom awaits even in ignorance. It's not just that these less savory traits can help us detect our own biases and imagine how the future will reproach our behaviors and attitudes, the horrors we take for granted. The future will be as outraged by our factory farms as we are by the past's slave markets. I love the unlovable in old books because of the shift of perspective it forces. Stare hard enough at this beloved thing, literature, and its imperfections and shortcomings rise and grow distinct, like the shapes in a *Magic Eye* illusion. Time may distance us from the "timeless classics," but the books, estranged in some ways, remain intimate and immediate in others. That tracks to the love we have for people. No mother or father, brother or sister, lover or spouse is irreproachable in every detail, but the love is no less real and deep simply because you perceive the unlovable parts. If anything, it's proof of how real and deep the love is. If you need a book to be a paragon of beauty *and* a paragon of moral rectitude, if you need perfection of every kind to permit yourself to love wholeheartedly and study deeply, it is not a book you seek but God, not the library where you belong but the cloister.

Though the monk's solitude in the cell may seem to resemble the reader's solitude in the library, it's an inexact parallel. The monk has only a single Book and takes it with him when he retreats from the mob. In a multitudinous, garrulous gallery of books, the reader engages with one at a time, one on one. Neither is quite alone; both arrive at intimacy and communion, with God or the author or the author's characters. But a reader seeks a wider variety of things from his many lowercase-b books: serenity, excitement, truths, fictions, worldly love and worldly despair, word-wizardry and a good yarn. Not God (or not *just* God), but all creation. Transcendence is just another mood. The only way to get there and back and everywhere else?

READ.

Because just as archangels command prophets to recite, muses command poets to read. Because burning libraries like Nalanda and Alexandria are Viking funerals that constellate the rivering of time. Because this communing with the innumerable and eloquent dead will set you apart, an ash mark on the forehead, words tattooed on your memory, your tongue pierced with a poem. Because this solitary pastime makes you part of the loftiest underground nation. Because the act of poring over a book pours you through a sieve of text that filters out the gold grit hidden within you. Because another meaning of "font" is "fountain," and the Pierian spring alone can cure the aging arthritic mind of inflexibility. Because distraction is always singing its siren song, and unless you plug your ears and read, you will not hear the music of the spheres that wants to sing you heavenward. Because some of the earliest Sanskrit manuscripts were written on birch bark, and "one could do worse than be a swinger of birches." Because when you live a full life, it's reading that leaves no time for everything else, not the other way around. Because the books that Prospero said he would drown have floated to the surface and become a fleet waiting to sail us deeper into ourselves. Because books, like newborns, love to be held, no matter how ancient they are. Because books respond to the brush of a gaze as newborns do to the stroke of a cheek: They turn toward attention and latch on. Because only raising a child can grow you up, and reading is how you raise your mind. Because radiology and literature are both arts that strive to see within, and the brain in a brain scan looks no different than any other brain, male or female, believer or infidel, white or black, except in the places it has bled. Because ultrasound sings a note and waits for an echo, conjuring its glittery guess at the world by this act of giving and receiving. Because life is so short that there is no time *not* to be reading, since the only way to increase our years here is by packing into them as many multigenerational Mahabharata-millennia and saga-centuries as possible, literary time nested in time time—or else to maximize one moment with poetic or Proustian dilation. Because we risk remaining mere character sketches, flat on a page, unless we read our way into personhood and stand three-dimensionally atop a library step stool, reaching for infinity. Because in antiquity, books used to be scrolls, and libraries looked like giant honeycombs. Because the soul is not located in the pineal gland as Descartes believed, but is divided between the pupils, which melt at the moment of death and trickle home to their author's inkwell. Because a row of books is no different than a row of readers, two kinds of spines that gather all the sensations of the world. Because a screen rivers into your eyes and a playlist rivers into your ears, but a book makes you the source of the visions and voices inside it. Because images cannot sing and music cannot paint but words do it all and then some. Because deckle edge and flyleaf and dogear. Because may they find my body face down in old book smell. Because my mother taught my daughter knitting, and the first thing she knit me was a bookmark out of orange yarn. Because it's so much more interesting than everything else. Because you need to. Because you need to "reason not the need." Because orphan line and proof and kerning, tree and pulp and seed. Because there's only one commandment when it comes to reading: *Read*.

The SILENCE
IS REST

1.

At the start of the pandemic, I too thought I might die of it. Statistically, I knew, mere misery was more likely than outright death. So what scared me most were reports of "brain fog," people saying they weren't able to think straight for weeks after infection.

Locked-in syndrome was the scariest thing I ever learned about in medical school. You stay conscious, but you can't express yourself in any way, not even a finger twitch. Less severe, speech-focused forms are known as aphasia.

No speech. Maurice Ravel got in a taxi accident, and he could not get his music out of his head forever after. He died while having brain surgery. His musical aphasia haunted me for years. I published a poem about it long ago (in *The Able Muse*) but never collected it.

THE MUSICAL APHASIA OF MAURICE RAVEL

Notes in his ear like motes in his eye,
This pencil a pin in pursuit of a fly—
Such were the secrets Maurice Ravel
In his last lost years was dumb to tell.

Aphasia, Parisian neurologists said,
From that taxi crash when you bumped your head.
The knock will dissolve like the clang from a bell,
And you'll be, once again, Maurice Ravel.

Notes afloat in the fog, in the air,
Boleros in mind too lively to bear
Unborn, unwritten, stilled by the spell
That quelled and ensorceled Maurice Ravel.

Begetting, forgetting themselves in his brain,
They were cats, and he patted his lap in vain.
An audience rose to applaud Ravel.
The Ravel they beheld was a wraith of himself.

Dementia, the doctors of Paris opined.
Old age has unraveled your musical mind.
The music you hear is the sea in a shell.
The music you wrote is forever Ravel.

He went to a surgeon, who would not cut.
He went to another, who gave a shrug,
Skeptical whether a scalpel would help
The music escape its cell in Ravel.

The roof of the prison was lifted off,
A bowler of bone incised and doffed.
With the sound of a radio dropped in a well,
The last lost works of Maurice Ravel

Floated aloft in the surgical suite,
Boleros unbound, too lovely to keep,
Ravel revealing, in surges and swells,
An oeuvre unrivalled by early Ravel—

Nocturnes that added a star to the night,
Impromptus that luck would be lucky to write
While his breathing slowed, and heart rate fell,
Releasing the soul of Maurice Ravel.

But here I am, still thinking about it, years later. Imagining, with a shudder, language stripped from me. Death or stroke or infectious brain fog: There are so many ways to be silenced.

2.

So the great voluntary silences in literature baffle me. Some really did just give this art up. For Gerard Manley Hopkins, burning his poems amounted to putting away childish things so he could focus on the priesthood. Philip Larkin felt the Muse had moved on and didn't write for the last ten years of his life. Virgil, on his deathbed, ordered the *Aeneid* burned. Kafka, in his will, asked the same manuscript-holocaust from Max Brod.

Voluntary silence, the bonfire of one's literary vanities—I would have to change profoundly before I got to that psychological place. For all my obsessive religious studies, literary immortality may be the only kind I really believe in. No meat, no alcohol, no caffeine, no smoking: ascetic self-restraints, but only the kinds I *like*. Do they even count? I am a lush when it comes to language.

3.

The most word-drunk, metaphorically euphoric poet of all went silent the last three years of his life. Shakespeare's biographers have documented his ignominious pursuit of respectability. Consider that made-up, touchily mottoed coat of arms: *Non Sanz Droict* ("Not Without Right"), as in, I really *do* deserve this. So what if I made my money among disreputable theater people in the big city? (Playwrights were considered lowlifes too; Ben Jonson had to read a "neck verse" to evade the noose, and Marlowe died in a bar fight.) Shakespeare, longing to be an upstanding citizen, dealt in grain and built his village's biggest house.

He wrote nothing after returning to Stratford-upon-Avon in early 1613. Just seven years before, he had written *King Lear*. And then he just . . . *retired*. No urge to see if he could match or outdo it; no imperative to map the abysses he had discovered; no impulse, even, to fool with the language. Forty-nine! Just seven years older than I am now. You could give me sharp vision and a fogless mind until ninety-four, and it wouldn't be enough to read and write all I want to.

Later that same year, the Globe theater burned down. Did he get word of it? During a performance, cannons were fired off, and the paper that stuffed them floated onto the theater's thatched roof.

> And, like the baseless fabric of this vision,
> The cloud-capp'd towers, the gorgeous palaces,
> The solemn temples, the great globe itself,
> Ye all which it inherit, shall dissolve
> And, like this insubstantial pageant faded,
> Leave not a rack behind.

Shakespeare's valedictory play, *The Tempest*, has that pun on the "globe," uncannily foreshadowing the fire. But *The Tempest* wasn't the last play he worked on. The latest text in the First Folio was a collaboration, *Henry VIII*— the play performed the day the Globe burned down. The playhouse lost its playwright the way a body loses its soul. It was a kind of cremation.

4.

"The rest is silence." Stare at Hamlet's last words long enough, and they start to seem strange. At first glance, "rest" is the remainder, what's left: eternity, that is, death. No verses there, no versus either, as in, no conflict. No iambs there, either. No "I am."

But then I wonder: isn't "rest" something you do before you work again? Another old meaning for "rest" is "stay" ("God rest ye" means "God keep ye"). Continuity, not completion. By 1570, the term "rest" had entered English musical parlance. The musical rest signifies the absence of sound. It is not silence, it is *a* silence, of a specified length, with a role in the ongoing composition. "If music be the food of love, play on."

The silence is a rest. The arrested sentence is a line break. The wood of the pyre gets repurposed for a cradle in another country. Forest fire feeds forest future. Max Brod never did burn Kafka's manuscripts. Nor did Augustus let Virgil's literary executors burn the lines that burned Troy. The ongoing immolation is time and neglect, but a few books flap their covers and take flight off the bonfire. From the ashes of the great Globe, a phoenix: stray quills flutter onto desks scattered in time. The feathers get up and dance a jig on the paper.

Whether abandoning or being abandoned by the Muse, that is a consolation devoutly to be wished: that even the silence of death may be only a musical rest.

In Shakespeare's day, the musicians struck up a tune after the end of every play at the Globe, even a play where Act Five was a slaughter. The characters covered in stage blood got up and danced a jig on the stage. It was a kind of rebirth.

CREDO

I've tried to talk about literature without talking about my religion, but I can't. It feels like talking about my religion without talking about my religion.

The premise is simple. You are you, and I am I, but at some level, you are I, and I am you, and at still another level, we are both simultaneously infinite mystic blissed-out godhead eternally blazing.

    Okay, maybe it's not simple. Let me backtrack.

For me, being a writer is saying to all other human beings, animals, plants, and inanimate objects on the earth:

    I don't know you, but I want to write you.

    By "inanimate objects," I am including the mirror.

From Merriam-Webster's definition of the word *know*:

    "*know* 1 a (3): To recognize the nature of."

Which is to say: You are really I. I am really you. We are by nature infinite. We are by nature all ablaze.

    I want to write you because I don't know you.

    "*know* 1 b (1): To recognize as being the same as something previously known."

One writer writes deeply about the self. "The self" is the standard English translation for the Sanskrit word "atman." We poets know it as "the lyric I."

Another writer writes characters who are nothing like him. "Madame Bovary, c'est moi." It is all the same, metaphysically; to study the self or to study the other is to study infinity.

I write poetry and I write fiction because I want to approach infinity from both sides.

I say *approach infinity*, of course, but I mean *know God*.

"*know* 2 a (1): to be aware of the truth or factuality of: be convinced or certain of."

This is supposed to be a credo, isn't it?

I believe.

I believe every role in Shakespeare spoken simultaneously will harmonically morph into the voice of God. I believe language trumps music and moving images in spite of considerable evidence to the contrary—*credo quia absurdum,* after all. I believe fiction is brain cocaine. I believe poetry is brain crack. I believe the system has never been anything but broken and that mind-blowing writers die unknown and forgotten, hell, are never discovered in the first place, and I mean *routinely*. I believe literature is how the brain has brainsex with the brains of strangers, brainsex as in "*know* 3 *archaic*: to have sexual intercourse with." I believe writing is so much like a religion that there is such a thing as the Blessed, the Elect, the Chosen, and that it is best not to envy them, and that for the rest of us there is still honest devotion and manual labor and the possibility of grace. I believe in doing everything at once. I believe the Epic Failure is better than the #1-*New-York-Times*-Bestselling Success, but that may just be because my books don't sell. I believe that credos are meant to be revised, so don't quote me. I believe that you are you and I am I and never we twain shall meet except in these poems, these novels, this common language made uncommon. I believe rhyme. I believe that in literature, universality and infinitude and unity are attained through infinite love of the specific and finite and multitudinous. I believe the hype. I believe religious scriptures are actually supremely powerful literary works and can be approached as literary works. I believe literary works are actually supremely powerful religious scriptures and can be approached as religious scriptures. I believe in approaching myself from opposite directions—call it a pincer action. I believe English is superior to binary code precisely because it is less precise. I believe I am a language lush whose favorite self-indulgence happens to be discipline. I believe we share language that we may know how completely we share being.

I believe.

NOTÈS

THE GREAT GAME

1. Huizinga, *Homo Ludens: A Study of the Play-Element in Culture*.
2. Frost, "Two Tramps in Mud Time."
3. "Match Point." *Newsweek*, 30 January 1956.
4. Shakespeare, *Macbeth*.
5. Dickinson, "The Soul Selects Her Own Society."

ON FORMAL RESTLESSNESS

1. Ryan, "Sharks' Teeth." Reprinted with permission of Grove/Atlantic.
2. Merwin, "The Asians Dying."
3. Goethe, *Roman Elegies*. Translated by Michael Hamburger.
4. Majmudar, *Godsong: A Verse Translation of the* Bhagavad-Gita *with Commentary*.
5. Browne, *Urn Burial*.

SISTER DISCIPLINES

1. *Nasadiya Sukta*. Translated by Basham.
2. Empedocles, *On Nature*. Translated by W. C. Lawton.
3. Rilke, "Black Cat." Translated by and reprinted with permission of Stephen Mitchell.
4. Milton, *Paradise Lost*.
5. Eliot, "Burnt Norton."
6. Wordsworth, "I Wandered Lonely as a Cloud."
7. Lucretius, *On the Nature of Things*, Book VI. Translated by Ian Johnston.
8. Virgil, *Georgics*, Book IV. Translated by A. S. Kline.
9. Shakespeare, *Henry IV*.

10. Dante, *The Divine Comedy*.
11. Goethe, *The Maxims and Reflections*. Translated by Bailey Saunders.
12. Goethe, "Metamorphosis of Animals." Translated by Christopher Middleton.
13. Larson, "Love at Thirty-Two Degrees."

TOWARD AN EVOLUTIONARY THEORY OF POETRY

1. *The Pocket Oxford Dictionary of Current English*.
2. Plath, "Metaphors."
3. Milton, *Paradise Lost*.

THE ANXIETY OF ORIGINALITY

1. "Original and Unoriginal: Matthew Welton on Plagiarism."

NOW THAT'S WHAT I CALL A TRAGEDY

1. Byron, *Sardanapalus*.
2. Tennyson, *Becket*.
3. Whitman, "Ventures, on an Old Theme."
4. Frost, "Introduction to King Jasper."

INTERLUDE / ESSAY ON REPETITION

1. Emerson, "The Poet."
2. Ibid.

POETIC STEM CELLS

1. Horace, *Odes III*.
2. Milton, *Paradise Lost*.

IT'S TIME TO TALK ABOUT LORD BYRON AGAIN

1. Lady Caroline Lamb, March 1812 diary entry.

KEPLER'S SNOWFLAKE

1. William Blake, "Auguries of Innocence."

VOYAGING WITH CHARLES DARWIN ON THE *BEAGLE*

1. Sørensen et al., "Multiple Sclerosis: A Study of CXCL10 and CXCR3 Co-Localization in the Inflamed Central Nervous System."

2. Henry, *The Voyage of the* Pequod *from the Book* Moby-Dick *by Herman Melville.*

THE MASTER AND EMILY

1. Dickinson, "I Went to Heaven."

2. Dickinson, 1863 letter to T. W. Higginson.

3. Dickinson, "Strong Draughts of Their Refreshing Minds."

4. Dickinson, "A Narrow Fellow in the Grass"; Dickinson, "It Might Be Lonelier."

5. Dickinson, "I Taste a Liquor Never Brewed."

6. Dickinson, "A Clock Stopped—."

7. Dickinson, "I Am Ashamed—I Hide."

8. Dickinson, "Prayer Is the Little Implement."

9. Keats, 9 April 1818 letter to John Hamilton Reynolds.

10. Keats, 6 August 1818 letter to Mrs. James Wylie.

11. Dickinson, "He Touched Me, So Live to Know."

12. Ibid.

13. Dickinson, "Love's Baptism."

14. Dickinson, "After Great Pain, a Formal Feeling Comes—"

15. Dickinson, "No Rack Can Torture Me—"

16. Dickinson, "Why Make It Doubt—It Hurts It So—"

17. Dickinson, "I Taste a Liquor Never Brewed."

18. Dickinson, 1861 "Master Letter."

19. Dickinson, "On This Long Storm the Rainbow Rose."

20. Dickinson, "Rearrange a Wife's Affection!"

21. Dickinson, undated letter to Susan Dickinson.

22. Dickinson, 1861 "Master Letter."

OUR HIDDEN CONTEMPORARIES

1. Byron, "The Bride of Abydos."

2. Swinburne, "A Ballad of Dreamland."

HER SEVEN INGENIOUS MASKS

1. Nash, "Eh?"

2. Ryan, "Sharks' Teeth." Reprinted with permission of Grove/Atlantic.

RAY BRADBURY, WORD WIZARD

1. Excerpt from "In Memoriam," T. S. Eliot, *Selected Essays*.
2. Bradbury, *Something Wicked This Way Comes*.
3. Ibid.

STOP LOOKING AT YOURSELF

1. Borges, "Mirrors." Translated by Alastair Reid.
2. Shakespeare, *The Rape of Lucrece*.
3. Alain Corbin, *A History of Private Life*, Volume IV.

PUBLICATION CREDITS

Able Muse:
It's Time to Talk about Lord Byron Again
Why Logue Works

Athenaeum Review:
Voyaging with Charles Darwin on the *Beagle*

Close Reading (Slant Books blog):
Poetic Stem Cells: On John Milton's Trinity Manuscript
The Silence Is Rest

The Dark Horse:
The Anxiety of Originality
Our Hidden Contemporaries

The Kenyon Review and *Poetry Daily*:
George Steiner, Last of the Europeans

The Kenyon Review Online:
The Ludlum Identity
Kepler's Snowflake
Credo

The Los Angeles Review of Books:
Essay on Repetition
Essay on Iron
The Great Game
Marginalia Review of Books:
Stop Looking at Yourself

The New Criterion:
On Formal Restlessness

Revel:
Compact and Dangerous

Think Magazine:
Notes on the Ghazal

The Threepenny Review and *Poetry Daily*:
Her Seven Ingenious Masks